There's a Revolution Outside, My Love

Edited by Tracy K. Smith and John Freeman

Tracy K. Smith is the author of four books of poetry, including *Life on Mars*, winner of the Pulitzer Prize. *Such Color: New and Selected Poems* will be published in October 2021. She is also the editor of an anthology, *American Journal: Fifty Poems for Our Time*, and co-translator (with Changtai Bi) of *My Name Will Grow Wide Like a Tree: Selected Poems* by Yi Lei. Smith's memoir, *Ordinary Light*, was named a finalist for the National Book Award. From 2017 to 2019, Smith served two terms as the twenty-second Poet Laureate of the United States. She is currently a chancellor of the Academy of American Poets.

John Freeman is the founder of *Freeman's*, the literary annual of new writing, and an executive editor at Alfred A. Knopf. The author of five books, including *The Park* and *Dictionary of the Undoing*, he has edited several other anthologies, including *Tales of Two Americas*, a book about inequality in America, and *Tales of Two Planets*, which examines the climate crisis globally. He teaches at New York University.

There's a Revolution Outside, My Love

There's a Revolution Outside, My Love

Letters from a Crisis

Edited by Tracy K. Smith
and John Freeman

VINTAGE BOOKS

A Division of Penguin Random House LLC

New York

A VINTAGE BOOKS ORIGINAL, MAY 2021

Copyright © 2021 by John Freeman and Tracy K. Smith
Preface copyright © 2021 by Tracy K. Smith

"The Red Wheelbarrow" by William Carlos Williams,
from *The Collected Poems: Volume I, 1909–1939*, copyright © 1938
by New Directions Publishing Corp. Reprinted by permission
of New Directions Publishing Corp.

The Cataloging-in-Publication Data is on file at the Library of Congress.

Vintage Books Trade Paperback ISBN: 978-0-593-31469-2
eBook ISBN: 978-0-593-31470-8

Book design by Nicholas Alguire

www.vintagebooks.com

Printed in the United States of America
10 9 8 7 6 5 4 3 2 1

Contents

Preface by Tracy K. Smith

I spent the summer of 2020 like many of my friends and loved ones near and far: worried, bothered, and gripped by uncertainty. How long would the pandemic last? Who would survive? How long would violence against unarmed Black citizens continue to claim lives? How far off were things like justice, safety, accountability, equity, truth? Were we as a nation heading toward them or in some other direction?

During the summer of 2020, held in place at home alongside everyone else in America, I experienced the feeling of having come to a crossroads. With it came the sensation of being pulled simultaneously forward and backward in time. We could move ahead into reconciliation and redress, or we could allow ourselves to be yanked back by our national denial of the ways that systemic racism impoverishes us all, no matter who we are.

It was this sense of a standstill, and the dire stakes of the decision at hand, that put me in mind of another iconic summer in American history: Freedom Summer of 1964, when northern and predominantly white college students traveled to Mississippi to participate in the effort to register Black voters.

A young John Lewis, at that time the chairman of the Student Nonviolent Coordinating Committee (SNCC), organized and conceived the endeavor with the dual aims of enfranchising Black citizens (at the time, fewer than 7 percent of Mississippi's Blacks were registered to vote) and educating northern whites as to the violent realities of southern racism. Among the other famous names associated with Freedom Summer are those of three volunteers slain by the Ku Klux Klan for their participation in the campaign: James Chaney, a Black civil rights worker from Meridian, Mississippi; Andrew Goodman, a New York City social worker and civil rights activist; and Michael "Mickey" Schwerner, a New York–based organizer for the Congress of Racial Equality (CORE). These martyrs, and the nearly one thousand Black and white volunteers serving beside them, endured violence at the hands of racist mobs and Mississippi law enforcement agents. They witnessed a state-sanctioned campaign of terror that included beatings of volunteers, burning and firebombing of Black homes and churches, and the murder of local Blacks who supported the civil rights movement.

As bold and unapologetic as Mississippi's violent campaign against Black voter registration was, there was also the widespread attempt to discredit the murders of Chaney, Goodman, and Schwerner as a hoax, a rumor perpetuated by a group of meddlesome outside agitators. A white Mississippian in a TV news clip repeated this theory, adding for good measure, "But if they're dead, it's because they asked for it." It is one of the great paradoxes of racism—one playing out in the summer of 2020 in acts of violence against protesters—that its agents are equally brazen in their aggression (driving into crowds, teargassing peacefully assembled protesters, kneeling on a man's neck for nearly nine minutes as he pleads for his life) and adamant in their insistence to be seen as the aggrieved (victims of lawless rioters, keepers of law and order, targets of insubordination or plausible threat). In the weeks leading up to the discovery of Chaney, Goodman, and Schwerner's remains, eight Black bodies were recovered from Mississippi rivers and swamps, one—that of fourteen-year-old Herbert Oarsby—wearing a CORE T-shirt. Perhaps the current analogy would be the deaths, at the hands of police, of Rayshard Brooks in Atlanta and David McAtee in Louisville, which occurred not just during but some might argue precisely because of a summer of calls for police accountability.

If measured by voter registrations alone, Freedom Summer failed. But the campaign raised national awareness of the organized and authorized nature of racial terror and oppression in Mississippi. And it served as an intensely compelling argument for the aims and the tactics of the civil rights movement. White northerners, witnessing coverage of these events on televised news, grew more sympathetic to the civil rights movement—perhaps because the young white activists volunteering in the foreign land of Mississippi allowed them to see their own children—in real or proxy form—as the protagonists in the effort for civil rights.

For the volunteers themselves, the summer was galvanizing not only because they saw themselves as agents of justice in the face of real evil, but because it cast them in positions of disenfranchisement that paralleled those of everyday Blacks in Mississippi, people who were often the targets of white mobs, whose homes were routinely shot at and firebombed by segregationists determined to keep the Black vote from interfering with the rule of white supremacy. In other words, for a few months during 1964, white participants were stripped of some of the privilege of their whiteness. The abstract concepts of civil rights and racial justice were transformed into actual lived experience and concrete embodied knowledge. These students went home eager to act upon their new knowledge, and to further the work of the civil rights movement from their communities and their college campuses.

Perhaps this is all well enough remembered. Perhaps there are also those who recall that the campus Free Speech Movement was one legacy of Freedom Summer, initiated by college students—among them Mario Savio at UC Berkeley—who returned home from Mississippi with the desire to keep organizing toward the goal of civil rights. In order to do so, they had to overcome institutional roadblocks to campus prohibitions on political organizing and demonstration.

But there is another legacy of 1964's Freedom Summer. That same year, student volunteers traveled throughout Mississippi registering Black and white residents as members of the fledgling Mississippi Freedom Democratic Party. Unlike standard voter registration, the MFDP's process did not require registrants to successfully interpret passages from the state constitution. And it was completely confidential; first and last names of registered voters were not published in the newspaper, a condition of general voter registration that deliberately opened Blacks and their families up to acts of retribution. The MFDP built up membership, crafted a platform, and sent a 68-person delegation to the Democratic National Convention in Atlantic City, where their intention was to challenge the validity of the state's all-white Democratic delegation, whose tactics obstructed Blacks from registering, let alone casting votes.

Martin Luther King, Jr., pledged his full support of the MFDP. But the remarks that captivated audiences were those of sharecropper and activist Fannie Lou Hamer, who described the harassment, beatings, threats, and firebombings to which she and other Black Mississippians seeking the vote were routinely subjected, concluding her remarks with the question, "Is this America, the land of the free and home of the brave, where we have to sleep with our telephones off the hooks because our lives be threatened daily, because we want to live as decent human beings, in America?" Those present in Atlantic City were so profoundly moved by Hamer's testimony that the MFDP received the necessary endorsement, naming them the legitimate Mississippi delegates to the national Democratic Party.

This was a moment of moral victory. A moment when the simple truth, told plainly, had penetrated the minds and hearts of listeners. Hamer's story, like the televised images of northern white college students braving police barricades and angry mobs in Mississippi, opened up a new capacity for compassion in the audience. Witnessing even just a glimmer of the reality confronting Black citizens, white people—Freedom Summer volunteers, audiences across the country, and the white Democratic delegates seated in the audience in Atlantic City—were moved to care.

Even all these decades later, the elation, captured in vintage news footage, is contagious. The hard-won victory. Justice genuinely triumphing over hatred—and not just any hatred, but the particular hatred of a state whose history of monstrous violence against Black voters goes all the way back to the era of Reconstruction. Miraculously, the hope that had been so brutally stolen by the murders of Chaney, Goodman, and Schwerner began again to return.

Watching the brave bodies of protesters in Minneapolis, New York, Washington, D.C., and elsewhere, I felt a similar feeling of victory. Fielding phone calls and emails from white friends claiming a sense of awakening to the reality of American racism, I was even tempted to believe change was not merely possible, but well-nigh imminent. But the summer of 2020 is a long time ago now. We have weathered a contested election and a lame-duck president's insurrectionist mob ransacking the United States Capitol. Nothing seems imminent to me now but the fact of more work, more struggle ahead. Struggle punctuated—thank God—by the occurrence of minor miracles, like Amanda Gorman's heart-filling and world-captivating delivery of the inaugural poem on January 20, 2021.

How will America respond to the decision it weighs? Will it invest in the project of national healing and racial justice? Or will it instead manufacture a means of protecting the age-old precedent of white supremacy? This question fits just as easily in the framework of 2020 as it does in that of 1964, when the Johnson administration wrestled with how to respond to the unlikely victory of the MFDP.

In 1964, a compromise was struck. The MFDP would be allowed to keep two essentially symbolic seats, and the regular Democratic delegation would be given the remaining sixty-eight. Hamer's reply— "We didn't come all this way for no two seats, 'cause all of us is tired"— speaks to the profound dismissal this compromise amounted to for Blacks in Mississippi, and those watching, and hoping, from elsewhere in the nation.

If there is unrest in America today, if some of us won't be quiet about the reality and the danger of this nation's racism, if we overstep the bounds of practicality in urging change—well, all of that fervor and duty and hope is the result in part of that fork in the road back in 1964, in Atlantic City. For if the Voting Rights Act of 1965 established the structural means by which Blacks in Mississippi and across the South could safely register and vote, it must also be acknowledged that it also arose at the cost of an unequivocal betrayal. It came about in such a way as to affirm that though America might be willing to enact laws to protect its processes, it remained firmly opposed to tampering with its hierarchies of power.

If there is unrest in America today, it is not because we cannot agree upon a definition of racism, as many who have argued against antiracist policies have suggested, but rather because power—especially contested power—will go to nearly any lengths to confuse, distort, and render muddily abstract terms that, when power is not called into question, remain as legible and distinct as black and white.

What I hear in this volume is some forty different records of the experience of America's most recent Freedom Summer; forty different missives to family, community, the world, and the self at a time when life versus death and hard-won unity versus irreparable division hung in the balance. Perhaps you will open this book and find solace during a time of consternation. Or perhaps it will serve a use for you like that of a road map for a nation that is no longer idling, but moving clearly in one or another direction.

—FEBRUARY 2021

There's a Revolution Outside, My Love

Salutation in Search Of

Patricia Smith

I.

Dear floaters, bloated kin. Dear flooded necks
and reckless leapers manic for the flow.
Though you are elegant in flight, your wrecks
distress the ocean's floor—the stark tableaus
of sliding skin and swarms of slither set
to drumbeat in your hollows. This is free
proclaimed by slavers' scourge—do you regret
rebutting scar with water? Dear debris,
that ocean mothers all your rampant funk
and spurts her undulating arms for you.
She likes to think that you are simply drunk
with purpose. Dear the voyage never knew

your name. You rise in pieces, loved to death,
at last unshackled. Time will hold your breath.

2.

Dear wild tumultuous, your mouth. Dear God.
Your mouth, in fevered skirmish with the tongue,
denying sound for rope or goldenrod.
Dear mouth, still bulging with Atlantic, wrung
into its new. Your tangled words are lash
into the back, intending to explain
the gritted teeth inspected for a flash
of rot, the hefted cock or breast, a chain
that's wrenched away with clinging shreds of skin.
Dear going to market, beauty on the block,
seed driven deep. Dear chartered womb, within
you squirms a tendency. A paradox.
You trusted voyage, trussed to kin, and found
the tongue through tumult. Now you need a sound.

3.

Dear mute contrivance, graceless drudge. Dear hexed,
Dear wily roots and conjures, Dear persist
with your existence—flaunting all that flexed
and bumptious brawn. Dear flagrantly dismissed,
the writhing in the cottonwood. Dear flail
and drip. Dear runaway who runs the hell
away. Dear prey for drooling cur. Dear veil

of Judas moon, its murmured decibel
of light. Dear cautious measurer of splay
and fury in a heedless star. (Dear we.)
Dear woman, who must now learn to unsay
her purpose as a mute machine. Dear be
that soft alive. Dear man, whose beating drum
was lost at sea. What nouns will you become?

4.

Dear lurch and pirouette, Dear flamed facade,
Dear eye that won't dissolve. Your audience,
obsessed with shrinkage, fancies to applaud
and whoop, but damn—that eye, and the suspense
and dogged smolder of its wide-aloud.
Identified (of course) and doomed to swing,
you vow to witness. Your enraptured crowd—
delighting in your noosing as a thing
to do, do not wish to be seen by you.
Dear languid rumba, freakish scorch and sway,
Dear blackened reckoning, Dear charred askew.
Dear stuff of nightmares seeping into day.
The fire has died—there's nothing of you there,
but they still see the fiction of your glare.

5.

Dear Langston, Zora, Louis, Josephine,
Dear Harlem, their rampaging stanzas, still

explosive whether they are sugar-lean
pronouncements from a horn, the thrill
of stories touting faces like the ones
who hallelujah every time they read
themselves, or—not to be undone—
a pure astonishment of women. Need
this nurture and this verve on dimming days.
Dear give you back your name. Dear higher ground.
Dear noontime strutter, balancing pince-nez
and being Negro all upside that town.
Dear swinger to a thicker harmony,
Dear every man they said you couldn't be.

6.

Dear migrant on a Greyhound, stunned upright,
or crammed into a wheezing Plymouth, or
bewildered by the rails soon to ignite
beneath your seat. Dear locked and shuttered door
with you on both the sides. Dear bound to be
more partial to the heat—folks say the chill
in ol' Chicago knows your bones. The key
is birthing your own sun and clutching 'til
it walks with you. Dear you, already done
surrendering magnolias, feigning shame
at chitlins, holding that amusing gun
to your own truant heart. Dear faultless aim,
Dear northern body scrubs at what it must,
that wily scarlet slap of southern dust.

7.

Dear edgy citizen, Dear crazed careen
through multitudes of all the same as you.
Your skittish eyes outstretch. Dear seen
and then—as if on cue—unseen. You knew
enough to heed the itchy siren song
that cooed you through the rusty yawning maws
of factories. Dear often in the wrong
direction. Dear Chicago digs its claws
in you. The rank air gorgeous with disease
and pay stubs. Mayor Daley's startling swell,
his pocked and blustered face an odd reprise
of those you thought you left behind. Dear bell
that keeps on ringing—blues that hit their mark
and make you dance all righteous in the dark.

8.

Dear still a nigger in all kinds of light,
Dear bullseye. Trees rise up on spindly toes
whenever all your skin strolls by. Dear quite
mistake of you. The way you dare expose
your neck and walk as if you own a thing.
Dear blue on you. And don't you wish there was
a ship, one chance to take a frenzied wing
into the ocean? Nothing but the buzz
of flashers pinning you against the past.
Dear suicide. Dear bullet in the back
Dear in the headlights. You're not tagged to last

until the morning. You are tagged to crack
beneath their weight. And don't you dare believe
that any one of them will let you breathe.

9.

Dear George, Trayvon, Breonna, Bree, Tamir,
Alatiana, Dominque, Jamel,
Antonio, DeAngelo, Romir,
Ashanti, Botham, Terence, John, Chanel,
Stephon, Philando, Kentry, Bee, Layleen,
Romelo, Emmett, Eleanor, Montay,
Jenisha, Kiki, Alton, Mack, Francine,
Tenisha, Eric, Dominick, Renee,
Michelle, Elijah, Nia, Amadou,
Akai, Monina, Cortez, Casey, Sean,
Alberta, Michael, Gabriella, Lou,
Natasha, Brooklyn, Walter, Lee, Laquan,
Ahmaud, Mohamed, Elray, Aura, Shane,
Rayshard, Denali, Sandra, Oscar, Blane.

10.

Dear someone who woke up without a son,
Dear damn the dawning. Echoes of a knock
with no boy crouched behind it, nothing done
to fix it. Dear reverberating shock,
Dear someone flailing, ripping at the air,
Dear hollow where he was. Dear someone who's
obsessed with resurrecting him, who dares

believe the muck of bullet hole and bruise
will ever breathe as anything but dead.
Dear someone loving body on its way
to being only body, just that red
and syrupy annoyance, hosed away
when street decorum says it will. Dear damn.
Dear chalk all washed to none. Dear traffic jam.

II.

Dear woman wounded by the things you've heard:
Dear angry all your days, Dear vibing wire
on top your head. Dear better watch the words
you say to white folk—don't make them tired
of you. Dear wish you'd pinch those nostrils down,
that nose is half your face. Dear talk too loud.
Dear stay out the sun—you fool around,
get blacker than you are. What, you too proud
to settle for that ordinary man?
Gon be too late real soon. Dear press
those naps. And don't you tell me that you plan
on yellin' bout that Black Lives Matter mess—
Dear who in the hell do you think you are?
Dear who in the hell do you think you are?

12.

Dear someone who woke up without a sun,
and spun the blues—the singer moaned so hard
the record skipped to save itself. Dear done

so wrong. Dear fryin' lettuce in the lard,
Dear wonder could a matchbox hold your clothes,
Your child's been scraped up off the boulevard.
Since then, ain't seen yourself—do you suppose
some rebel yell can find you, hit you hard?
Dear someone who has chosen just to rust
instead of breathe—here's how they lied to you:
Your child will keep on dying, and you must
keep punching play to watch him blue and blue
until he trends. Then he's a photograph
who laughs at you and rips himself in half.

—————————

I rip another page in half.

Dear—

Dear—

And start again.

Dear floaters, bloated kin, Dear flooded necks—
Dear wild tumultuous, your mouth. Dear God.
Dear mute contrivance, graceless drudge. Dear hexed—
Dear lurch and pirouette, Dear flamed facade—
Dear Langston, Zora, Louis, Josephine—
Dear migrant on a Greyhound, stunned upright—
Dear edgy citizen, Dear crazed careen—
Dear still a nigger in the neon's night—

Dear George, Trayvon, Breonna, Bree, Tamir—
Dear someone who woke up without a son—
Dear woman, wounded by the things you hear—
Dear anyone who wakes without a sun.

—JULY 16, 2020

Learning from the Ghosts of the Civil War

Randall Kenan

Dear ones,

’Tis the season for toppling Confederate monuments.

And this particular location feels as if it were the epicenter, the beginning, when students tore down the "iconic" statue at the front gates of the University of North Carolina on the evening of August 20, 2018, leading to the confrontation between Klansmen and right-wing activists and fresh-faced students, and the firing of our chancellor. Looking at the videos of cops manhandling and clashing with young people—black, white, and Asian—feels prescient. But I can't help thinking of the lithe Bree Newsome, who climbed the flagpole in Columbia, South Carolina, in 2015, and ripped down the Confederate flag as a galvanizing and generative moment. Yes, Black Lives Matter was a full-fledged movement by that point, but a certain focus had already begun to take over the young folk, and the memorialization of the Confederacy felt absolutely galling. It was galling before, but the idea that something could be done about the celebration of the "Lost Cause" had become imaginable. But it wasn't only about the Civil War. It was about Jim Crow. It was about UpSouth Chicago and Detroit. It was about gentrification.

I was an undergraduate here at UNC in the 1980s and walked past Silent Sam every day. It is not that I didn't see it or know its history—on the day of its dedication a local millionaire, Julian Carr, who paid for it, bragged about whipping a black "wench" until he shredded her clothes. Every black student I knew knew that story, and it cut us to our core, yet imagining it actually coming down was not considered a possibility; the fact that it would stand so arrogantly, well into the twenty-first century, seemed an inevitability. That such righteous destruction would one day happen in Charlotte, Durham, Fayetteville, New Orleans, and ultimately Richmond, the capital of the Confederacy, would have struck me as science fiction in 1984. That the names of racist generals would be stripped from hundred-year-old buildings the least possible.

Still, what I most would have struggled to imagine is that certain people would be up in arms were it to ever happen. That they would quite literally take over a state capitol building, bearing arms, in anger to keep monuments up. That we might have another civil war over the matter.

For me—a poor black boy from the swamps of Eastern North Carolina—the Civil War was far from a lost cause, let alone a done war. I had underestimated how unfinished. Most southern states are host to many Civil War reenactors—many of them quite literate, supposedly sticklers for historical accuracy who can argue about geography all night—but the fantasies these monuments and symbols represent don't embarrass them. I find this mystifying. They still defend these murderous, enslaving individuals, these traitors. Even though—being such students of "the War of Northern Aggression"—they know full well these monuments were erected decades after the war had been won to bolster the Big Brother eyes of Jim Crow, to reinforce the notion of racial superiority. These statues are monuments to that war, not to the war of Lee and Sherman and Grant.

The coming war will not be about the monuments, but the mentalities. Let's be clear on what that future war will be about. Why hold on to these antiquated notions of skin color signifying some type of superiority? Why cling to a past of loss and degradation? (Those who fought for the Confederacy clearly had their backs broken in the end.) Why was holding other human beings in bondage a cause worth fighting for, other than money? When most of the white men who died for the Confederacy were as poor as church mice?

Yes, it is hard to imagine we have come to this moment in the early years of the twenty-first century. I'm a lifelong fan of *Star Trek* who lived to see the first black Vulcan elected to the presidency of the United States, so this entire situation feels very like something out of the back of Gene Roddenberry's mind. (I love that MLK exhorted Nichelle Nichols to keep her job as Lieutenant Nyota Uhura because she was the only black woman on television who represented black women in a position that was not a maid. It is fun and amazing to speculate on what MLK would have thought of Kamala Harris.)

Roddenberry might have imagined such a 2020, but I never might have imagined it. Today is impossible. The convergence of Donald J. Trump, the coronavirus pandemic, the unrest over police abuse, and the tumbling of Confederate monuments were all unimaginable decades back. Can we seize the moment? We all must now readjust our thinking. The war has only just begun.

Chapel Hill is a truly spooky place right now. It feels like a ghost town where 50,000 young folk used to play. Now only one or two students amble about the halls. The large, long campus is populated by a small percentage of its once-robust population, where thousands thronged among the century-old Federal-style buildings. There is nothing but grass where the silent statue once stood. The public safety officers who once wrangled teenagers to the ground like military police in a war zone are now herding them apart when they gather in crowds. The not-knowing keeps everyone on edge. But the country's oldest public university is truly haunted by its mythical Confederate past. Even ghosts can teach us a thing or two.

—AUGUST 13, 2020

Mourning

Edwidge Danticat

My neighbor died last night. I saw the ambulance arrive. The red and blue strobes bounced off every glass surface on both sides of our block. She was eighty years old, and ambulances have come for her before. There was that time she broke her arm in her backyard, and already accustomed to osteoporotic and arthritis pain, she treated herself until her movements led to other fractures. She ended up staying in the hospital for several days because her blood pressure wouldn't go down; then she spent a few weeks at a rehab center.

She was among the first people we met when we moved to Miami's Little Haiti eighteen years before. We had an avocado tree in our yard, and one day we saw her standing outside the gate looking at it. The gate had been "locked" with a metal coat hanger that allowed easy access to the avocado tree. For years, when the house was empty, everyone on our block could come into the yard to get avocados. Our buying the house changed that.

My husband gave her some avocados. She suggested a few neighbors who had benefited from previous harvests. My husband gave them some, too.

"See," she told my husband, "I've made you popular on the block."

It's hard to figure out how to mourn during a pandemic. Our mourning rituals have all been disrupted or taken away: the home visits, the festive wakes, the funerals, and post-burial repasts. My husband walked to our neighbor's front yard after we first saw the ambulance lights through our bedroom window. Usually I would have gone with him, but the city we live in, Miami, is one of the many epicenters of the pandemic this summer, so we take turns at being exposed to the elements.

My two daughters, my mother-in-law, and I waited inside. My husband returned a few minutes after the ambulance pulled away. Our neighbor had no pulse, he said, but the emergency medical technician told our neighbor's daughter, who lives with her, that they were taking her to the hospital. The daughter was told she couldn't come in the ambulance, nor would it be a good idea for her to go to the hospital. It sounded to me like my neighbor was already dead. Maybe the EMT thought it was best not to pronounce her yet, in front of her family.

My neighbor's death was not, as far as I know, a Covid-19 death. She'd had gallbladder surgery and had been in the hospital for two weeks. When she came home, she no longer had any appetite or thirst. I had visited her in the hospital during previous stays, but this time we were not even aware that she was sick. I suppose her daughter figured, why tell, since no one, including family members, would be able to visit her.

When my mother died of ovarian cancer in our house, this neighbor came over to sit with us that same night. She came over to pray with us when my mother was near death. We attended the same small church, and sometimes I gave her and her slightly younger sister a ride home. She loved to hand out cookies and hard candy to the kids at church. She cooed over both my daughters when they were just a few days old.

A few weeks before, for her eightieth birthday, her daughter had organized a "drive-by." Over a dozen cars—she was the matriarch of a large family—streamed by her house. Her friends and family members honked their horns while waving *Happy Birthday* banners and blasting loud celebratory music. We all went outside—all wearing masks—to wish her a happy birthday, watching as she swayed to the different types of music—hip-hop, Haitian konpa, gospel—that was played for her. She was wearing a beautiful pink suit and had a Miss America–type sash across her chest. She looked very happy.

The next day I called her to more formally wish her a happy birthday. She said her children had been planning a lavish party pre-Covid. They'd rented a banquet hall and friends and family members were supposed to come from all over the world, including Haiti and the Bahamas, where she'd spent her youth.

I think back now to my neighbor's description of her birthday party plans. Her party sounded like a dream my mother-in-law had described to me a week before our neighbor died. There was a lavish banquet at church. People were singing and dancing, rejoicing that they could finally be together again. That same day, my mother-in-law learned that two of her friends had died.

In dreams, a feast signifies death, my mother-in-law had explained. Might it be because death is a kind of celebration in some other realm? I was tempted to ask her. But lately there had been too much death in our realm, and too few opportunities to celebrate the lives the dead had lived.

Four of my parents' friends died from Covid-19 in New York. Their funerals were streamed on Zoom and Facebook. I watched one of the funerals, but couldn't bear to watch the others. My parents' octogenarian minister told me that thirty members of another Haitian church in Brooklyn had died, and in each case only ten people were allowed to attend their services in person. A historian friend told me that she thinks more Caribbean people have died of Covid-19 in New York than in the entire Caribbean so far.

"Since we can't mourn in person now," my parents' minister said, "we'll have a massive memorial when this is all over. Whenever that is."

After our neighbor's death was confirmed by another friend, my mother-in-law and I walked over to her front yard and knocked on the window of her living room, where a family meeting was taking place. Our neighbor's daughter stood in the doorway and said, "My mother left us. She left us tonight."

I remember having to announce my mother's death over and over to family members and friends. I recently had to do it again, five years later, to an old friend I haven't spoken to in some time.

"She's gone," I would say. "She's gone," leading some to think that my mother had left Miami while she was sick and returned to New York, where she'd spent most of her life.

As my mother-in-law and I were standing in front of our neighbor's house, a sprinkle of rain began falling; it felt as though the God our neighbor loved so much was weeping for her. We could not touch or hug her daughter. We could not even shake her hand. We could not go inside and sit with her and her siblings, so we stood out in the rain for a few minutes and while looking up at the daughter kept muttering, "*Kondoleyans*. Sorry. We are so sorry. Very very sorry."

Recently while sitting with my family at dusk, on a beach near our home, I looked up at the sky and was in awe. Perhaps it was because I had been inside for weeks. It's also possible that in quarantine, my eyes had grown unused to having unobstructed views of sunsets, but that afternoon on the beach, the sky looked the most luminous I had ever seen it. Swirls of cirrus, cumulus, and altostratus clouds appeared to have been set aflame. What I didn't realize then was that I was looking at a Saharan dust sunset. The fact that a plume of dust from the Sahara Desert could be hovering over the sky in Miami the same week that I, and many others, were finally allowed to go to the beach reminded me that colors, like viruses, could mutate. That afternoon, it was as if the sky had become a colossal color field painting, with layers upon layers of hues and shades, pigments and shapes, dipping into the horizon.

What were these flaming skies trying to tell us in the midst of our plague? I took it as a sign that the world is still very much alive. Aristotle thought that colors—which he linked to the four essential elements of earth, water, fire, and air—came to us directly from the heavens. Leonardo da Vinci observed that between shadows are other shadows, a phrase that reminds me of the Haitian proverb *Dèyè mòn gen mòn,* or beyond mountains are more mountains, which is something I overheard my neighbor saying to her younger sister more than once when I gave them rides home from church.

My husband calls from the car to tell me that a notary friend he spent a half hour with (both masked) in an office the day before—the same day that my neighbor died, the same day my husband was outside watching her body being taken away—has tested positive for Covid-19. The friend is routinely tested at his job and is asymptomatic. The friend's results, incredulously, came back two weeks after he took the test. For two weeks, he had been at work. He had been in close contact with his family. He might have even made love to his wife. He came to an office to meet with my husband, which he wouldn't have done had his results come back sooner. This is where my mind immediately goes: I hope we don't all get this thing now. I hope we're not all about to die.

My husband's test is negative, as were eventually all of his friend's family members. My husband paid seventy-five dollars to get the results in forty-eight hours, rather than two weeks. My mind also goes to how many people might have caught the virus and died because someone didn't have the necessary dollars to pay for the quicker test. Though I'm glad my husband tested negative, I find it hard to fully trust the results. What if it's a false negative? According to the local news, 15 percent of the tests give false negatives.

In the midst of all of this, a wire pops in my older daughter's braces, cutting into the inside of her cheek. This requires an emergency run to the orthodontist. The terror I feel at imagining my daughter's mouth being wide open while another person pokes inside it makes my body shake.

Dental visits are a lot more complicated these days. You drop your child off at the front door after you've both been grilled about your recent travels and whether anyone in the family has had a fever, cough, or shortness of breath. The child's temperature is taken before she's escorted inside by a masked and shielded dental assistant. You wait, far away from other parents, on a bench outside, or in your car. Whenever I think of anyone in my family falling ill right now, this is all I think about: child or adult, they will have to face every horror alone, without anyone they know or love nearby.

While waiting for my daughter to come out of the dentist's office, I keep thinking about my neighbor. Since she died, there are always at least half a dozen cars parked in front of her house. My mother-in-law keeps insisting that we go pay our proper respects to the family. I can't imagine sitting in my neighbor's living room, as I have done a few times before, and drinking her daughter's tea right now.

In lieu of flowers, the family asks, via texts, that donations be made to a church she supports in Haiti. They also send a Zoom link for the funeral. My husband and I debate whether sending some restaurant food over might also be a good idea. When my mother died, our neighbors sent over enough food for us to eat for weeks, but now we fear that whoever would be delivering the large plates of hot Haitian food might potentially be putting our neighbor's family or themselves in danger. My husband hand-delivers a box of Haitian patties and beverages to my neighbor's house. On her front gate is a sign that reads: PLEASE WEAR A MASK FOR YOUR SAFETY.

When I sit down at the end of the week to watch my neighbor's funeral, the Zoom link does not work. I don't want to text her daughter in the middle of her mother's service to ask for the right code. *Maybe we were not meant to watch,* I think. Maybe my neighbor did not want us to.

That afternoon, while my neighbor is being buried, some new neighbors, people who have moved to the neighborhood during the pandemic, blast loud rock and roll music at the highest possible volume, just as they have nearly every weekend since they arrived. At first their booming serenade seemed defiant and necessary. They are young and can't go out and party in one of the party capitals of the world.

I imagine that they'd decided to come to Miami at a time when our governor was still bragging that, in spite of festivals and open bars and beaches, our infection and death rates were minimal. At that time, people with license plates from New York—the previous epicenter— were being stopped by state troopers at the Florida state line as though they were smugglers of the virus or its possible cures. My young neighbors might have been among those fleeing the virus elsewhere, only to find that it had followed them, at an accelerated pace, here. The pandemic has further eliminated that ritual of even thinking of walking to a new neighbor's door and introducing yourself, so we will never know.

As our new neighbors' loud music thumped throughout the whole block, their din the aural equivalent of strobe lights, my mother-in-law and I walked to our front gate and tried to scold them from a distance with our stares.

"Why would they not silence that music for this one day?" my mother-in-law said. "A neighbor's pain is the same as your own. They should be mourning, too."

Standing there, I realize that they could also be mourning. This might just be their way of doing it.

A few hours later, in the middle of the night, yet another ambulance siren startles me awake. In my groggy state, I beseech it to keep going. *Let us have no need for you to ever stop here again.* I walk to my bedroom window and watch the ambulance turn and stop a few blocks farther down. Another neighbor, another friend, another life, another dream.

—JULY 31, 2020

Why the Rebellion Had to Begin Here

Su Hwang

Like so many of us, after two months of quarantine, I often wake up not knowing what day it is.

Memorial Day weekend came and went unceremoniously, I thought, until disturbing headlines peppered my news feed the next morning: the Minneapolis police had killed another Black man. At the intersection of Cup Foods and a Speedway gas station, a mile or so up on Chicago Avenue where I currently live, George Floyd's life was extinguished over a contested twenty-dollar bill. Twenty fucking dollars. And like many, I did not have to watch the viral video to know what went down by the bus stop that Monday evening. Sadly, a lot of us in the Twin Cities recognize this script all too well after the deaths of Jamar Clark, Philando Castile, and countless others without hashtags. The screenshot of Derek Chauvin's knee on George Floyd's neck as he lay handcuffed on hot asphalt was all I needed to see to grasp that this was another egregious, violent, racist act perpetrated by the MPD.

And yet the tenor this time was different: this white cop's smug mug, his hands shoved in his pockets as if he didn't have a care in the world, the sheer audacity of his hate. It didn't matter it was still light out. It didn't matter he was being videotaped. It didn't matter there were bystanders, many of them begging for him to stop, to show a little mercy. It didn't matter there was a global pandemic. It didn't matter that George Floyd called out for his late mother. To Chauvin and the other three officers, a Black life didn't matter enough, which in effect made their own lives not matter, because they were willing to risk it all. Nothing mattered because they believed they were going to get away with murder.

I'm not a native Minnesotan, but South Minneapolis has been my home for the last seven years. By most standards, I'm still a relative outsider, a transplant, so I must acknowledge that I am hardly the definitive voice on all that is happening here—just one in a kaleidoscope of perspectives.

Having grown up in New York, then spending much of my adult life seesawing from there to San Francisco and Oakland, I was an insufferable bicoastal snob when I first arrived in the Twin Cities. I had packed what little I owned into my jalopy and moved to the Midwest in the fall of 2013 to attend the MFA program at the University of Minnesota. Back then, I complained a lot about seemingly endless winter months, shoveling so much snow, feeling landlocked, Minnesota Nice. As an Asian American woman, I had trepidations about living in a flyover state because race is a constant companion I travel with, as it is for so many of us, and I really had no idea what to expect in the Land of 10,000 Lakes. It was no secret that Minnesota is a super white place, and I vowed to return to California after graduate school. But then the socioeconomics of the Bay Area became untenable for a forty-something poet like me, and perhaps more surprisingly, I found community here. For the first time in my wayward life, I began setting down roots.

Stunning sight on the sixth day of protests: a sea of people from all races and walks of life flooding both sides of the I-35W bridge on a sun-drenched afternoon (incidentally, the same bridge that collapsed into the Mississippi River in 2007). Momentum grew as the crowd swelled into the thousands when suddenly from the bottom of my computer screen, a tanker truck barreled down the roadway, cleaving the crowd in half like a broken zipper. It was nothing short of a miracle that no one was seriously hurt. The truck driver, pulled out of his vehicle and beaten by a handful of protesters (and magnanimously protected by other protesters), was placed in custody, then later released. I had immediate flashbacks of the 1992 Los Angeles riots, having watched a similar scene unfold on television as a teenager, and it was hard to ignore the eerie echoes.

Almost thirty years ago, four white LAPD officers were acquitted of brutally beating Rodney King. The horrific scene was captured on video and aired around the world long before iPhones and social media. I watched live broadcasts of widespread protests, violence, fires, and civil unrest mostly in and around Koreatown, where dozens died and thousands were injured or arrested. What many may not realize is that a year before, a Korean store owner shot and killed a Black ninth grader named Latasha Harlins, whom she suspected of shoplifting, and was only sentenced to probation and community service. This case was the exclamation point in a long chain of vitriolic, often deadly volleys between Korean merchants and those within the Black communities that they served. Cultural biases and language barriers as well as stark economic disparities fueled distrust and blame from both sides, but these issues did not crop up in a vacuum or manifest out of thin air.

Now retired and living in Southern California, at the time of the riots my Korean immigrant parents used to own a cramped corner store in the Queensbridge projects in the shadows of the Manhattan skyline. They sold pagers, batteries, baseball caps, T-shirts, handbags, and toys, among other knickknacks. When I helped out during summer breaks, I was tasked with copying keys on the old screeching machine and getting lunch next door from the Chinese takeout place with thick bulletproof glass coated in grease.

Much of my debut poetry collection, *Bodega,* was inspired by this place and period; and there, the realities of life for Black Americans came into very clear focus for me. White cops patrolled the area around the clock, but they never made anyone feel safe. They were uniformed bullies on the prowl, and it was abundantly clear they only cared about protecting and serving whiteness. Sirens were a constant fixture, as were the undercurrents of deprivation, desperation, fear, and grief brought on by centuries of systemic racism and abject poverty.

My family experienced discrimination and prejudice, yes, and dished it back, yes, but nowhere on the scale that the police and other white monoliths have and continue to inflict on Black communities all across the United States. And in our attempt at white adjacency to achieve the myth of the "model minority," however subconsciously or explicitly, my family was complicit in anti-Blackness, too. White supremacy, whether internalized or not, pervades every interaction within marginalized communities in this way, pitting one ethnic group against another so we can in essence cancel each other out.

It was not always an us-versus-them situation by any means, but then again, white supremacy does not allow for nuance. What wasn't being told on the nightly news was that my parents had regular customers they knew by name, their preferred brands of this or that, and their individual stories. In return, they were affectionately called Suzy and Mister H. by many members of the community. They shared jokes and good tidings, mostly through hand gestures, because my parents barely spoke English. I witnessed countless acts of kindness and mutual respect from both sides of the counter, human to human. And by virtue of our corner store having high elevated counters and windows chock-full of merchandise, my parents offered sanctuary to many young men selling the occasional dime bag or whatever else in the name of commerce. Even in this fraught urban food chain of haves and have-nots, there was also a kind of intimacy—an unspoken camaraderie in doing our best to survive and thrive. When many Korean-owned businesses in Los Angeles burned to the ground, my parents' store on the other side of the country remained unscathed, for our version of protection went both ways.

Seven years after the L.A. riots, a twenty-three-year-old Guinean immigrant named Amadou Diallo was killed in a hail of forty-one bullets in front of his apartment building in the Bronx. Four plainclothes NYPD officers were later acquitted of executing an innocent man walking home from dinner because he vaguely fit the description of a suspect. What officials claimed was a gun was in fact Diallo's wallet.

I'm a late bloomer to poetry, so landing in Minnesota has been a blessing in a multitude of ways. Minneapolis is a world-class literary hub, the arts funding here is the best in the country bar none, and as far as I can tell, you can't throw a rock without gently tapping a brilliant and inspiring BIPOC/LGBTQIA/white-ally writer, artist, musician, dancer, elder, educator, arts administrator, filmmaker, scholar, curator, grassroots activist, healer, hospitality worker, civil servant, social justice warrior, or sometimes a combination of these—many of whom I call my friends, mentors, and colleagues. There are strong, multigenerational Somali and Hmong refugee communities, as well as the highest concentration of Korean adoptees in the country. Minneapolis and St. Paul politics tend to err on the progressive side compared to other major U.S. cities, but like every state in this country, Minnesota has a very dark, sinister side.

First and foremost, we occupy stolen Dakota and Ojibwe land, and the largest mass execution in U.S. history occurred in 1862 when thirty-eight Dakota men were publicly hanged in Mankato, Minnesota. On June 15, 1920, exactly a hundred years ago in Duluth, three Black men, named Elias Clayton, Elmer Jackson, and Isaac McGhie, who were wrongfully accused of rape, were taken from jail and lynched by a white mob of thousands. Since then, government officials and shady developers have sanctioned the destruction of predominantly ethnic neighborhoods for white capitalistic agendas, reinforcing a passive-aggressive culture of exclusion and double standards. Not to mention the disturbing history of racist deed covenants that prohibited people of color from buying homes or owning land. Fast-forward to the present: Minnesota ranks second in the nation for worst median income and homeownership gaps between white and Black residents, and is forty-fifth out of all the states when it comes to racial integration—making it one of the most segregated places in the entire country. The MPD continues to kill Black Minnesotans at an alarming rate and with total impunity because of unapologetic racists and Trump enthu-

siasts at the top like Bob Kroll, president of the police union, and
Hennepin County attorney Mike Freeman. Don't even get me started
on incarceration rates for people of color in Minnesota.

Many white Minnesotans are married to this squeaky-clean image
of bike-friendly paths, the home of Prince, pristine parks, Swedish
meatballs, cheese curds and hotdish, and pontoons on shimmering
cabin-dotted lakes befitting those "The Best of" lists that get published
every year, but the reality is far from these sanitized archetypes. High
quality of life in this country has always been colonial and conditional.
Finally, the fragile white veneer of Minnesota Nice has been hammered
into a million pieces with the world as witness because this nebulous
sense of fake politeness and notions of not wanting to rock the boat are
just as detrimental as overt hostilities against people of color. If Minnesota were a person, I'd imagine the Amy Coopers of the world would
fit the bill, and Chauvin's knee is the final line in the sand—either you
are on the right side of history or you will be left behind.

In light of all these deep-seated issues, there seems to be a shift
in energies. People are finally waking up, some forcibly so; it's hard to
look away when there's an enormous conflagration on your street, the
literal burning down of centuries of apathy, willful ignorance, hoarded
privilege, and misplaced entitlement. Days after George Floyd's murder, the University of Minnesota, the Minnesota public school system,
and the Minneapolis Park and Recreation Board have announced that
they've cut ties with the Minneapolis Police Department. In addi-
tion, the state of Minnesota has filed a civil rights lawsuit against the
MPD, and the Minneapolis City Council made a pledge to a massive
crowd at Powderhorn Park that they will begin taking concrete steps
to disband the police, thanks to grassroots organizations like MPD150,
Black Visions Collective, and Reclaim the Block.

Meanwhile, thousands of citizens continue to fill the streets to protest, mourn, clean, paint murals, and dream of a better future. Even at the height of violence and raging fires, the majority of which were intentionally set by white supremacists, huge, diverse throngs spontaneously gathered at numerous sites with brooms and buckets to assist in the aftermath, day after day after day. Bleary-eyed, over-caffeinated bands of neighbors and community leaders continue to come together to offer mutual aid, mobilize supply drop-offs, and organize neighborhood patrols. In the embers, something truly beautiful seems to be coming to life.

Let's be very clear: Minneapolis and St. Paul, so-called bastions of white liberalism, are under attack. We are in the crosshairs of white nationalist maniacs looking to fan hate and fear, but what they don't realize is that legions of lovers and warriors have been laying the groundwork toward resistance and true equity for generations. From the outside looking in, the depth and breadth of these sweeping changes may seem radical in their swiftness, but they are the result of decades of community-based activism by BIPOC individuals, collectives, and organizations working tirelessly to dismantle white supremacy in Minnesota for a very long time. Also, youth movements including nonprofit media collectives like Unicorn Riot have been instrumental in disseminating the truth. So as much as we ache for the destruction of cultural landmarks and essential businesses in our backyards—the traumatic toll yet to be fully processed—groups of visionary artists, civil servants, activists, healers, and builders are already on the scene. They've been here all along.

Many are calling this an "inflection point" in American history, myself included, but the more I think about it, the less this sentiment holds water. Inflection implies singularity, of one musculature or a single stream of consciousness, when there have been multiple inflections since the looting of this land from Native Americans to the founding of the country on the backs of Black lives. I believe we are at a point of convergence. Convergence denotes multiplicity and cumulativeness—a cacophony of voices and perspectives. In this semantic distinction, we honor the lingering ghosts of all our ancestors. We can no longer afford to pivot from one point to another and call it progress or justice; the weight of our collective histories can no longer support these blatant disparities between what is deemed progress and justice versus the lived realities of marginalized peoples. What we're seeing and experiencing is a cavalcade of centuries of protest, of deaths and rebirths, the final heave for human decency for all.

And yet we still live in the throes of a global pandemic, and the current backlash against people who look like me, an Asian American woman, clearly demonstrates that people of color are always at risk from the insidious exclusion of the white supremacist gaze. K-pop fans crashing hate-filled hashtags and calls by Asian American organizations and individuals to support Black Lives Matter bring me solace—making amends for the many years we participated in anti-Blackness—but there is so much more work to do. White supremacy and white complacency can't hide anymore. There is no longer the cloak of ignorance to reason away truth. Cameras are rolling. Every marginalized human is exhausted and fucking pissed. The global pandemic has disproportionately affected Black and brown communities, but this virus has proven to be the great equalizer in many respects, showing 99 percent of us that we are not immune from the evils of capitalism or the ineptitude of those who are supposed to protect and serve the people.

George Floyd was a transplant like me; I'll be forty-six years old later this year. George was known as Perry or Big Floyd by his loved ones; some dear friends call me Su Bear. Like me, he was a Libra with a Taurus moon, and made his way from Houston for better opportunities and started to set down some roots in Minnesota. He was working two jobs while building his community when the pandemic hit. He worked security at a restaurant. I've worked in hospitality for over a decade. We could have been coworkers, perhaps even friends. George Floyd was murdered a mile up from where I live on Chicago Avenue, at the intersection I drive past every damn day. And just like any other Minnesotan, George Floyd had the right to complain about the weather and bad drivers who can't merge for shit, eat cheese curds dipped in chocolate at the Minnesota State Fair, get photographed holding a humongous fish.

There's a lot more to say, but my thoughts are in shards. My heart is broken for my city, for George Floyd's family, for Breonna Taylor's family, for Tony McDade's family, for Ahmaud Arbery's family, and for the many other lives lost, but I also believe in goodness and the goodness of the people I know and love. So, I will end this rambling missive with the prophetic words of an incredible writer, artist, goddess and friend, Junauda Petrus-Nasah. In her recent contribution to the *Minneapolis Star Tribune* feature with two other amazing souls, Michael Kleber-Diggs and Shannon Gibney, Petrus-Nasah writes:

> Overnight, our city became a phoenix, glowing and rebirthing something unstoppable and irresistible for the world. On Dakota land, in the midst of a global pandemic, the wounds of white supremacy, oppression, police violence, erasure and

parasitic capitalism caught flame. And amid the fire, grief, confusion and property loss, there was a transformation crystallizing.

Black Lives Matter.

—JUNE 8, 2020

On the Complex Flavors
of Black Joy

Michael Kleber-Diggs

> Ay, just cashed the check
> And I'm 'bout to blow it all on chocolate
> —Big Boi, "Chocolate" (feat. Troze)

During the disquieting days and violent nights of early June 2020, Big Boi saved my life.

I work from home these days. My house is ten miles or about fifteen minutes northeast of where police killed George Floyd on Memorial Day, two miles southeast of where police killed Philando Castile in 2016.

I'm a middle-aged dad with a pandemic mini-'fro and a plague beard, both of which grow grayer by the day. My wife and I have a daughter who came home early from her second semester at college. She arrived right after I started working from home. We have two cats, Curly and Mocha, and two miniature goldendoodles, Ziggy and Jasper. The dogs demand breaks often, more often than I'd like, so several times a day we walk our neighborhood in St. Paul. The skies are clear now. The sounds of sirens are rare here again. The curfew was lifted, and the phased opening makes the coronavirus seem illusory at times. As Minnesota's shelter-in-place order was eased and ended, vehicle traffic increased. As the more obvious aspects of the uprising tapered off, white nationalists in menacing trucks and cars quit zooming around town without license plates and stopped causing mayhem every night. Reports about Proud Boys and Boogaloo Bois have been replaced by amplified stories of more common summer violence.

When I survey the sky around me, I don't see towers of smoke. I see something resembling the way things were. I wonder what the country would be like if George Floyd hadn't been killed or if we had sheltered in place a little longer. But he was, and we didn't.

In the immediate aftermath of George Floyd's murder—when we were still shocked by his slow assassination, when we were stunned to see eight minutes and forty-six seconds of inhumanity dispatched with nonchalance—friends checked on me to ask how I was doing. Some check-ins were friends who already know the multiple ways state murders affect Black survivors, the ways in which sadness, anger, disappointment, frustration, worry, fear, past trauma, and fatigue affect our bodies and spirits. Other check-ins were friends becoming more aware of racism and its daily wage. Some wanted to know my family was safe from far-right instigators, from agitators and accelerationists.

Sometimes I spoke the general truth: "I feel all the feels all the time, in various ways and amounts," I said. Sometimes I offered the kindest lie: "I'm fine." And in many ways, I was. Being Black in an anti-Black country is like being handed a stone at birth, an object you have to carry and can never throw. It's manageable but wearying; it gets heavier the longer you hold it. You know you can't put it down, so you try to get used to it. From time to time, when people notice the stone, when they remember your burden, when it occurs to them that hauling a stone all the time might weigh a person down, when they recognize how unfair it is, you can almost feel seen or validated.

I didn't say what I wanted to say; I held back the full truth.

Often, when I do this, I wonder if I can love my white friends without being candid with them. I wonder if they can love me if I hold them at a distance, if race and racism function as a veneer, a layer between us obscuring any substance underneath. When I don't answer fully, am I not saying I don't trust you to do anything about it?

What I wanted to say and didn't say was this: "I'm fine today; the hard part will begin soon. The hard part for me starts when things get comfortable for you again. The hard part begins the day you return to your normal routines."

I don't remember the first time I was called nigger. I know it was on a playground at an elementary school in Kansas City, Kansas. I know it was before I turned eight years old. I know I'd already been taught to say, "I ain't no nigger, I'm a negro. When I become a nigger, I'll let you know." I know I didn't understand what any of it really meant. The last time I was called a nigger was 1990. I was in college. Some men in a truck yelled it out as they drove by. No one else was around but me. I remember thinking they were idiots; I remember walking around on high alert for several days.

The last time I saw someone else called a nigger was this morning, in a video on Twitter, some white man at a grocery store mad about a sandwich error or a mask mandate or both. The man wanted to get back at the essential worker making his lunch. He paused for several seconds before he said it. I couldn't tell if he was fighting a base impulse or considering what might happen if he spoke from his heart.

Modern racism is usually subtle; it's often expressed through a violent politeness. I often see it in confined expectations. You're not expected to be in this classroom; you are expected to be in a particular negative circumstance, like an underperforming school or a school-to-prison pipeline or its designated destination. You're not expected to walk around in certain neighborhoods. Your ideas for how we might achieve racial equity and social justice or your ideas on how we might reimagine policing aren't expected to be thoughtful. They are expected to result only from anger—a brick thrown through the window of a pawnshop—not from scholarship or context, not from critical theory. Overt racism hasn't gone away, but it has lost favor, so covert forms have emerged to replace it. The courtesies that the majority extended George Floyd were strategic. They started to disintegrate the day he was buried.

June 9. Fifteen days after he was killed. Pro-police propaganda began in earnest. Today, Floyd's character assassination is well under way. While activists seek major reforms, the establishment hopes symbolic changes will be enough to allow a return to business as usual. Those who favor the status quo are saying so, but not directly, never directly. They're not articulating why; they're not saying the real reason why.

Fifteen days after George Floyd's death, a familiar hopelessness descended upon me. I returned to believing nothing would change. I felt reminded that most Americans don't want things to change. Not really. I was reminded some folks need things not to change, or feel they do. Breonna Taylor was murdered in her sleep. Rayshard Brooks was shot in the back—twice. Elijah McClain's murder was almost covered up by darkness; Ahmaud Arbery's murder was almost covered up in bright daylight. I drove by a Thin Blue Line flag as I ran a few errands. The head of the Minneapolis Police Union appeared on national television to talk about George Floyd's murder and stand up for his officers. He cautioned against a rush to judgment. Eight minutes and forty-six seconds. As I walked Ziggy and Jasper around the neighborhood, many passersby viewed us with concern. The overeager smiles of late May and early June—smiles communicating concern for my well-being, smiles that said you are welcome here—succumbed to a familiar consternation, suspicious eyes, some friendliness, but also long wary looks from people I've lived among more than ten years now. My steps grew leaden and sad. You see, I am carrying this stone.

This was where Big Boi came in, with his song "Chocolate" (feat. Troze). For three weeks, maybe more, "Chocolate" was my bop. My theme song. I had "Chocolate" in heavy rotation. I listened to it whenever we went outside; I listened to it about six times a day. When it was on, I floated.

The song begins with Big Boi's sweet tooth bothering him. He's craving chocolate. He addresses an unknown Black woman and asks her to back it up, which I received as a reference to the 1999 hit "Back That Azz Up" by Juvenile, featuring Mannie Fresh and Lil Wayne. Later in that same verse, Big Boi raps about standing up and makes a reference to Standing Rock.

"Chocolate" is a club song, set to a club beat. It's about club culture. It's sex positive. It's pro-joy. It pulses like a youthful heart, vibrant and alive. It begins with driving beats and a call and response that is maintained throughout. Early on, there are a crescendo and a decrescendo of a cymbal sound. Hit the hi-hat seven times. In the background, there is an occasional whoop or whoot; they echo a bit and return in intervals. The bass seems like it's singing *we are choc-late* and *we're choc-o-late*. The wood block sounds like the pitter-patter of rain. Hit the hi-hat eight times. Rest. Hit the hi-hat six times (wanting seven).

I left my house, fresh from a cleansing cry (social media ignorance, the TV news, a word from a friend, some particular worry, or a general malaise), and, within seconds of hitting play, found myself pulled toward a dance floor that doesn't exist. I started to shimmy and shake on the sidewalk, on my neighbors' lawns, in the park one block north of my house, all while Ziggy and Jasper and goodness knows who else watched me quizzically.

I'm shy in ways and shy about my body. I don't have much rhythm and overuse the same four dance moves. Where I live, my skin, bittersweet like 70 percent chocolate, is conspicuous on good days but felt notorious then, still does. I danced anyway. I felt like I was supposed to show sadness or mourning, and I was sad. I do mourn. I danced anyway. It felt revolutionary, so I won't let it feel wrong.

The music would hit just right, and I'd stop. I'd throw my head back. I'd roll my arm like I was learning how to hit a speed bag, slow like that. I swayed left and right. Sometimes I thought about second-wave feminism. I thought about how the personal is political, how the lived experiences of people suffering within inhumane systems are inherently political, can spark an uprising. Then both arms, my hips, my feet, their pattern no longer a forward gait, more like a crip walk, or what a crip walk would have looked like if I knew how to crip walk.

Sometimes I thought about Paul Laurence Dunbar's "We Wear the Mask":

> *We smile, but, O great Christ, our cries*
> *To thee from tortured souls arise.*

> *We sing, but oh the clay is vile*
> *Beneath our feet, and long the mile . . .*

and how Maya Angelou's adaptation in "The Mask" honors Dunbar:

> *My life has been one great big joke!*
> *A dance that's walked a song that's spoke.*
> *I laugh so hard HA! HA! I almos' choke*

So, you see, my dance was a knowing dance. My dance was my truth, and my dance was my lie. I already knew that where I live—the tree-lined streets, the middle-class people in houses that are mostly well maintained, the park one block away, the lake, the golf course, the few other Black families anywhere nearby—where I live my dance can never be just a dance. Not during a summer of race hate and rising up.

My dance was also a mask. In the white gaze, it will always either confirm or disrupt some expectation. My dance was conspicuous and aware it was observed, aware of context. My dance was derived from the art of survival—spirituals and chain gangs, poems and the wobble. My dance reminded me I'm here. It gave me strength to go the length. My dance was resilient and defiant, righteous and right, powered by joy, powered by Big Boi, who asked if I had ever found myself between a rock and a dark place or if I've ever gone to sleep just to claim a chance to dream.

"Chocolate" came out in 2017. I heard it for the first time in early June 2020, while watching a Seth Rogen and Charlize Theron movie. It's easy to explain how I missed the song's ascendancy and zenith; I listen to a lot of public radio and books on tape. Music is a big part of my life, but my daughter is often embarrassed by my tendency to obsess over songs two or more years after their moment.

I was deep into the music video for "Chocolate," too. It begins, we're told, at 8:37 p.m. in Atlanta, Georgia, with Big Boi playfully disguised as a driver from a ride-sharing app. He's behind the wheel of a high-end, late-model sedan and picking up three Black women who are dressed provocatively, as one would for a night at a voluptuary club in a libertine city. When asked, the women say they're going to shoot a music video for Big Boi. Then begins a series of orgasmic jump cuts featuring rap video bodies in rap video costumes doing rap video calisthenics—twerks, drops, displays of limberness—often with kaleidoscopic swirls and distortions. The jewelry in the video is spectacular and so is the chocolate. There are chocolate-covered bananas. There is liquid chocolate—dark and white—sometimes thrown against near-nude bodies and sometimes bouncing up as if on a subwoofer. There are painted bodies and hands slapping chocolate-covered asses. Also, there's a chocolate-colored pug that mouths "chocolate" and a few lines from the song. Then, midway through, a vivid yellow bicycle makes a confusing cameo. At one point, a woman in white undergarments and white thigh-high boots dances as Big Boi explains that the goal of the evening isn't to throw rice as one would at a wedding, it's to throw moves as one would in the bedroom.

(Translation: Bridal attire aside, I don't want to marry you. I just want to have sex with you.)

The phrase ends with Big Boi expressing an enduring goal beyond the more immediate one: "making music for people that be feeling me," he says.

In the kitchen, listening to "Chocolate," my daughter asked if the song is about what she thought it was about. I said yes kinda quickly—

too quickly. After I answered, a thought crossed my mind: If it's a club song and only a club song, how does it mean so much to me? Why?

I listened again. I felt joy within a broader sorrow. I floated. I was light. I stopped. I threw my head back. I closed my eyes in ecstasy, like I was tasting for the first time a dessert many people have loved for years. Sometimes I said, "I deserve pleasure." I said it out loud. Whenever I listened to "Chocolate," I felt connected to something older and vaster than the moment or me. I decided that:

> *Ay, just cashed the check*
> *And I'm 'bout to blow it all on chocolate*

is a utopian manifesto on Black separatism. It's about the pleasure of payday and the value of spending money in our community. It's about Black folks supporting each other. Many of the businesses that burned down in Minneapolis and St. Paul and cities all over America were Black-owned or owned by people of color. The overwhelming majority of the fires weren't started by us, although a few were. We'll need to rebuild, like our parents did and their parents did and theirs and theirs.

But it's payday, and I have coins for the cause now. In that moment, Big Boi goes on to say he's going to make his money stretch, and I feel committed to making my dollars go as far as they can in our community, too.

I decided when Big Boi raps about backing it up, he's imploring Black people to follow through on our commitment to meaningful change.

And yes, in America, in Minnesota, in St. Paul, on the street where

I live, I have found myself stuck in between a rock and a dark place. I have felt like all of my options are bad here. I have realized I don't feel comfortable anywhere. And I have slept for a dream and shuffled for one and bobbed my head to one, all knowingly.

When Big Boi mentions standing up and Standing Rock, I decided it was because we're still here.

In spite of everything, we're still on our feet. And yeah, "standing rock" is doing a lot of work. I saw its connection to sexual readiness, but at first, for me, it connected the Black experience with injustice to Indigenous people's experience with injustice, to a broader injustice. It made the song intersectional. In early listening, before I got the innuendo, the reference to Standing Rock seemed like a quick aside, like bringing politics to the party. It made me think even our play is serious. We're bringing sorrow to our joy now; we're multitasking emotionally, like always, because we don't have a choice.

More than anything, one line in "Chocolate" stood out for me. It's a line connected to a life preserver that arrived when I felt I couldn't tread water much longer, when I was tired and felt alone, like there was no safe harbor in sight. It wasn't that I wanted to let go and sink. It was that it was hard to keep my head above water and carry my stone at the same time. I wanted a place to rest. Okay? I wanted to float, just for a little while. There's the line that says this song is just for you, Michael. All my songs are for you and for us—people born into it and people who opt in. The line always arrived right on time. Whenever Big Boi said:

> *Making music for the people that be feeling me . . .*

my pulse rate elevated. My heart beat hard—vibrant and alive. We are vibrant and alive. See? He said:

Making music for the people that be feeling me . . .

and I had the same thought every time: "Chocolate" is a club song, and I am in the club.

"Chocolate" is pro-joy, even though our club is bittersweet. We dance anyway.

"We deserve pleasure." I say it out loud.

I can bring the club wherever I go. We can spark a revolution just by walking down the street.

The club is a place where I belong.

I'm never alone, I realized. The club is with me wherever I go.

—JULY 2020

Letter from the Fault Lines of Midwestern Racism

Amaud Jamaul Johnson

Dear Wisconsin—

Dear swing state: Dear battleground and infinite presidential visit: Dear broken-heartland: Dear flyover: Dear Packer fan and Brewer fan and anti-labor leader: Dear Act 10: Dear apple orchard and cranberry bog: Dear Tammy and Ron: Dear Cheesehead: Dear Butter Burger: Dear diabetes and high cholesterol and Ironman: Dear Supermax and overcrowded county lockup: Dear red tape and yellow tape, supper club and polka mixtape: Dear bottle glass and chalk silhouette: Dear cell phone footage: Dear seventh bullet in my back: Dear Tony Robinson and now dearest Kyla: Dear Governor Evers, Lieutenant Governor and Brother Mandela, and former Governor comb-over: Dear Jacob Blake: Dear ghost of the dead Koch brother: Dear fried cheese curd and frozen custard: Dear Ho-Chunk Gaming: Dear Epic Systems and Trek Bicycle and outside agitator: Dear "Berkeley of the Midwest": Dear Harley-Davidson and Bud Selig: Dear polar vortex and Canada Goose: Dear Ed Gein and Jeffrey Dahmer: Dear Frank Lloyd Wright and death at Taliesin: Dear grandchild of a hidden war criminal: Dear Brat Fest: Dear "I don't see race": Dear legacy of Joseph McCarthy: Dear Brett Favre and Aaron Rodgers and Russell Wilson and Colin Kaepernick: Dear dairy farmer and *That '70s Show*: Dear "not my tax dollars": Dear coasties: Dear "I can't understand why they can't get over it": Dear gerrymandered majority: Dear Don't Tread on Me: Dear OshKosh B'gosh and You Betcha: Dear Fuck 'Em Bucky, "Jump Around," and "Sweet Caroline": Dear State Supreme Court: Dear frat house and functional alcoholic: Dear public urination: Dear Rust Belt and buckle: Dear achievement gap and infant mortality: Dear "you must be from Chicago" or "another country": Dear conspiracy theory and living off the grid: Dear Pewaukee and Waukesha and Oconomowoc: Dear preschool-to-prison pipeline: Dear home brew and Brandy Old Fashioned: Dear fish boil and "Cape Cod of the Midwest": Dear Miller High Life and lake house: Dear walleye and kayak: Dear why I'll never hunt or ice fish: Dear Chancellor Becky and Robin Vos: Dear statistically worse than Mississippi (sorry, Mississippi): Dear popular vote versus electoral college: Dear Driftless: Dear Buck: Dear Greek Freak and Sterling Brown: Dear passive-aggressiveness and aggressiveness: Dear Richie and Potsie and Ralph Malph, and Mr. and Mrs. Cunningham, and *Joanie Loves Chachi*, and *Laverne & Shirley*, Lenny and Squiggy: Dear Mr. Arthur Fonzarelli:

I've lived in Milwaukee for two decades, and despite my best efforts, I'm still a stranger. Growing up in Compton, I loved *Happy Days*, which was based here. If you would have asked me, I couldn't have pointed out Wisconsin on a map. This didn't matter because the show became an imagined place where the homes in every neighborhood were Arts and Crafts or split-level black and white American Colonials. The teenagers ate hamburgers and drank malts every afternoon, wearing two-tone cardigan letterman sweaters or poodle skirts. They didn't have sex, but there was necking and sometimes heavy petting at the drive-in or at Picnic Point. The only trouble in this world was eating those Salisbury steak TV dinners or the stress behind cramming for the next big exam. Fonzie, an unmarried itinerant motorcycle mechanic, renting a room above the Cunninghams' garage, offered this world its sole point of tension. He is supposed to represent an "outside element," and now that I think about it, I can't remember how he made money. We are led to imagine that he's a reformed member of some bike gang, an outcast from the film *Easy Rider*. The Cunningham children are so innocent, even as teenagers, and Fonzie hovers around them as an educator of and a protector from "street life."

Happy Days was a guilty pleasure. It trafficked in a nostalgia that didn't have any connection to my life in Compton, particularly in the late seventies and early eighties. Its world was uncomplicated. Diversity on the show was about personality, about the assumptions made about blondes, brunettes, and redheads. I didn't think of this as a segregated world. Sure, Compton was segregated, but segregation seemed both a part of our distant past and our everyday existence.

Richie was an all-American boy. He was a "good person," and because he was the protagonist of the sitcom, we saw the world through his eyes. We laughed with him and hesitated when he found himself in uncomfortable situations or when he felt the need to be protective of his little sister, Joanie. Richie had red hair and freckles. I think we were supposed to pity him because these traits didn't make him conventionally handsome. We hoped that his "good character" would shine through and everyone around him would love him, would see him as a natural leader. Maybe he'd grow up to become the owner of a small business or perhaps our next president.

Back then, some of my cousins criticized me for being so obsessed with the show. As a Black suburb of Los Angeles, Compton shouldn't be classified as an "inner city." I felt like we were living on an island. We had our own rules, our own dress codes, our unique sound. Deep segregation allows one space for strange fantasies. I enjoyed a perverse form of freedom. No one would have called me white or thought I wanted to be white for enjoying these shows. At the time, I don't know if it occurred to me that *Happy Days* was set in the midfifties and early sixties, the heart of the civil rights era. What did I know about life in Middle America? The Cunninghams lived in a suburb; we lived in a suburb, a bubble. And what did I know about Freud or Jung or Deleuze or Fanon? *Happy Days* was just popular.

We also all loved *The Dukes of Hazzard,* and one Christmas somebody bought me a model car of the General Lee. (The nostalgia connected to that toy, and the time I spent "whistling Dixie" in our backyard as a child are as complicated as the eroticism attached to Daisy Duke.) We had other options that attempted to portray inner-city Black life. We had *Good Times,* of course; *The Jeffersons, Sanford and Son,* and *What's Happening!!,* a show about a Black family in Watts, the community that neighbored Compton, where my mother was born. Those shows were problematic in many ways, but I can't overstate the importance of representations of race in popular media.

I consumed obscene amounts of television when I was young. I wasn't much of a reader, so my early imaginary life was drawn through screens. This was like a slow drum roll leading up to the significance of

The Cosby Show. Learning to let go of my love of *The Cosby Show* still feels like an open wound. But before the Cosbys, I had the Cunninghams. Their life seemed perfect. Who wouldn't love banana splits with extra cherries, roller skates, hula parties, and Perry Como?

I remember an episode of *Happy Days* entitled "Fonzie's New Friend," when Richie forms a band with Potsie and Ralph, and they are planning to perform at a Hawaiian-themed party in the Cunninghams' basement. Richie realizes that they need a drummer, and Fonzie recommends one of his good friends, Sticks. The scene opens at Arnold's, the after-school hangout burger joint. Richie wants to invite more girls to his party. He's interested in a particular young woman, whom he refers to as "dollface." She rebuffs Richie's advances because her girlfriend wouldn't have a date. Richie, while waiting for Fonzie's "new friend" to arrive, suggests that Sticks would make a great blind date. Sticks walks in. Yes, he's Black, which triggers the first laugh track. The girls see him before Richie, and there's a look of disgust and outrage on their faces. Richie glances back at Sticks and at first dismisses him as if he's swatting a fly from his shoulder; then Sticks introduces himself. This is the cue for another big laugh. The girls accuse Richie of being cruel and storm off. Within a three-minute scene we get jokes about basketball, fried chicken, watermelon, and rhythm. Richie is clearly confused and befuddled, which provides a window for Fonzie's moral assistance.

Ironically, Sticks foreshadowed my adult life. I moved to Madison, Wisconsin, in the fall of 2000. My wife was starting a teaching position, and I was still trying to "find myself" as a writer. *Money* magazine had recently named Madison the number one place to live in the United States, so it seemed to us like a great place to land. After leaving Compton for college, I crisscrossed the country, living in D.C., New

York, Atlanta, and Oakland. The Midwest was the frontier. I've lived in deeply segregated communities my whole life, but I rarely experienced being the only Black person in a room. For me, the opposite was true: the white world was elsewhere, in other neighborhoods or on TV.

Wisconsin is a lovely state. We actually live in our dream home, a lovely Colonial. I bike and hike; I ice-skate and cross-country ski; I've become an amateur sommelier of craft beer. But I'm also a kind of mascot, a pet Negro, that one Black body in the coffee shop or at the private pool; I've become everyone's one Black friend, the anchor of every "one drop" diversity initiative, everything short of a drummer. Maybe a year ago, I was out alone having lunch, and a woman approached me. She placed her hand on my shoulder and said, "I'm so glad you're here." I felt like Sticks walking into Arnold's. I'm concerned that I exist to improve the political capital of my neighbors. Is the purpose of my life the cultural enrichment of a white community? Was that my grandmother's dream when I left for college?

Similar to Sticks, I smile when nothing's funny. I speak before I'm spoken to. I've mastered the early exit, a Black version of an Irish goodbye. And I learned from Malcolm X and my grandfathers to never sit with my back to a door, but that's not enough to keep me safe or protect my sons. My palms sweat and I can't remember the last time I had a good night's sleep. I've traded one form of segregation for another. But I'm an anomaly.

In Wisconsin, the domination of Black bodies has been so complete, white conservatives started feeding on white liberals. Like Iowa, Wisconsin is a sort of test kitchen, a political science laboratory, a cultural barometer for our nation. The term *heartland* is more than a metaphor. Poison the internal organs; then watch the eyes turn jaundiced; then wait for the extremities to change color: red to blue, blue to red, purple as a bruise. Anyone living here, navigating the political landscape of the Dairyland over the last few years, could see Donald Trump coming.

When I moved here, the local news was delightfully boring. Now I admit, as a child I fell asleep to sounds of sirens and helicopters, and I still miss the buzz of street traffic. Nothing used to happen here. Most nights, the lead news stories were about bake sales and canned food drives. (I write this without sarcasm.) If you are from Wisconsin and you are white, maybe *Happy Days* wasn't fiction. We bought a new house a few years ago, and none of the locks worked. Our real estate agent didn't understand why this was a serious problem. Almost every house in my old neighborhood was blanketed with bars.

Politically, Madison and Milwaukee are deep blue dots in an otherwise red state. But like Portland and Seattle, progressive communities in Wisconsin have blind spots regarding race. Midwesterners are classically passive-aggressive, so no one would dare say the things you might hear in rural Georgia or Alabama. People here take great pride in being pleasant, and any confrontation would compromise a true Wisconsinite's dignity. At first I found it strange that I didn't see people of color anywhere—not as bank tellers or as grocery clerks, not as postal workers or in construction. What added to my confusion, I noticed the public schools were very diverse.

I learned quickly that Madison is a heavily policed bubble with fragmented Black communities on the fringes of the city, struggling to survive. As it turns out, compared to Compton, the odds are greater that a Black child in Madison will drop out of school and end up incarcerated. Five years ago, during that horrible string of deaths, exposing the brutal vulgarity of police violence directed at Black bodies, when we learned the names Michael Brown, Jr., Freddie Gray, Jr., Walter Scott, Sean Bell, Sandra Bland, and Philando Castile, in Madison, on

March 6, 2015, a nineteen-year-old named Tony Terrell Robinson, Jr., was shot and killed by Officer Matt Kenny. Kenny was responding to a well-check call because Robinson suffered from a mental health condition. Kenny shot an unarmed teenager because he was afraid for his life. Now these stories are painfully pedestrian, but Robinson's death was a wake-up call for the city. Our bubble burst, and it was almost as if people here lost their innocence. Unfortunately, guilt is an unsustainable emotion, and Robinson's death intensified fault lines running across the state.

It's difficult not to think of the nostalgia shaping those *Happy Days* episodes as the evidence of a crime. The show debuted in 1974, the year Richard Nixon resigned, when the country was still reeling from Vietnam and the fallout from the riots after King's assassination. Black communities were entering a period of reconstruction. I don't think *Happy Days* is another *Gone with the Wind*, but this ran in the years hip-hop and punk were born. Given its timing, *Happy Days* was more pernicious than any bloodred MAGA cap.

At the conclusion of "Fonzie's New Friend," after Richie spends the bulk of the episode searching his spirit, trying to decide if Sticks joining the band is worth the risk of ostracism, we're left with an image of integrated musicians playing to an empty room. Over eleven seasons, Sticks was featured in three episodes. Ron Howard, who played Richie, would go on to have a long career as a film director, eventually winning two Academy Awards for *A Beautiful Mind* in 2001. John Bailey, Sticks, changed his name to Jack Baker and starred in a series of pornographic films in the mideighties. He died of bladder cancer at forty-seven.

—SEPTEMBER 22, 2020

I Cannot Stop: A Response to the Murder of George Floyd

Layli Long Soldier

For George Floyd, his family, and all who are deeply affected

Today, after two months of Covid-19 lockdown and four days after the murder of George Floyd, I'm flooded. Tossing in the waves. I have cried many times in the last few days over the injustice, and now I'm strung out. And I don't trust nobody. Except for my closest friends and relatives, I don't trust nobody. Except for the land, as I have said before, I don't trust nobody. Though you and I both know how the double negative works. "I do not trust nobody" unravels to mean I do trust some bodies. Yes, I do trust some bodies and I don't trust anyone either. This is a paradox: two seemingly opposing truths that exist within a single statement.

Under these conditions, I want to share a few things that I've been thinking about. Most of those things are memories.

O

First, I remembered something my daughter told me in the car one day, after I picked her up from school. As soon as she slid into the front seat, she said, "Mommy, we dissected an elk's eyeball in science class today." She was beaming.

"No way! Really?"

"Yes," she said, "and guess what I found out?"

I was feeling the excitement. "What?"

"Guess what was inside the pupil when we cut into it?"

"Oh my god, what?!"

"There was nothing."

O

My second memory is a collective memory, prompted by a text that Dr. Craig Howe shared with several Lakota artists, myself included, in preparation for an exhibit—Takuwe, which means *why* in Lakota—dedicated to the Wounded Knee Massacre. If you do not know about the Wounded Knee Massacre, I kindly recommend an online search to learn more. But what is important to know here is that it occurred on December 29, 1890. Dr. Howe organized a day-by-day report of accounts from our Lakota ancestors preceding and following the massacre. Mrs. Mosseau recounted what happened on December 28, the evening before our grandfathers and grandmothers were murdered:

They made up camp at Wounded Knee Creek about four o'clock in the afternoon with soldiers all around us. The soldiers brought Big Foot in an ambulance because he was sick. When we came to camp, the soldiers brought him from the ambulance and put him into an army tent. After we made camp, they gave us coffee, sugar, hardtack, and a small piece of breakfast bacon.

About midnight we wanted to get some water, but the soldiers refused to let us get it. After refusing to let us get water, the soldiers called all the women together and let them go by twos, a soldier with a gun going behind each two women. At this time Joe Horncloud was interpreter, but at daylight Philip Wells was interpreter. At this time [daylight] a herald cried out that the soldiers would take us to the agency and take good care of us. The soldiers marched round in single file round the hill and told us to break up the camp.

Another of our ancestors, Iron Hail (Wasu Maza), recalled:

Some time near evening we arrived at Wounded Knee. When we arrived, they gave us rations of sugar, coffee, crackers, and bacon. I myself distributed these rations to the people. We had supper. While we were doing this, the soldiers guarded round our camp. Then they put Hotchkiss guns where the cemetery is now. There were so many guns all around us I could hardly sleep at all that night. I was rather afraid and worried in my mind about those guns.

After the distribution of sugar, coffee, crackers, and bacon to Lakota prisoners, their evening supper, and a sleepless night, at daybreak the next morning on December 29, the massacre ensued. Sunrise was at 7:22 A.M. The high temperature that day was 66 degrees; the low was 30. Dr. Howe could not provide a number of texts about what happened that day because, as he explained, they were hard to read. But among those provided, Alice War Bonnet recounted the hours after sunset, in the aftermath:

> The soldiers started to get active and the noisy wagons were moving. The sun had set, and the guns seemed to get quiet. In the meantime, we moved to the north, and a child was asking for water. There were dead horses scattered about, and there were wounded crying out, but it was dark and we could see black objects here and there, but we did try to recognize the objects.

And finally, I share one last account from Mrs. Mosseau. This is what she remembered from December 30, the day after the massacre:

> In this place of many pines, west of Wounded Knee Creek, we stayed that night. I had one blanket and I was wearing several dresses. I had to tear up part of them to make bandages for my wounds. At least I had three dresses on and it was very cold when the storm came on.

I refer to this as a collective memory because, as a people, we remember who we are from our families, from this land, from stories within the community, and from our senses. Yes, from our senses, we remember what's stored within us already. Maybe, sometimes, I/we cannot put words to it, but we feel something. I might call it instinct. It's an old sensation that cannot be named, for which there is no textual record or language to help us understand. Yet it is there just below the skin and just like that. I feel it here today.

o

I might note that I am especially drawn to women's stories and accounts, perhaps because I am a woman and I make natural connections. For example, the following day after surviving the Wounded Knee Massacre, Mrs. Mosseau wore three dresses—this image has hooked me, years after reading her account. I think about being a woman in this world, in this country to be specific, and the lengths to which I have been stretched. Yet our grandmothers, they endured more. I know this so I keep going, sometimes only because I can. And I have learned that along the way—en route, when there is time—a dress can be ripped up to bandage.

o

Yet the older I get, as a woman, I feel unable to endure much. It's not like when I was younger, when I had more physical strength. I feel fragile and I berate myself, every now and then, for what I perceive as growing weakness. Even mentally and emotionally, I have less tolerance—only because I simply cannot tolerate. Like the sapling that bends and quickly bounces back to form, I could "take it" when I was young. Now I'm a full-grown tree, a storm comes, and my branches break. I'm all broken up! And it takes so much more time to mend! That's how it feels.

Throughout my life, intimate relationships with men have broken me the most, I confess. Cracked me right in half. I remember someone I once dated. It was a relatively short relationship. Who he was and when I dated him are not important, so much as what was at work internally. There were many qualities I loved about him, and I cared about him deeply. But I did not love him, and this created much confusion and conflict inside me. I felt I had no choice but to end it. I cried and lingered in depression for months, long after he'd moved on. I'd lie awake at night, agonizing, Why? After all the thought I gave to it, even now I cannot say why—except that it was instinct that prevented my heart from opening to his love. I knew something that I could not put words to. And without the words to define and make sense, I had no revelation, no epiphany, no shimmering thought to release me from the pain and let go. It has only been over time, with age and experience, that I have come to accept instinct as the light-ning rod through which I know, energetically. Instinct is strong in me, despite all other perceived weaknesses. It is all I have sometimes, and it is always enough.

o

Instinct tells me when danger is here, even when everyone tells me it is not. I remember that man, he was a relative; everyone around me—even common sense—would say that I was safe with him. Still, I locked my bedroom door automatically, without thinking. Instinct makes me reach for a bag, ready to pack it and leave, when I "know" I should not. As we walk along the sidewalk, instinct moves my hand quickly to my mother's arm; I think I saw, though I'm not sure, an uneven balance in her step. And you might agree with me—instinct is not the same as intuition, though I believe they are cousins. In intuition, there is room for planning and negotiation. Let's say I have an intuition that my nephew has a crush on someone. There is time for me to watch, to talk to him about it—room to guide. Yes, usually my intuition is right about these things. But instinct is much older than me and it will not let me negotiate. I can't ignore its command, so I frequently submit. I listen to my elder.

o

If you're like me, you may have a tendency to skim over historical passages. I don't know why I do this, and I don't like my habit. But I ask you, warmly, to return to accounts from our Lakota ancestors, quoted previously. Take your time. Because, in their words, you may sense an old yet very present energy when you read, "A herald cried out that the soldiers would take us to the agency and take good care of us."

You may taste that present energy in "They gave us rations of sugar, coffee, crackers, and bacon."

You may see it in "While we were doing this, the soldiers guarded round our camp. Then they put Hotchkiss guns where the cemetery is now. There were so many guns all around us I could hardly sleep."

Hear it in "The guns seemed to get quiet. In the meantime, we moved to the north, and a child was asking for water [. . .] there were wounded crying out."

Feel it in "It was very cold when the storm came on."

This is instinct.

o

U.S. president Benjamin Harrison was in office during the Wounded Knee Massacre in 1890. This is what he had to say, following the murder of nearly three hundred Lakota men, women, and children. Again, I gently urge you to take your time reading:

> That these Indians had some complaints, especially in the matter of the reduction of the appropriation for rations and in the delays attending the enactment of laws to enable the Department to perform the engagements entered into with them, is probably true; but the Sioux tribes are naturally warlike and turbulent, and their warriors were excited by their medicine men and chiefs, who preached the coming of an Indian messiah who was to give them power to destroy their enemies. In view of the alarm that prevailed among the white settlers near the reservation and of the fatal consequences that would have resulted from an Indian incursion, I placed at the disposal of General Miles . . . all such forces as were thought by him to be required. He is entitled to the credit of having given thorough protection to the settlers and of bringing the hostiles into subjection with the least possible loss of life.

I want to bold or highlight certain moments that speak to me in the above passage to make sure that you don't miss them. But I know that you will glean and perceive what's important to you. Mostly I am thinking about the empowering beliefs among certain Lakota people that created "the alarm that prevailed among white settlers." Their beliefs caused alarm, not actions. The U.S. president placed into the hands of the general "all such forces thought by him to be required" for the protection of white settlers with the "least possible loss of life."

Those are the president's words, not mine. This "protection" is now
called a massacre.

○

Often, when I think of Minneapolis, the first thing that comes to mind
is an afternoon ride that I took with my poet friend Heid Erdrich some
years ago. I was visiting Minneapolis for just one day and she gave me
a mini-tour of the city. We visited Birchbark Books and the Minneapolis American Indian Center. Heid is Turtle Mountain Ojibwe, and
as we drove, she shared her knowledge of the area. She told me that
several of the old roads running through Minneapolis were originally
trade routes (ancient routes, one could say) among our people, inter-
tribally. And those old trade routes aligned with our star maps. Not
many people are aware of this here, she told me. I was astounded. I felt
so humbled and grateful to Heid for sharing this gift of knowledge.
And though I hesitate to be so honest—it suddenly felt holy, driving
in her car, on those streets, knowing they aligned with our star maps.

I spent considerable time reading and writing about the Minnesota region—or Mni Sota, as we also know it. I wrote a poem titled
"38," in which I unfolded an event referred to as the "Sioux Uprising,"
motivated by deprivation and violated agreements with the Dakota
people.

And when I think of Minneapolis, I also remember that this is
where the American Indian Movement (AIM) was founded. Here I
begin to make connections. Among other things, AIM is well known
for the takeover of Wounded Knee in 1973. For seventy-one days, AIM
occupied this site as a push against police brutality and glaringly unjust
government policies with Indian affairs.

And now I just cannot stop thinking about Minneapolis.

I cannot stop.

O

A few years ago, my daughter and I drove up north to the Lakota Summer Institute in Standing Rock, North Dakota. This was in 2016, early summer, and the sun had set. It was very late. We were trying to make it to Prairie Knights Casino and Resort before midnight. We had reservations to stay there, along with other students. Though we were determined not to stop, I had to pee. Holding my breath, I finally spotted a little town off the highway. I saw glowing streetlamps. I took a right turn onto the town's main street. I wanted to find an open restaurant or gas station. Nothing. The town was asleep. We drove to the end of the town, which took approximately five minutes. We turned around and drove back to the main highway. Just as I turned onto the highway, a cop flashed his lights and pulled me over. I had no idea why I was being stopped. And now, I'm sorry to say, I cannot remember the reason the policeman gave. Maybe I was speeding? But this is what little I do remember: He came to the driver's window. He asked for my license, registration, and so forth. I opened my wallet to find my license. And my stomach dropped. I'd just applied for a new driver's license and I'd forgotten the 8½ x 11-inch piece of paper—my temporary license—on our kitchen counter. I apologized and explained my situation to the officer. I gave him my old license, and I knew that if he searched, he'd surely find me in the system. The officer asked me to step out and accompany him to his patrol car. I looked at my ten-year-old daughter in the passenger seat and told her I'd be back. He escorted me to the back of his car. It was pitch-black outside on the

North Dakota plains, except for his patrol lights. I cannot remember what he was doing exactly—there was an upright computer screen in the front, he was typing information, he was calling things in. Then he began questioning. I can't remember what he asked, either, except for one particular question: Are you transporting drugs in your car? Yes, point-blank, he asked that. I was taken aback. No, I'm not. You're free to search my car, I said. We're on the way to Lakota language camp in Standing Rock, I told him, hoping to alleviate suspicion. I was detained in the patrol car somewhere between thirty minutes to an hour. It was strange. I'd done nothing wrong that I could think of. I began to feel a dreadful sick energy in me. It wasn't so much because of the cop, but now, I know, I could feel my daughter. Finally I was "released" and allowed to return to my car. When I opened the driver's door, my daughter was in hysterics. I had no idea what was going to happen to you, she cried. As I write this, I'm asking my daughter what she remembers. The first fifteen minutes that you were gone, I was fine, she says. But after a while, I started panicking. I thought you were in trouble. I started worrying that he was going to drive off with you. I nod my head. I could feel it, I tell her. Maternal instinct. And when we returned home and recounted what happened to our family, they ranted and yelled in anger, asserting that the policeman was not allowed to do that. I did not know my rights, I admitted. Yet I'm still not sure that I do. After an internet search, I cannot verify whether that procedure was legal. And even had I known, I was alone with my daughter out on the prairie in the dark. The cop was big. Staring up at him, I found myself locked into his power, like a trance. My brain was a walnut. I did as I was told. I'm shaking my head because I know that my story is mild as milk. It's plain. I'm sorry. Still, there's one thing I know. From now until forever, I will not drive alone with my daughter past sunset on a road trip. Not because of the black night but because of the Blue.

o

Out of curiosity, I googled the anatomy of an elk's eye. It's true, what my daughter said. There's nothing in the pupil. It's a hole through which light passes and is absorbed into the iris. And in that tiny space, countless reflections.

o

Horror, fear, anger, terror, outrage, panic—I felt this as I witnessed. Through the pupil to my throat into my chest. Like an arrow, the images of George Floyd pierced my soul. I have no other way to describe it. I wanted to rage! This country, the structure—if it were a dinner table, I'd flip it. But as I considered how big this structure is, my adrenaline quickly synthesized to poisonous dread. Timeless dread, older-than-you-and-me dread, from the grave and born again. For days, I could not stop my tears. There was nowhere for this sickly energy to go except back to the source, my eyes. With water and salt, my soul cleanses naturally. But I want to tell you what dread does to me. It makes me feel impotent. Like I have no arms or legs. Not even a mouth to open, cry out, or bite.

But I forgave myself for all those responses, even feeling impotent, because I'm sure it's instinctual. Iron Hail could not sleep; neither could I. It's the knowing, without words, that something is here. More is coming. I've been so shaken, I even asked my teenage daughter, who craves independence, to sleep with me this week. Why? I cling to my child to ensure her safety. I am obliterated emotionally. Why? George Floyd and I—we are from different communities, different backgrounds, different genders. On this land, our histories overlap, but in some ways, they are distinct. I have no words for why, though I can say with certainty that George Floyd's murder hit me to my core, as if he were my brother, my own, my blood. His death—along with the recent chain of violations and murders of Black people—makes me feel desperate for the respect owed to them. Absolute respect. Not one more violation.

I must do something, that elder instinct says. But I don't know what, I answer. Forgive me, elder, the only way out of my desperation is to write. And forgive me for the gaps in this essay, there's so much I don't know and much more to include. Though I believe the adage that "the pen is mightier than the sword," I also believe that words are meager. For my paradoxes and contradictions, forgive me. But I empty my pockets—here are personal memories, something from our ancestors' words and Lakota history, knowledge about this land, a nod to our modern-day AIM warriors, love for my daughter and family, mention of a pitiful love life, my experience as a woman—it's all that I have. Even if it's meager, I give it to Mr. Floyd, his family and anyone affected.

I don't know nothing, but I do know something. I give, knowing that my offering is one of many. What is the opposite of impotent? Capable, potent, or powerful. What is the most powerful thing I can think of? The sun. Its light. Look at its power to reflect in incalculable directions, in the darkest places.

—JUNE 2020

Notes

I thank Dr. Craig Howe for providing accounts from the Lakota survivors of the Wounded Knee Massacre, and giving me permission to quote them in this essay. He has noted that Mrs. Mosseau's account can be found in an article by Arthur C. Parker, "The Truth of the Wounded Knee Massacre," The American Indian Magazine, *vol. 5, no. 4 (1917): 240–52.*

I would also like to thank Heid Erdrich for sharing her knowledge about Minneapolis and allowing me to likewise share it here.

Be Safe Out There
(And Other American Delusions,
Rhetorical and Otherwise)

Sofian Merabet

I didn't speak English properly until I crossed the Atlantic westward for graduate studies in 1996. I was twenty-three years old, and it was the first time I'd crossed the northern part of that ocean. I had been to most countries in South America, had lived on both shores of the Mediterranean, had traveled throughout the Middle East, but had never gone to North America.

I landed in Upstate New York, near the Pennsylvania border. So much of what I saw upon arrival intrigued me. Binghamton, where I would study for two years, was not only a quintessential example of a Rust Belt town experiencing economic agony, the socio-racial tensions I witnessed there stayed with me a long time before I even began to understand or experience what constitutes discrimination and racism in the United States.

It was in Binghamton that I heard, for the first time, expressions such as "play it safe," "be on the safe side," and "be safe out there," which were generally said with what was, to me, an unsettlingly big and phony smile. Back then, I grasped neither the obsession with ceaseless cheerfulness some Americans displayed, nor the meaning of the rhetorical preoccupation with safety, for translating it directly into the other languages I knew didn't make any sense.

In Arabic, for example, people might say *allah ma'ak* ("God be with you") or *bes'lama* ("with peace"); in French, they say *bon voyage*, thus simply wishing you a "good trip" before embarking on a journey. Germans often use the term *alles Gute* ("all the best") and Spanish-speaking South Americans just say *Que te vaya bien,* which loosely translates as "have a good one." None of these, however, deal in imagined conceptions of space or, for that matter, in obsessions with safety.

But it quickly dawned on me that for those who used these expressions in America, safety had not only a spatial but also a conceptual component to it. Safety was one's own imagined blissful and bulwarked castle, whereas anything outside of it was conceived as potentially dangerous. A threat, even. This imagined danger could be coming for a neighborhood, a city, or even the entire country, where American parochialism pits a national dreamland—fueled by a patriotism in perpetual need of "national security"—against a perilous world "out there" not many citizens know anything about.

After two years in Upstate New York, I moved to New York City to pursue my doctorate in anthropology. While navigating the privileged bubbles of Manhattan's Morningside Heights, I encountered the exact same expressions around "being safe" I had gotten used to in Binghamton. In the Big Apple, the complex social divisions that characterized the city flabbergasted me. For instance, the racial division of labor and space on the Columbia University campus was one thing that demarcated how one could "be on the safe side." Crossing Morningside Park was quite another experience, however. Harlem at that time wasn't the gentrified utopia it would turn into shortly thereafter. On its streets and avenues, boarded-up brownstone buildings testified to black precarity. The only visible presence of the state was limited to police cars patrolling the streets, driven by hulking, gimlet-eyed white men.

I never assumed they were coming for me, but I was extremely wary. As the son of a white mother and a mixed-black father, I have experienced plenty of racism throughout my life, with different histories attached to discrimination and prejudice in the two countries of my upbringing, Germany and Algeria. Even my sister, who has blond hair and blue eyes and passes as white, has been the subject of racist bigotry. I am her "dark" brother, a difference that, to our chagrin, regularly leads to puzzled faces and the occasional offensive remarks questioning the actuality of our full siblinghood. Now, as a U.S.-based academic, I am typically identified by others as "African American."

My study of how gender and sexuality are impacted by socio-racial factors and vice versa is primarily focused on places such as the Middle East and Latin America; despite this, I am plainly aware of how "race" works here in the United States. It is a complicated awareness, because the African American man I am perceived to be doesn't actually deliver when it comes to prefigured notions of racial embodiment and performance. I have "an accent" (as if those who say this with their regional drawl do not), and due to the different cultural realities in which I have been socialized, I exhibit a bodily and affective habitus that is not expected from an African American man.

My students at the university where I teach often struggle to place me, to know how to make sense of me. They tend to be fully conditioned by the script of their American socio-racial experiences. This script tends to say, a black man does this, he speaks like this, he might care about this. To them, any performance off that script is disorienting. In the community at large, this confusion in turn marks me as a threat to the entire system that brought those students to the classroom.

Being marked as a danger is dangerous. When I walk in most neighborhoods of Austin, Texas, the college town in which I have been living over the past eleven years, I am never "on the safe side." Rather, I am often viewed suspiciously as a black man by my mostly white fellow Austinites. On occasion, the suspicion ranges from hostile furtive glances, sometimes covered up with an unmistakably rehearsed toothpaste smile, to being followed by a white man in a car just a few streets away from my apartment who apparently thinks that the only reason I am walking past his house is that I want to rob him.

Most acts of racism and prejudice are seemingly trivial, so that some people (perpetrators and victims among them) end up now and again naturalizing them. But it is those acts that form the bedrock of a structure ensured by state-sanctioned violence. This violence is systematically enforced against those who do not fit the dominant societal mold and who happen not to be white. The space and the people "out there" who jeopardize white perceptions of "safety" in the United States are far beyond the conceptual—are in fact a physical landscape that is heavily policed.

If the pervasive presence of uniformed white men with their rehearsed violent masculinity isn't enough, their exorbitant armament always leaves one staggered. Police departments in the United States are a domestic window into U.S. military might abroad, into what is happening every day in countries such as Iraq, Afghanistan, and (by Israeli proxy) Palestine. It is a reminder how the military-industrial complex has strong connections to local "law enforcement" agencies, including city and university police departments.

In most countries around the globe, one would be hard pressed to find a metropolitan police unit as highly equipped in weaponry as any of the university police forces of the five U.S. institutions of higher education (public and private) with which I have been affiliated over the past twenty-four years. Let's not even mention the municipal police forces of the different American cities—small, medium, and large—I have lived in.

Moreover, in racially segregated America, what is called "law enforcement" is rarely patrolling in white neighborhoods because it isn't needed there to uphold the status quo. However, on the "other side of the tracks" (or more accurately, highways), the parts of town where black and brown people live that are, for many whites, akin to foreign lands, "safety" is imposed by systemic force and, as too many recent videos have captured, abuse. Under such circumstances where black and brown bodies are always seen to be suspicious and a threat to the system, it becomes impossible for anybody to "play it safe." Along with pandemic vulnerability, the ordinary state of surveillance in marginalized neighborhoods goes hand in hand with a general divestment of the state and, therefore, a notoriously underfunded social infrastructure that results in the closing of schools, expensive and inadequate supermarkets, and the general difficulty of accessing economic and health resources. Add to that what has been euphemistically referred to as "gentrification," what you get is a hopeless situation where white "friendly smiles" displace anybody who doesn't fit the cheerful equation.

As long as socio-racial segregation and discrimination persist, and as long as the presence of the state is limited to the increasingly armed police force, then neither the biggest smile nor the use of any hollow expressions of "America Nice" is going to remedy what for a very long time most people of color have lived as a daily experience of injustice in this country. How can we step out of this infernal logic, of which the proliferation of arms among civilians only exacerbates the situation? How can we break the cycle of violence that leads to the death of black and brown women, men, and trans-identified individuals?

One essential first step is to recognize that the fantasy of "safety" that too many Americans use to define the United States is in actuality an attempt to hide away the dire reality of being one of the most violent societies anywhere on the globe. In spite of pervasive nationalist rhetoric, our society remains not a heroic one that protects the vulnerable, but a nation of dominant settlers built on a dreadful history of genocide, slavery, and racial segregation.

The police violence we are witnessing now and which the global Black Lives Matter protests are denouncing is not an aberration, but a continuation of this nation's well-documented history. It is a continuation in need of being ruptured, not to keep white people "on the safe side" of history, but so that the very notion of safety—equal protection under the law—might finally be tested, and at last expanded to include everyone who lives in a country whose official name, often reduced to a euphemism, needs to be taken to task by its citizens.

—AUGUST 20, 2020

I Hated That I Had to See Your Face Through Plexiglass

Nyle Fort

Dear ███,

I never told you how we met. On May 11, 2008, as the sun scaled the sky, a New Jersey Transit train smashed into my big brother at 80 miles per hour. We don't know what made him run across the tracks. We just know he'd drunk a bottle of Hennessy on his way to the halfway house where he was living at the time. Luckily, Chad survived. But his body took a beating.

Your mom was on nurse duty the day the doctors amputated his left leg. My other brother bumped into her outside the emergency room. They hadn't seen each other since high school, where they went from sweethearts to bittersweet. But it took them only a few minutes to settle the score.

You were fourteen then, when we found out you were my nephew. I can't believe it's been twelve years.

I was anxious the first time I visited you in jail. What could I say to comfort you? How could I explain, in thirty minutes, that your ten-year sentence testified to centuries of racial bondage? I didn't want to lecture you, but I wanted you to know that the system didn't fail you. It's rigged against you. I wanted you to see how your choices are shaped by what Saidiya Hartman calls a "political arithmetic" that multiplies the chance you'll end up dead or in prison. I wanted you to understand that your inmate number marks our government's criminal history, not yours. More than anything, I wanted you to know that I love you.

We ended up rapping about Pusha T versus Drake and how cold your cell gets at night. I loved seeing your face. I hated that I had to see it through plexiglass.

The city of Newark established Union County Jail in 1811. According to the facility's website, white authorities used the courthouse basement to "hold runaway slaves, beggars and the insane." Some inmates were under ten years old. Between the year Black people were declared legally free and when W.E.B. Du Bois penned *The Study of the Negro Problems,* jailers there hanged four prisoners.

Meanwhile, European settlers were battling for political power, stealing Indigenous land, and struggling to keep rebellious slaves in their place. Your neighborhood, where my mom went to high school and your father learned to hustle, was once home to the Lenni Lenape Indians and later a middle-class Jewish community that raised the famous novelist Philip Roth.

So much and so little has changed since then. We've had a Black mayor for the last fifty years. All nine city council members are people of color. Six of the nine school board officials are Black. Even downtown, which features a new Whole Foods and a Prudential headquarters building, smells like incense and Muslim oils.

But Black presence hasn't meant Black progress.

Don't take my word for it. Just walk down the number blocks, see who's standing in line outside the welfare office, pay attention to who travels through and who sleeps at Penn Station, and notice the complexion of the families in the visiting room at Northern State Prison. Then visit Port Newark and watch who gets the good jobs. Then drive down Market Street after a Devils game or before a K-pop concert and notice whom the police are there to protect.

Then peruse the city budget and let the money talk. Listen to who gets tax breaks and who gets motivational speeches. Ask yourself what it means for the mayor, son of the late activist and poet Amiri Baraka, to march with protesters one day and kneel with cops the other.

You know better than I do about the limits of reforms from politicians, Black and otherwise, however well intentioned. It may get you a slightly bigger cell, more time on the yard, better books in the library, and a job that pays $3 instead of 87 cents per hour. But none of that addresses the forces that stand between the outside world and you. Your cell is just as locked. The basketball court is still wrapped in barbed wire. Your gig is still a form of legalized slave labor. Please don't get me wrong. I'm glad you have a tablet to send emails and listen to music. I'm happy you can watch TMZ after lunch. I'll never stop sending you money to buy Power Up deodorant and sour cream and onion chips. But, ███, I don't want you there at all. I want you home, where you're loved and where you belong.

I'm writing this letter beside my favorite window. The air is brisk. Ambulances have been hauling potential coronavirus victims since dawn. Hanging above me is a *Life* magazine I bought from a black-owned artist collective a few months ago. The cover depicts a wounded twelve-year-old Joe Bass, Jr., whom local police shot in July 1967. The summer Newark exploded.

The rebellion responded to a menacing experience for Americans

like you and me: a minor traffic stop. Police assaulted and arrested
a Black cabdriver. Residents of Hayes Homes saw the incident and
headed down 17th Avenue toward the 4th Precinct. Officers draped in
full riot gear met the unruly crowd with pistols and billy clubs. A five-
day battle ensued. Twenty-six people died. And over seven hundred
were injured.

The uprising caused nearly $10 million in damages, $80 million in
today's dollars. Even now, the city has yet to fully recover. As development penetrates downtown, you can still see abandoned lots that were
once bustling streets.

I used to go back-to-school shopping not far from where little
Joe's wounded body lay over fifty years ago. Back when Avirex jackets
and Sean John Velour were hot. I wanted to be like your father. He
was flossy and intelligent. He was also angry. I remember when he
ran away from home. He must've been sixteen or seventeen years old.
He and my father were scuffling on the second-floor banister. I don't
know what or who started the fight, but I know that your father's
anger had nothing to do with my father and everything to do with his.
He was ashamed of the way AIDS had begun to eat away at the man
who brought him into the world. And he was ashamed we didn't have
enough money to buy nice clothes or order from certain parts of the
menu or travel beyond the Jersey Shore.

The next time I saw him he could afford much more than the nice
clothes, including the Mercedes-Benz CLK-Class he pulled into the
driveway. That day he bought me two pairs of Timbs and a Tommy
Hilfiger T-shirt. It was one of the happiest days of my life.

Trauma has a way of bringing us together and keeping us apart.
Sometimes at the same time.

I haven't seen your face since the beginning of March. The week quarantine orders were put in place. Now we can talk only over the phone. Still, our conversations always make my day. Me hiking on your hairline. You hating on my clothes. Me asking you what you're reading and if anyone is bothering you. You assuring me that everything is all good. Me reminding you that you are loved. You responding, "I love you, too."

I've missed your last three calls. I can't call you back. You can't leave me a voice mail. GlobalTel Link leaves one on your behalf. The corporation controls half of the $1.2 billion prison telecommunications industry. It's a fraudulent enterprise that does more than take our money. It robs us of tenderness. No "call me back." No "I love you." No laughs, no tears. Just an automated voice notifying me that the call is being recorded.

The last time we talked I asked you about the protests. You said you were proud. I could hear it in your voice. I'm proud, too. But can I be honest? I'm also terrified. No empire falls without a fight. Ask Haiti or Cuba or Algeria. But if there's ever a time to slay Goliath, the time is now. And I'm talking about much more than defunding the police and toppling racist statues. I'm talking about dismantling a society that thinks it needs police, or prisons, or war, or guns, or borders, or fossil fuels, or private property, or the lie that some of God's children matter more than others.

I'm talking about building the New Ark, whence our city bears its name. Not just an exclusive vessel to withstand a storm. But a new way of journeying together.

It's going to take everything we've got. But everything we need is already inside us. We are the descendants of Maroons and share-croppers. We are the great-great-great-grandchildren of mighty people who worked the land and made the blues. We are the substance of things hoped for, the evidence of things our ancestors died for the world to see.

Love, and I hope to hear from you soon:

Uncle Nyle

—JULY 1, 2020

Let These Protests Bring Light to America

Daniel Peña

The news of George Floyd and Christian Cooper in the same day brings a clicking to your jaw, right at the back of your mandible. The sound is indigenous to your body, rooted in rage, though you haven't heard it in some years. Last time you clenched your jaw that hard was in Mexico City when you were twenty-six and you were marching and everyone you knew was healthy.

That riot in which you found yourself was by accident, which is to say it was planned: a Mexican plainclothes cop amid a peaceful demonstration threw a bottle toward his colleagues in riot gear, allowing them to spring into action. Suddenly everyone could be detained.

And then a second bottle is thrown.

When that bottle explodes, you're near enough to the fire to feel it. Close enough to smell the Molotov cocktail's black plume, to glimpse the wooden doors of the presidential palace set ablaze in the Zócalo of

Mexico City. You do not see the person who does it, but you hear the whistles and jeers of supporters, a small crowd anxious to provoke a fight with police, who dance in and around the flames.

The police avoid the worst of the shrapnel. They look weird inside of their skin, their faces somehow not theirs. And then the riot uncoils. They swarm from every direction. The meat connections of billy clubs on backs, skulls, skin. The wet crack of bottles on stone. The chemical rot of synthetic flame accelerant. And then the dry swish and grind of acrylic and rubber in action. Riot gear clacking on riot gear. Blood pounding your ears. Banners torn asunder. A Chinese sky lantern flickering into the green night.

Somebody has been releasing those lanterns all night. All night you've been naively thinking, wouldn't it be a fire hazard if they landed in the wrong place, should the mysterious atmospheres of Mexico City at more than 7,000 feet pull the lanterns back to earth?

You're a lapsed pilot, but you still think of these things—air density, altitude, gravity, combustion. All of the lanterns are inscribed in Sharpie with the number 43 written on their sides. That number in commemoration of the forty-three normalista teachers from Ayotzinapa—Indigenous students—who were kidnapped and murdered. The cover-up was facilitated by the Mexican government. Even then, the government's complicity was apparent. And that's why you're here.

Everyone knows they were murdered, but no one says murdered. Not the government, not the demonstrators. They say *disappeared*. Like there's a person-shaped hole missing in the world. And that's the first time you think of those holes walking around. Not like ghosts— the way an American would see it—but like an echo. There but not there. Nowhere but everywhere. Not so much remembered as felt.

Between English and Spanish, you wonder if there's a third language that connects the Mexican to American by way of trauma—a kind of cultural legibility. You think of the encuentro between the Zapatistas and the Black Panther Party. You think of Acteal, you think of Birmingham. And it's in a riot you come to the horizon of this epiphany: that in both countries, the darker you are and the poorer you are, the more disposable you are to that country.

You remember that in the chaos you find an open lane. It is clear of bodies. You run hard into it. It is out of sheer luck that you are not confronted by a single riot cop. Or swung at, for all you know. Or pinned down by a plainclothes cop of whom there are many.

You remember that someone kicks a trash bag. A thousand mice are startled. They panic out into the street. They're fast. You've never seen mice so fast. Not in Houston or in Union City. And they run between the plunging steps of protesters fleeing everywhere, into the lane that you're running. And you kind of love them because it's like they're rioting, too. Though you've always loved pests—they can't be killed, someone has to love them. And their backs are so shiny with what you can only imagine makes the streets in Mexico City shiny— diesel particles and bits of tire and sun and oil and soot. The mice flow like water running under halogen light.

There's a blue jay called Fred that visits your window in Houston during quarantine. He sits atop a squirrel-sized picnic bench (nailed to a fence post) you ordered from Etsy to support a guy who you read had been laid off during quarantine. Fifteen bucks for a fully built squirrel bench. Ten bucks for just the pieces in a media mail envelope. You opted for the envelope. You want to support the guy, but you also like a deal.

The pieces came in a manila envelope along with soggy instructions and a bunch of nickel screws taped together. You had time on your hands. You were finished teaching and it was late May and the cicadas were coming out of their seventeen-year hibernation and rattling us into summer, which in Houston smells like benzene pouring in off the Ship Channel. The tang of chemical in the air. That feeling in the back of your throat like you accidentally ingested aerosolized deodorant.

The bench was only two or three pieces, but you got to use a power drill, which made you look cool in front of your neighbors.

"Wutchya working on?" your conservative neighbor asked from twelve feet away. The one who drives a Corvette. He never wears a mask.

You didn't know if you should say or not. The slightest hint of granola sets him off. And on top of that, you're a brown man in a red state with a professor gig and a German wife, and you're basically a Republican nightmare. And maybe it's because you could die today or tomorrow—such is the feeling of quarantine—you're just like, fuck it, man, and so you draw your line in the sand.

You're building a squirrel picnic table.

What? he says. It's like a picnic table for squirrels, you say. What? he says again. He tells you they're pests. They're going to invade our attics. He just looks at the bits of wood and screws and the little red cup you're supposed to bolt into the middle of the table.

Some things are just simply outside the realm of imagination. This includes squirrels, too, who don't know what to do with the bench. But that's how you find Fred, who knows what's up. A picnic bench, some peanuts, an open invitation.

Fred visits twice a day. Once in the early morning and once in the early afternoon. On Saturdays he hangs around and watches Bundesliga through the window and you wonder what his little side eye sees. Fred's got a cool haircut. Wings so blue they're almost purple. But he can be ugly, too. He makes this kind of predatory screech to announce his arrival, to scare off other animals about to take his peanuts. Nobody is coming for his peanuts. Either way, the sound is ugly and frightening and silly at the same time, and you like it. You wonder if Fred's got a crew. You wish you could do this everywhere.

It's late May and you're new to birding. Or bird-noticing, as Jenny Odell might call it. Because that's all it really is. Noticing a sound. Darting your eyes toward the source of that sound. Noticing birds. Mostly a judgment-free zone. A way of slowing down, being present, recognizing oneself as part of one's bioregion, which is just a fancy way of saying recognizing oneself as part of the land that you're standing on. An idea Odell attributes to Peter Berg in her book, *How to Do Nothing: Resisting the Attention Economy,* which you're digging, and there's only so much bad news you can take in a day. You gotta step outside. You have to enjoy the light when it comes. And so you step into the sun, take the heat. You watch your goddamn birds.

You've avoided birding thus far for the simple reason that America does not know what to do with the sight of six-foot brown men staring out into the sky in public. Just like America does not know what to do with buzzed brown or black men period (or even sober brown or black men). Or brown or black men in my neighborhood who run at night (thanks, Nest Cam and Glock-armed Karens of Nextdoor.com).

It didn't terribly surprise you, for example, what happened to

Christian Cooper in Central Park in New York City. Though it angered you just the same. A white woman weaponizing her whiteness to sic the cops on a black man for the sin of exercising his full citizenry.

It was maybe a week before that you saw a Cooper's hawk devouring a baby Bachman's sparrow on the ground. The baby bird's mother was dive-bombing the hawk, who kept batting her away. You'd never seen that before—a songbird dive-bombing a bird of prey. A songbird suddenly becoming a bird of prey to save its baby.

You stepped in to scare the hawk with your size. The hawk made itself big. Up close you could see the baby was already dead. And as you got closer, the hawk pivoted and flew off, the carcass dangling from its talons.

The next day you saw a horned owl trying to poach a nest of baby robins in Garden Oaks, where you live, where you own a home. Just as you were about to try to scare the owl off, a white couple, your age, came up to you. Demanded to know where you belonged, what you were doing, why you were looking into that tree. Were you going to climb the tree? Why were you going to climb the tree? Why did you notice there was an owl in that tree? Are you here often?

You let your white wife handle it. She knows how to disarm them with conversation and a smile. Her privilege gets you out of things sometimes. People like that she's German. They hear her accent, and they like that they've visited where she's from. She can always bend them to see what we see. Oh yeah, the dude says, HOA should do something about these owls.

In a way that white lady was right, because you were gonna fucking climb that tree. But only for the babies, though.

————————

You're built for the heat of your native Texas. Hair so coarse that it sticks out like a broom to vent. Copper skin that's never betrayed you with a sunburn. To be frank, you have zero connection with your Coahuiltecan heritage outside of living with the vague knowledge that technically you're living in the homeland of your ancestors—they're buried here. And Karens aside, you were here before anyone.

Where is a person from, anyway? How do you lay claim to a place? Is it just being there? Is it, as a drunk guy told you in Mexico City once, having been somewhere long enough to have buried a relative in the ground? Or is it, as the Texas Parks and Wildlife PDF on migratory birds suggests, just passing through? Nearctic-neotropical migration. That means going south when it gets too cold, going north when it gets too warm. Going to where it's just right. Where you can momentarily blip across a park ranger's radar and suddenly you're native to Texas and Mexico and California at the same time. Like the red-bellied summer tanager. Or Danny Trejo.

You don't know why, but you take a day trip with your wife out to the San Jacinto Monument east of Houston. Where Texas gained its independence from Mexico in the Battle of San Jacinto, which was less a battle than a massacre.

It's hot, you overhydrate, and you have to take a whiz. There are picnic benches everywhere but no bathrooms you can find. It's either you or your wife who decides to venture farther into the Mexican encampment, past the breastworks where Houston's army invaded. You think if you go far enough that maybe you can find a place in the woods.

You walk until eventually there's a placard that says END OF CAR-NAGE, and you feel at peace taking a whiz there, beyond the battlefield, maybe a dozen yards past the sign, which feels less sacrilegious. In front of you there's a marsh. Just fish and more picnic benches on the other side (who the fuck picnics on a battleground?) and the irides-cent slick of petrochemical runoff from the Intercontinental Terminals facility, which burned down last year and soaked the city of Houston in a plume of benzene. They drenched the fire in flame retardant, but the fire kept spontaneously reigniting. Everyone gets cancer around these refineries. The city, though, rationalizes that only Mexicans live around them.

The sign says END OF CARNAGE, but really it was where the carnage began. You only learn this after reading the small print under END OF CARNAGE on the placard. Six hundred Mexican soldiers retreated into the marshland behind them, which still appears as solid land at first glance. Bogged down to the knee, they were essentially executed. Picked off one by one even after having thrown down their weapons to surrender, stuck in place. Everyone waited their turn. This went on for six hours.

Their bodies are still in that marsh. Still in uniform. In Spanish, you pray for them, you pray with them. You ask them for forgiveness—you didn't know. You're so incredibly sorry.

And it's then you realize you don't even know their names. None of the Mexican dead have names. They were never taught to you in school. There was no need to remember them.

Across the way, by the battleship *Texas,* a Mexican family is fishing in the petrochemical waters. You wave to them, they wave to you. You say in Spanish, it's hot. They say yes, it's hot. And overhead a crane flies into the marsh where the salt water meets the freshwater.

For seventy days you've been so good at quarantine. You wear your mask. You wipe down your groceries. You cook dinner. You're really good at compromising with your wife on shows. You feed Fred and watch him through the window. Sometimes he comes with a friend. Sometimes he comes alone. Sometimes you're not there and your wife says Fred came. And you realize that the days start blending together. Not so much disassociation as disconnection. Your instinct to look away, numb yourself from the rage. About Trump. About how this was preventable. About George Floyd's murder, even as he was whispering with his last breaths that he couldn't breathe, even as he cried out for his mother.

One day Fred comes and nearly flies into the window. His beak clinks against the glass like, *Snap the fuck out of it.* And you do.

For more than seventy days you're surrounded by no one but your wife. Then you're surrounded by more than 60,000 people in the streets of downtown Houston accompanying George Floyd's family from Discovery Green to City Hall. And though you're a germophobe and deathly scared of falling ill, you march anyway. Your family came to this country for this exact reason, for you to exercise these exact rights. And though you come with rage, you see how everyone around you has converted that rage into light. Everywhere there's light. And in a single moment, a cacophony of moments of experiences distilled into this march, this moment opening up into infinity (as Jenny Odell might put it).

No one talks about that aspect of a march—the light. That light is not a miracle. Or accidental. That light is superhuman. Something greater than grace.

And this brings you to the second epiphany you've ever had in a march: who better to save America from itself than the black and brown people who still believe in it?

—JUNE 12, 2020

Letter from a Seattle Protest

Claudia Castro Luna

I write these lines from Seattle, sitting at my kitchen table, where on a normal day I can see Puget Sound and the Vashon Island ferry like an elegant paper boat sailing back and forth on its daily runs. But today is not a normal day. Today is day four that I am trapped at home as forest fires raging over the West render our air thick yellow and hazardous to breathe. Even so, this September lockdown offers a chance to consider the months that preceded it.

When Washington's governor issued the official stay-at-home order in late March, schools and many businesses in the Seattle area had already been closed for weeks. Public life had slowed to a near standstill. Legions of us took to walking at all hours of the day: the early risers, the midday power walkers, the evening strollers. On my own daily walks, I saw shy crocuses peering at the sky awakening from their winter slumber and daffodil clumps waving their buttery faces auguring spring.

Mid-April brought a cavalcade of tulips, and soon after, cherry, apple, and plum blossoms exploded on bare branches. Lilacs released their scent coyly at first, then with sultry passion. I watched a couple stand on a corner sniffing a flowering bush that spilled over a fence. It was comical, the two of them turning to each other to acknowledge something, then back to the fence for more sniffing. It was funny until inadvertently I walked past the same fence on my return home. Then I, like them, planted myself in front of the fence and filled myself with the glorious scent.

Spring wore on, and the rhododendrons, the state flower, flamed up against their deep green leaves. Teddy bears, even as they were unable to deliver the hugs for which they were designed, showed up in windows as a friendly gesture to the little ones who could not be in school. I dug out an old teddy bear from a closet and arranged it in our living room window but promptly took it down when my three teenagers, independently of one another, snarled at me: *What are you doing?*

Yet, neither the promise of longer days after months of dark skies and cheerless cold rain, nor the poetry of fallen cherry petals prettily mounding on streets dispelled the dread that defined this spring. The first incident of coronavirus infection was detected here in late January, and it was here on February 26 that Covid-19 claimed its first victim in the United States. By early May the virus was everywhere. The afternoon I realized the death toll from Covid-19 reached 70,000, I became sick to my stomach. The figure echoed another from the place where I was born. Seventy thousand is the low estimate of the number killed in the Salvadoran civil war. It took over a decade for El Salvador to claim that tragic number; here in the United States we reached the staggering figure in a matter of weeks.

Then May twenty-fifth happened. I walked in on my oldest, two weeks away from her high school graduation, sitting on her bed, staring into her phone, her face contorted, whether from anger, sadness, or disbelief, I could not tell. She looked up at me and said something like, "What the fuck, Ahmaud Arbery just happened and now this!"

My daughter spent her last two years of high school as part of a group she co-founded and named the Change Coalition, successfully bringing attention and demanding changes to curricular biases and equitable outcomes for students of color at her school. George Floyd's murder galvanized her into community activism. Through endless Zoom meetings she expanded the Change Coalition, and with youth from across the city, organized a youth-led march. On June ninth we watched her give a prerecorded speech to her high school graduating class while balloons bobbed from our five dining room chairs. The next day she was out on the streets leading the march she'd planned, which drew thousands.

I grew up watching my parents, both of whom were teachers in El Salvador, putting their lives on the line for economic and political reform. For years, demonstrations took place all over the country. I remember my shock at seeing my father's photograph on the front page of the national newspaper. He was one of the leaders holding a sign with eight others that stretched the width of the street as thousands behind them marched through the streets of San Salvador.

Over the past twenty years I've watched El Salvador and the United States share more in common: the violence of hunger, the violence of guns and drugs, and now massive demonstrations demanding social change. When I dwell a little longer on that last similarity, something nuanced and intangible surfaces. In El Salvador then, and in the

U.S. now, sorrow and an immense sense of loss permeates the demonstrations. I lived in El Salvador when an estimated 150,000 attended the funeral of Monseñor Romero, the country's archbishop, who was killed in 1980 while officiating mass. People marched, at a time of extreme state repression, at great personal risk, wearing their pain and sorrow, thinking of him and of all those who had already died. These days, in streets across the United States we see the outpouring of grief over George Floyd's murder and Black lives lost.

June was no doubt an intense month, and for me the events of the past continued to converge with the present. At the university where I teach, one section of the syllabus I'd developed months before came up for discussion while protests in support of BLM broke out across the country. My plan with the students was to explore the events of November 1999, what is known as the Battle of Seattle, when participants from over seven hundred organizations from around the world shut down the World Trade Organization ministerial meeting in Seattle. Between 40,000 and 60,000 people are estimated to have arrived, part of a global justice movement against corporate globalization.

The TV footage from 1999 shows police in full riot gear, launching tear gas into standing crowds, spraying mace at protesters' faces, their demeanor designed to intimidate, rather than de-escalate. My students commented how constant brutal police behavior had remained in the twenty-one years since the WTO meeting. They also noted that then, as now, the protests and marches were overwhelmingly peaceful. Participants engaged in nonviolent tactics, wore colorful costumes, made giant puppets that ambled through the streets. But the media focused only on the clashes that erupted, made worse by police overreaction and aggressive crowd control tactics.

Without articulating it, the media coverage of Seattle's marches in

June of this year folded neatly over the images incessantly beamed to the world twenty-one years ago. Smoke-filled streets, people peacefully locking arms, raised fists. The coverage reinforced the notion, planted decades earlier in the collective imagination, that Seattle is a socialist, anarchist haven. In late June my children made cardboard signs to carry at a silent BLM march that drew an estimated 60,000. Not a single scratch was reported. The march did not show up on TV screens nationwide.

As the city reeled in controversy over demands calling for the resignation of our police chief, peonies broke out from their thick buds. On my early walks, I'd find their splendid heavy heads collapsed on the ground, their scent wafting gently about. By then the concentration of Covid-19 cases in Washington had shifted east, over the Cascade Range, finding fertile ground in meat-packing and large apple-processing plants, both places with overwhelming Latino workforces.

Latinx people in Washington State are underrepresented in almost any measure: K-12 and higher education outcomes, political office, white-collar employment. The coronavirus changed that. In this respect we are a hair above parity, as we make up 13 percent of the population and account for 14 percent of Covid-19 deaths statewide. Native Americans are 1 percent of the state's population and account for 3 percent of our dead.

Seattle is named for Chief Si'ahl of the Duwamish and Suquamish people, who for millennia called what is now Elliott Bay and Bainbridge Island their home. Chief Si'ahl foretold that at night streets would forever "throng with the returning hosts that once filled them and still love this beautiful land." And so they do. His departed people observe the thousands marching for peace and justice, for Black people to be accorded their dignity, the full measure of their humanity. They watch and remember springs and Junes of yesteryear absent lilacs, peonies, and cherry blossoms. They remember, using their own ancient names, snowy trilliums along stream banks, florid salmonberry shrubs, swaths of waxy yellow skunk cabbage lilies on damp forest floors.

—SEPTEMBER 10, 2020

Finding Justice in the Streets

Pitchaya Sudbanthad

All day and all night, rotor blades whop-whop the sky over Brooklyn. Sometimes one of the helicopters hovers somewhere above my apartment for what feels like hours. I put on my headphones and turn up the volume, hoping for the sound to go away, but it rarely does.

I live not too far away from Barclays Center, where the major avenues Atlantic and Flatbush crisscross and roving carnivals of discontent have gathered nearly every day. Marchers from north Brooklyn arrive to join marchers from southeast Brooklyn. Marchers from Grand Army Plaza stop under the arena's oculus and rally before heading off again, maybe across one of the bridges to City Hall, or maybe eastward through the neighborhoods of Fort Greene and Crown Heights. Wherever the protesting masses go, so go the helicopters.

I wonder what the pilots are watching from up there. Technically, some of the helicopters are equipped for omniscience—with surveillance systems that can capture thermal and infrared night-vision footage, and high-powered optics that can focus on a license plate from a thousand feet away.

But can they hear the shouts and chants through the blade noise? Do they recognize the names evoked? George Floyd, Breonna Taylor, Eric Garner, and too many more. Do they understand the demands being made? *Defund the NYPD. Hey, hey, ho, ho—racist police has gotta go. No justice, no peace.* Are they recording the clapping that spreads through the crowds in waves, as drivers in passing cars honk in support and window after street-facing window opens for someone to stick out their head and cheer? Do their cameras zoom in on the lines of evenly spaced riot-geared cops whose faces crease behind their ballistic face shields as protesters yell in unison for them to quit their jobs?

Weeks before, Brooklyn didn't sound like this. It didn't sound much like anything other than the constant heartbreaking wails of ambulance sirens. I left my apartment only when supplies ran low, walking through eerily calm and empty streets to get to the supermarket and then retreating back. The coronavirus pandemic had brought silence to the borough that couldn't and wouldn't shut up, and I was getting used to a new kind of New York not unlike the one often depicted in post-apocalyptic movies' prologue scenes, where something terrible was beginning to unfold.

In this New York, my apartment—a sealed-off one-person biosphere—became the center of my universe, and it was here that I observed the world beyond my window through whatever screen I held in my hand. That world arrived as video clips: the strangeness of unpeopled Times Square and Grand Central. The morgue trucks in hospital parking lots and mass graves on an island a gull's flight off the Bronx. The recorded incidents of anti-Asian racism against people who looked like me, as an unfit president inflamed his loyalists with conspiracy theories and xenophobic misinformation. It all felt so distant and unreal, yet it was a reality in which I also existed, somewhere out there.

When news of George Floyd's murder reached me, I couldn't bear to watch the full video, the same way I wasn't able to completely view the one of Ahmaud Arbery's killing that appeared online two weeks earlier to its ultimate lethal conclusion. Like many other similar incidents of racist violence, it was all too likely that this news would capture and exit the speedy cycle of American attention.

But it didn't.

The reckoning had to happen sometime or another. In New York, the pandemic had made it all too clear whose lives were always endangered and whose were protected from all peril. The coronavirus outbreak was taking a toll on minority neighborhoods at significantly higher proportions than on more affluent, predominantly white ones. Many Black workers took on greater risk of infection at jobs deemed essential at medical centers, supermarkets, and restaurants, laboring long hours and often for thankless pay, where "essential" only felt like capitalism's euphemistic camouflage thrown over "disposable."

It's fitting that protests now regularly happen at Barclays Center, a bait-and-switch scheme realized by the razing of a largely Black and Brown neighborhood by virtue of eminent domain, all for the eventual profits of a white real estate developer. In New York City, policing worked hand in hand with a real estate industry that generously donated to its foundations. More police presence made the city's white residents and newcomers feel safer in neighborhoods abandoned by white flight in the American postwar period. In Black communities, real estate opportunism displaced longtime residents. Housing values skyrocketed to unprecedented heights as communities fell apart and homelessness grew. In a metropolis that over the past few decades had seen exponential growth in capital wealth, hospitals, schools, and other services in Black neighborhoods underwent catastrophic budget cuts while police head counts steadily rose.

It was very clear that the notion of law and order applied to some more than others. The number of stop-and-frisks by the NYPD grew sevenfold to nearly 700,000 from 2002 until 2011, when it was scaled back because of civil liberties unions' lawsuits; to no one's surprise, reports showed that young Black and Latino males were disproportionately targeted.

So Floyd's murder in Minneapolis lit up cities all over the country within a matter of days. Or rather, it ignited smoldering fires that had been kept off-camera and ignored for very long.

On my phone, I watched angry protests erupt all over New York City. After a curfew was called, friends posted videos from defiant nighttime marches and bike rides. I told them to keep an eye on the cops. Since 9/11, the already massive NYPD budget has almost doubled to $6 billion. Much of it went to a steadily increasing personnel and overtime pay, and huge sums were spent on surveillance and militarization, with equipment meant for America's imperial wars quickly repurposed for use by domestic law agencies.

Friends and relatives in Bangkok ask what's happening in America. They catch only glimpses of the protesters; most video clips they see are of violent confrontations and looting. A few who may not have ever talked to an actual Black person ask me to be careful of angry Black people. They've tuned in to CNN and Fox News. They've seen the TV shows and the movies. In the kinds of footage—both news images and Hollywood entertainment—transmitted overseas, the global scale of the partnership between American white supremacy and capitalism becomes fully visible. The struggle for racial justice and equality is not profitable, so it must be distorted and obscured to fit the standard script. White hat, black hat. Pale skin, dark skin. Heroes, villains.

The rebellion, however, refuses obfuscation. Too many cameras to count—like the one Darnella Frazier tapped on her phone to record Floyd's last moments—now point at the true sources of violence.

In Brooklyn, arriving at a protest could be as easy as stepping out the door. I throw some precautionary items into a backpack—antacids to neutralize tear gas, a vial of vinegar to stabilize pepper spray, just in case—don my face mask, and head to the nearest protest site I'd jotted down from social media. Thousands of participants are usually already there. I make my way toward the back, where the crowd is thinner and I can at least keep some social distance, and wait for the people holding the megaphones to tell us to start walking. We know we're moving when the chanting and cheering begins.

We march. We're Black, Brown, Asian, White, Whatever. We're the church group kids dressed in fashionable all-black. We're the freelancer army in plaid and jean shorts. We're still wearing our white coats or monocolored scrubs. We're families with a stroller-bound kid holding a sign. We're hunched on our bikes. We're zipping forward in our wheelchairs. We push out. We keep arriving in large numbers. We say, "What the hell . . ." and join from our grocery run. We march. We hold up hand-markered signs made from now-plentiful packaging cardboard. We clap between chants and wave back to passersby and those standing at the curb, holding up their phones to show their friends what they oughta have seen with their own eyes. We take bottled water from neighbors who hand them from their stoop. We thank volunteers giving out face masks and energy bars. We wind through stopped traffic, as truck drivers blast their horn in salute and bus passengers inaudibly cheer behind glass. We give elbow bumps to people leaning halfway out of their car windows. We snap photos and start live feeds. We shout. We raise hell and a lone finger at the menacing helicopter above. We march.

New protests pop up every day. The vast majority proceed peacefully. If there's any riotous chaos, it usually comes after dark at the instigation of a police force chomping to use the curfew as an excuse to attack protesters, kettling trapped crowds, pushing riders off bikes, ripping off masks and macing without provocation, arresting clearly identified journalists and even throwing legal observers against cars. The city's mayor and police commissioner deny what's happening, but our cameras are recording.

I don't own actual athletic shoes. My ankles hurt after a couple of marches. When I stay in, I keep on marching in my own way. I repost others' images and accounts of huge marches happening everywhere. I send out articles on racism in police violence, pointing out how defunding bloated police budgets can actually reduce crime and strengthen communities. Sometimes I can pull up a map and tap on a live outdoor camera to watch protests moving through Brooklyn in real time. I keep track of what's happening on the police scanner and warn friends if, say, an eardrum-bursting LRAD sound cannon—one of the crowd-control weapons adapted from the theater of imperial war—is being readied near the Manhattan Bridge.

Progress is happening and will continue, I hope. In New York, protesters have already convinced the state senate to repeal 50-A, a decades-old law that shielded police disciplinary records from public view and stood in the way of accountability. Talk of significant cuts to the NYPD budget is gaining momentum within the city council, with as much as $1 billion in talks of being shifted to healthcare, education, housing, social services, and other underfunded vital programs.

The ill-advised curfew has been lifted, and cops appear to be standing down. The mayor seems afraid to show his face anywhere, after massive calls for his resignation.

They know we're watching, and we're not going to stay quiet anymore, because Black lives matter.

Eventually, I get used to the NYPD helicopter noise. The sound becomes no different from the thumping car stereo bass or pigeons squabbling outside my window—just another fixture of Brooklyn's music. Soon, for all our sakes, it will be gone.

—JUNE 11, 2020

A Riotous Anodyne

Indigo Moor

Dear Sacramento,

Yes, I have heard about the protests, trouble scarring your body. I can only imagine your fear. You are entering your summer phase, casting your calm heat across the fields. The tranquil streams and rivers. Open sky from horizon to horizon. My God, you are beautiful. And now all of that has changed, hasn't it? One man's killing in another city has brought you to this reckoning. His pain flutters city to city like a wounded bird, raising arms city to suburb. No, it is not your fault. You are the third most diverse city in the country, and you should be proud of that.

But let us be open and honest. After twenty-three years together, we owe that to each other. You have had your problems. Your skeletons refuse to stay hidden. You have such a luscious landscape of multicultural, ethnically diverse schools. It is easy to forget some parts of your rainbow shine brighter. Some of the bends are thinner, more ethereal than they should be.

No, I am not writing to kick you as you face another night of fire and anger. I love you. Even as you kneel on the edge of this precipice, wondering which way rolls you into oblivion. I can't promise you the morning will not bring more pain, craters in your beautiful skin. There are many folks ready for some things to burn. And they will not be stopped by public condemnation, the cries for peaceful protests. None of this is your fault. But protesters and people of color have the same problem: how others treat them is not their fault.

I am working in Philadelphia, and I have seen the same pain churning across this city like a dust devil swelling to a storm. You must be frightened. Fearful of coming rage. The shouts and screams reverberating across your streets and neighborhoods. Yes, there will be many peaceful protests. But I have issue with that term. Its passivity too easily turned away and ignored. Martin Luther King, Jr., said, "A riot is the voice of the unheard." I do not speak for everyone. Nor do I want to do so. I am only saying I have learned repeatedly that a gentle voice is easy to ignore.

When I was in the eighth grade, still making my way through the literature of a country divided in my thoughts, I was introduced to the funniest poem imaginable to my carefully sheltered mind. As an African American male bused to a white school, I struggled with what was supposed to be relevant. Much of what I read was outside of my understanding, not intellectually, but emotionally. I felt that to be literate meant not to be me.

Here was a poem that spoke of the scarce Sundays on my Aunt Jane's farm, where pigs and moonshine cut with lemonade were the difference between existence or not. The long, lazy afternoons where the sun seemed pinned to a spot on the sky. My brother and I chased the piglets that squeezed out of the pen. We chased butterflies and June bugs as our elders talked inside, the doors and windows open. We chased summer, always a step away from its heavy arms crushing our chests. Mostly we fled from boredom. From the knowledge that this was our entire world. That it must be all that was real. From that moment until the day we would die, far away from what we saw on the three channels of our TV. We ran. We drank water from the hose. Ate slices of watermelon.

And yes, we chased chickens. Swaddled in the cracked-wire frames of black-boy bodies, we were still no match for them. Their lightning-quick change of direction. Their pronged claws that never slipped in the dirt. Catching one was more than an unfulfilled wish. It was Excalibur magicked. It was the sorcerer's stone. Jesus nailed to a barn. We knew this. Still, we could not, would not stop trying to have a piece of the magic that would take us away from this place where we could not see the edges. Once I chased a chicken for so long, it crossed the street and ran into deep woods. I wanted to go after it, convinced that it would get lost. My brother stopped me. He insisted we would get hit crossing the road. The chicken would find its way back. I do not know if it ever did. They all looked the same to me. I still dream of never crossing that street.

Until I read that poem in class, I had forgotten the rusted cart sitting under the kitchen window in the shade of the afternoons. It was anchored to the ground and disdainful of Carolina drought. In my memory, it was always half filled with rainwater. Oh, and the startlingly white chickens forever pecking in the dirt beside it. William Carlos Williams, whom I immediately imagined as Black, leaning over his desk, communicated to me the only way to catch a chicken unaware. The patience necessary to stand for hours until they forgot I was human. Until they imagined me as a part of the farm. A part of the wheelbarrow. And if I could find that one moment, that single instant where everything aligned, I could change my fate. I could do something no one else could have done. For me, there is a love and a sense of panic that rises when I think of the South so deep in its prison that the bars are cloud, woods, and distance. Even in my memories, I am desperate to break the hermetically sealed hourglass of lackadaisical heat and humidity of those days. Jonesing for that one miracle that would release the people I love, and loved, from that small patch of so little. I would stand holding those cracked wheelbarrow handles for as long as it took, knowing that

> so much depends
> upon
>
> a red wheel
> barrow
>
> glazed with rain
> water
>
> beside the white
> chickens.

When the teacher read the poem, I laughed out loud. What can I tell you? I was in love. It was the funniest poem I had ever heard. And it spoke to the real world, my world, in such sensuous, concentrated language.

Unfortunately, the accepted understanding of Williams's poem was not mine, and the response to my interpretation was argument from all corners. Williams was a modernist. A minimalist. His work, while simple in language, contains worlds and multitudes. The crux of my teacher's argument was "I don't think it was written with you in mind."

I gave protest. But I did not have the momentous words or language to say that my life was as wide and deep as Williams's. My interpretation had no merit. There was no room for the acceptance of a minority experience into the discussion.

Outside my window, police helicopters are circling. Sirens ebbing and falling like waves, so many of them. Smoke rises around the corner of the building and sifts through my open window. Not close to me, but very present. Sacramento, love, parts of you may burn over the next few days. But not because protesters, peaceful or riotous, are ugly. They are like me, tired of hearing that their world is not the poetic one. Sick of being told they are not the poems that need to be read. They are beautiful and refuse to be ignored. And we protest. And we riot. And even if it is not material, a lot of old notions will burn.

Stay strong, Sacramento.

So much depends . . .

—JUNE 23, 2020

A Letter to Black America

Tracy K. Smith

Dear Black America—

We are many things, aren't we? We are hair. God yes, we are hair. And song. And memory. We are a language so deep it has no need for words. And we are words that feint, dart, and wheel like birds. Like James Brown, we feel good. Like Fannie Lou Hamer, we are sick and tired. We are fearsome. We are fire. Like God, we are that we are.

I've always felt great freedom in the countless territories making up the realm of Blackness. So many routes to wholeness. So many versions of joy. In Blackness I am local. In Blackness I am also distant kin. Indigenous and immigrant at once. Host and welcome guest.

But in the country of America—the physical and psychic territory in which the physical and psychic domain of Black America is situated—we are made to huddle together. By force. By the feelings of rage, threat, exhaustion, disappointment, and long-suffering that swarm us in this nation that loathes, fears, regrets, and cannot yet fully bear to accept the fact of us.

And I hear my uncles saying, "Tell me something I don't know," with laughter in their throats. And it is that laughter—our laughter—that I cleave to.

We revel in the depth and the flair and the belief and the secrecy of Blackness. We are lucky to be who we are, and we know it. And I hear my aunts saying, "Amen," and their deep intaking of breath, followed by a steep exhalation.

Black, we revel in the resourcefulness and the resilience and the poise and the know-how and the grace and the anger and the prayers to all manner of beings that have kept us alive. Alive despite attempt after concerted attempt to annihilate us.

I see you in all your forms, Black America, and I feel inside me a welling up of pride, reverence, and fierce protection. These threats we live subjected to—these ceaseless, baseless, unending, and uneradicated threats to our Black bodies, spirits, and minds—do you know what I think they are? They are the grotesque and perverse ends to which a nation founded in shame has gone in order to avoid atoning for its crimes. They are defensive acts, based on the belief that if we were allowed to dwell in our full power, what we would bestow upon this nation would be vengeance.

But we know better, don't we? Look what we do with our voices. Look what we build with our hands. Look what we hold together with just our arms.

Once a friend told me, "I think we came to this earth to save it."

Once I wrote in a notebook, "Maybe we are operating at a heightened spiritual frequency."

Why else do we call it Soul?

Black America, I feel myself cradled by this thing we share. When I call it race, I'm told that race is false. When I call it a movement, I'm reminded that we have moved through countless other movements before now. When I call it culture, I feel the seams of the word splitting at the great moving heft it attempts to contain.

We are here in America now as we have been in America always. When we are struck down and held back. When our bodies are corrupted by the violence of others. When we love. When, as now, we are trapped inside of finitude and flesh. During all of this and then some, Black America, we are agents of the eternal.

—JULY 2, 2020

Where Is Black Life Lived?

Joshua Bennett

The plot of ill-gotten land where my grandparents first locked eyes was 116 miles away from the town of Lillington, North Carolina. A place so named for the man that claimed legal ownership over my grand-mother's grandmother, as well as the rest of her kin. In spite of the bru-tal absurdity of this fact, and indeed, in spite of a social and juridical order founded and built from the ground up by such facts, such bru-tality, my grandmother and grandfather, Charlotte and Levi, persisted.

In 1944, they moved from North Carolina to New York. There my grandmother opened and operated three beauty salons within the boundaries of that irreducibly hip, invincibly Black cultural mecca: Har-lem. Over forty years, and seven children, and more than three times that number of grand- and great-grandchildren later, I emerged into the world of one of her beauty shops, shimmering from the summertime heat.

I was seven years old. I did not yet know how to spell the word *cosmetologist,* but I loved that it reminded me of both comic books and comets. My grandmother spent her life making strangers and friends alike feel beautiful. The older women in the salon would pay me a dollar whenever I spelled a word three syllables or longer: *malfeasance, indubitable, recalcitrant, loquacious.* When I went on an especially good run, I could walk into the neighborhood bodega with eight dollars of cold hard cash, stuffed as if contraband into my freshly ironed khaki shorts. Do you know how many Peanut Chews and Swedish Fish you can buy with eight dollars? A lot. To borrow a phrase from June Jordan: I was a millionaire in love.

This was where I fell in love with language. I learned to maneuver it, to appreciate its strength. I came to adore the salon for the robust social life it held within its four blue walls. Yes, I was small and still wore high socks. I had a high voice and a high-top fade, a laugh too big for my body. Yes, I was a Black American child in a country that despised us and reminded us of that ire quite often, most frequently in the bodies of security guards at our school, or bus drivers who called the police on us when we acted up, or the prison wardens presiding over the cells holding our cousins, parents, big brothers.

There was no death in the salon, though. There was only the latest gossip and Motown-era Marvin Gaye on the radio, an entire atmosphere of sounds and smells too perfect to have been engineered on planet Earth. You could have filled a hundred beauty shops with what I didn't know back then. But I was acutely aware of a certain truth I have not forgotten since those days: what we built in that space was indeed a refuge, but it was also something infinitely greater than that. It was a world on and in our own terms. A haven and a home.

This past March, at the outset of the Covid-19 pandemic, my grandmother, Charlotte Elizabeth Ballard, left this earthly realm. She died with her daughter, my mother, right beside her bed. In the same apartment in the South Bronx projects where she hosted Christmas every year, reciting folktales and Harlem Renaissance–era poems from memory. At that point, we did not yet know what the shape of the historical moment would be. We were unprepared. I went to Grandma's funeral via Zoom. When that link failed, several of the distant attending moved to cousin Jennifer's Facebook Live. The director of the funeral home was a man named Isaiah, whose voice and image now adorn a recent profile from *The New York Times* entitled "Coronavirus 'Ripped a Hole' in N.Y.C.'s Black Community." I remember arguing with him over protocols for social distancing only days before the ceremony. I regret it now. The impossible distance between my Massachusetts apartment and a New York City building packed to the walls with the pandemic dead—an expanse mediated by this invisible tether between us, connecting our voices—made a simpler version of the encounter impossible. For much of the service, I could not see my grandmother's face. The angle of my sister's tablet, my cousin's iPhone, would not allow it. They did their best. It was all we had available. The commitment to care for our people means you make do with what you have at hand. I wrote her obituary on the same laptop I used to write this letter. The last sentence of it was "She was loved."

Outside, or perhaps alongside, the litany of losses we have all experienced during the Covid-19 pandemic, what new ways of feeling close to one another have we cultivated? When I think of the past four months, I see both a sequence of tragedies and an ongoing refusal to be destroyed by them, relayed through a screen: the funeral; the news of the deaths of Ahmaud Arbery, Breonna Taylor, George Floyd, Tony McDade, Elijah McClain, and so many others; numerous family members diagnosed with the virus; not being able to remember the last time I held a friend or even spoke to one as we sat in the same room.

Adjacent to these more difficult moments, somehow, is the process of my becoming a parent, seeing my child grow as the landscape transforms around us. In honor of that surreal and yet wonderful occasion, I thought it might make sense to take some time today and share at least one of the pieces of writing that has taken on new meaning for me, given my particular experience of grief and celebration in this period. I was witnessing on the one hand the state of emergency caused by the converging pandemics currently engulfing our planet (and not only Covid-19, of course, but anti-Blackness, that perennial ecological catastrophe), and on the other, the emergence of my son into the realm of the living.

The most human thing I could do here, I realized, was to provide a window into the varying forms of mediation that have shaped my days, as well as the varied forms of human sociality that strain against and emerge through those forms of distance. The laptop screen, the BabyCenter app on my phone, the revolving glass door at the hospital. Seeing a colleague on the street and raising our elbows in solidarity, our masks failing to cover our smiles entirely. This letter ends in a poem, is what I'm trying to say. It's from a sequence that is at the core of a new book I'm writing about Black disposability, environmental degradation, and fatherhood. It recalls a world before the pandemic, and gestures toward the one we are building together, even now, in the midst of it.

One more thing: I've been thinking quite a bit recently about the role of air in African American letters. The people that could fly. Eric Garner. Christina Sharpe highlighting the link between anti-Black racism and the weather. It bears remembering. For the legal studies scholar and foundational critical race theorist Derrick Bell, one of the first characteristics of the Black utopia he describes in his classic vignette "The Afrolantica Awakening" is that it is simply a place where we can breathe. A space of celebration and retreat, somehow flourishing both inside and beyond the constraints of the present order. The sanctuary; the dance hall; my grandmother's salon, glistening at a distance.

When we turn to the written page, where is Black life lived? Anywhere. Everywhere. Underwater, outer space, underground. Even where there is no air at all. We imagine it as if it were otherwise. We conjure a world that is worthy of us. And then we gather there: unbowed, unburied, unabashed in our joy.

Benediction

God bless the lightning
bolt in my little
brother's hair.
God bless our neighborhood
barber, the patience it takes
to make a man
you've just met
beautiful. God bless
every beautiful thing
called monstrous
since the dawn
of a colonizer's time.
God bless the arms
of the mother
on the cross
-town bus, the sterling silver
cross at the crux
of her collarbone, its shine

barely visible beneath
her nightshade
navy, New York
Yankees hoodie.
God bless the baby boy
kept precious
in her embrace.
His wail turning
my entire row
into an opera house.
God bless the vulnerable
ones. How they call us
toward love & its infinite,
unthinkable costs.
God bless the floss.
The flash. The brash
& bare-knuckle brawl
of the South Bronx girls
that raised my mother
to grease knuckles, cut eyes,
get fly as any fugitive dream
on the lam,
on the run
from the Law
as any & all of us are
who dare to wake
& walk in this
skin & you
best believe
God blessed

this skin
The shimmer & slick
of it, the wherewithal
to bear the rage of sisters,
brothers, slain & still function
each morning, still
sit at a desk, send
an email, take an order,
dream a world, some heaven
big enough for Black life
to flourish, to grow God
bless the no, my story
is not for sale
the no, this body
belongs to me & the earth
alone the see, the thing
about souls
is they by definition
cannot be owned God
bless the beloved flesh
our refusal calls
home God bless the unkillable
interior bless the uprising
bless the rebellion bless
the overflow God
bless everything that survives
the fire

—JULY 21, 2020

On the Endless Mourning of the Present

Honorée Fanonne Jeffers

NORMAN, OKLAHOMA

Dear John,

I prayed before writing you this letter, on this evening, when young African American folks have taken to the streets to protest Derek Chauvin murdering George Floyd in Minneapolis. Once again, a white police officer has killed a Black person. This is a scary moment for me, a southern Black woman who has tended historical altars for thirty years. This is a burning time, and I am quite familiar with fire.

I suspect you want me to offer you some wisdom over the events of the past week. In saying that, I don't mean to accuse you of any crime. Our friendship is rare, that between a white man of ancestral privilege and a Black woman at intersectional crossroads. I dearly want to communicate my profound agape love for you. To let you know that I consider you my true brother. And yet, at the same time, I am enraged at some folks who look like you.

I'm writing you from my house in Norman, twenty miles from Oklahoma City, the capital of the state. This is a university town, home to the flagship institution at which I've taught for eighteen years. Norman used to be a "sundown" town, where Black folks could not live or even stand around in, after the setting of the sun. This same town is 130 miles from Tulsa, the site of the 1921 race massacre, when white men descended upon the Black residents of the Greenwood district. Those men murdered around 3,000 African American women, men, and children. Planes flew over the neighborhood and dropped firebombs. Sometimes, I imagine the terror of my people, as they tried to shield the small bodies of their young.

I moved here in the summer of 2002, driving west past an exit for Okemah, Oklahoma. It's a town familiar to me from Terrance Hayes's poem "A Postcard from Okemah" about a white mob that lynched Laura and L. D. Nelson, a Black mother and son, in 1911. Whenever I drive back to visit my family in Alabama and Georgia, I say prayers as I pass the Okemah exit sign.

Different white colleagues have asked me why I moved to Oklahoma, since I don't have family here. When I've said, I came for the job, they replied with understanding about why I'd left the South. That region being so racist, and everything. But these micro-aggressive encounters have been inconsequential, compared to those other Black folks have faced. After all, I'm still alive.

I've weathered other cuts: the insulting comments on my semester evaluations from students who were "tired of talking about race." The diversity workshops where white faculty members insisted that white male students "were being persecuted." The yearly racist scandals involving white students—and this year, involving white faculty. Through the years, I've told myself I have survived. I've paid my bills. Fifteen years ago, when I bought a home in this town, I sat in my used car and cried with gratitude for the sacrifices of my ancestors. What a blessing: to own a home, instead of being owned.

The tragedies of this state—of Okemah and Tulsa—began to echo, however, with the growing numbers of police killings of Black folks. Even when Barack Obama became our first African American president, the names of the recent dead haunted my sleep. A biblical litany. In 2016, when Donald Trump was elected, my rage finally awakened, like a usually placid creature prodded in its den.

I understood that hidden within the mass of supposedly kind, white "progressives" who had voted for Obama were those who literally turned around and voted for Donald Trump. Not a few, but actually many white college-educated middle- and upper-class elites who viewed themselves as politically progressive voted for Trump, the man who took out a full-page advertisement calling for the execution of five Black teenagers. Trump, who didn't even apologize when, years after those Black boys had been brutalized in prison, they were exonerated by DNA evidence. This week, instead of offering comfort to Black folks for the constant violent transgressions against our people and communities, Trump is hiding in the White House bunker, calling for the National Guard to use "dominance" toward (mostly) Black protesters, people who are supposed to be citizens of this country.

John, the only wisdom I can offer you is, this moment is not new. It didn't begin with the policeman who kneeled on the neck of somebody for nearly nine minutes, ignoring frantic pleas for air and humanity. Yes, Derek Chauvin is a murderer, but he's an opportunist of the times, a sharp-eyed vulture who saw vulnerable flesh.

Those white progressives who supported Trump are opportunists as well. When they voted for Obama, they believed that absolved them of the racist history of this country, that this history was no longer their concern. This betrayal by white progressives is one reason why Black folks are so angry right now. Our rage is not simply at the racist police or the current racist occupant of the White House. So much of our anger is directed at those who we thought were our true friends.

At best, white progressives abandoned Black folks because they believed if they ignored our fear and anger, that would make racism evaporate. At worst, white progressives took the opportunity to discard the strenuous antiracist work that (eventually) will unite this country. But it doesn't really matter why they voted for Trump. He's in the White House, we are living with that reality, and the past four years have proven that, as usual, African Americans are on our own.

At least we knew who—what—Derek Chauvin was when we saw him casually murder George Floyd and discard his body. But tonight, as I consider the endless list of my murdered kindred, as I try and fail to sleep in this house, I wonder, whom can I trust?

Which one of my white friends offered me their Judas kiss?

Love,

Honorée

—JUNE 1, 2020

On Protest, Laughter, and Finding Breath

Ali Black

A week ago, I was up during the middle of the night trying to figure out if I was really having chest pains or if I was just tripping. Until now, I didn't realize that these chest pains could have been attributed to the murder of Ahmaud Arbery or the exhausting situation between Amy Cooper and Christian Cooper. And before that, I felt more panic and pressure from trying to help a Black mother help her son finish an English assignment minutes before the deadline to make sure he'd graduate from high school. And before that, I was in a panic because no one had heard from my brother for hours after he got off work, his phone consistently shooting straight to voicemail, which rarely happens. Before that, I was panicking about a shortage of hydroxychloroquine because I, in fact, need it for lupus.

This was all before I learned about the murder of George Floyd.

The chest pains came back immediately after a small back-and-forth I had with my husband because he decided to travel to Buffalo, New York, to photograph an illegal dirt bike ride out. And yes, I can pretend to blame it all on the coronavirus, but here's the reality: I worry about the Black men who are closest to me all day, every day. So honestly, my biggest fear about this trip was that my husband could have another one of these unnecessarily dangerous-ass encounters with a police officer and never come back home.

Two days after my chest pains subsided, on May 26, I saw a few seconds of the video of George Floyd getting murdered on someone's Instagram feed. The chest pain came back. This time I didn't need to figure out if I was tripping or not. Oh, I felt what I felt—a dull ache. Tightness. Pain. I swiped out of Instagram, hit the side button on my phone, and watched my screen go black. I stared at the blackness until I felt a big lump rise in my throat. I knew this recipe all too well and I didn't want to begin crying the way I know all of this can make me cry, so I pushed the lump down and tried to—I don't know—pretend everything was okay.

But let me also show you how joy inserts itself into my life. Keep in mind I'm a native Clevelander—meaning, according to a recent study, I'm living in one of the worst cities to live in for a Black woman. And perhaps you know my city's history or you've seen the headlines about our infant mortality rate and our violence and our public education system and our current need to declare racism as a public health crisis. And you know his name: Tamir Rice. Google Timothy Russell and Malissa Williams. Google Desmond Franklin. Then type Tanisha Anderson's name into your search and you'll discover that the Cleveland police murdered all of these people. And this is how fast joy slips away from me.

But, back to joy. I can't tell you how many times I've burst into uncontrollable laughter in the past week. For example, on the afternoon of May 27 I received one of the best emails of my life. I cried so hard at the good news my tears spilled into an uncontrollable laughter.

Out of nowhere, I keep finding myself laughing about a recent Zoom session I had with my college girlfriends. My girl Joni recently started interviewing her friends and family and posting the interviews on her Facebook page because she's using virtual platforms as an opportunity to connect with others during the pandemic. For our interview, Joni wanted to discuss friendship. During the interview, we laughed so hard with and at each other that Joni could barely ask us the questions she had lined up. My girl Tish was wearing a silver cami, which looked to be made out of velvet, so her sexy Zoom swag became the humorous center of everything we said.

These days, laughter lasts only a little while. By Friday, May 28, I was glued to the news. Minneapolis continued to burn. Other cities joined. My mentee told me Cleveland's protest was going to be held on Saturday, May 29, at two P.M. And I'm not going to lie, my first reaction was one of annoyance, because where was this same protest energy when any of the aforementioned Clevelanders were murdered? But I don't like to get stuck in the past, so I asked my mentee about the location. She said she heard everyone was to meet downtown at the Free Stamp (a thirty-five-ton sculpture that makes a nod toward the Civil War), which is problematic, but that's an entirely different conversation that I don't care to get into right now. Anyway, the lump in my throat returned because I knew what was next—my husband and I would be in another back-and-forth about his attending the protest. I knew he'd want to go. The same worry made its way back into my chest. Once again, this could be another dangerous-ass encounter with the police, so I did not want him to go.

On the morning of Cleveland's protest, I woke up to my husband saying, "I'ma go shoot." "What about the coronavirus?" I quickly replied. I still don't know how or why this was my first response. I wanted to tell him not to go. But then again, I wanted him to go. I wanted him to witness and capture history. I wanted him to be a part of history. And because of the way my husband is "built," it didn't even make sense for me to think he wouldn't go to the protest. By noon, my husband's cameras were charged and he was on his way out the door.

"I think I want to go, too," I told my husband. I had been thinking about going since Friday, but I was torn. A part of me felt obligated to go. A part of me recognized this obligation as pressure, and it didn't feel smart to place more pressure on top of my preexisting chest pains. But that still didn't stop my mind from swinging back and forth from *go* to *don't go*. Every time I decided on not going, I remembered all the names on all the lists. "Naw, if you go, I won't be able to focus because I'ma be trying to make sure you good," my husband replied. And just like that, I wasn't going.

And then I sent my mentee a text telling her my husband was going to the protest. She replied, "I wanna go, too!" And just like that, I was going again. There was no way I could low-key be afraid to go while my twenty-two-year-old mentee showed no hesitation. Plus, I felt a responsibility to be there with her while she witnessed history and took a stand. So I told my husband I was going, and we made a simple plan. "I'll FaceTime you when I get down there," my husband said. We kissed and he left.

———

As soon as I arrived at the protest, all of my senses heightened. Once Na-Te' (my mentee) and I reached the thick crowd of people, we climbed up on a platform and faced the street. A Black man walked past us, stopped, faced our direction, and thanked three white women for being there. I got annoyed. Another Black man stood on top of a small school bus painted black and waved the Pan-African flag. My eyes flashed toward three Black men who had climbed the almost thirty-foot-high Free Stamp. I could feel the hot red of the stamp on their Black skin. I saw so many people I knew—former colleagues, other mentees, artists, local activists, and friends. I searched the crowd for my husband, but I couldn't find him.

I quickly realized that the protest lacked leadership. One minute the crowd was chanting, "Black Lives Matter!" and then, before we knew it, "No Justice. No Peace!" Then the crowd began walking toward the Justice Center. In the middle of thousands of people, I found Black (my husband). It was a bit surreal. I did not expect to find him in the crowd. As we approached the Justice Center, people started to lower themselves down on one knee. Then they quickly got up. It felt like a flash round of Simon Says. I was confused. But things got intense as we stood facing the Justice Center and people began throwing plastic water bottles at the windows. At one point, the crowd up front, about a hundred feet away, began running back toward where Na-Te' and I were standing because the police started to mace them. Black locked eyes with us and yelled, "Pole! Pole! Pole! Barricade! Get behind a pole or a car!" My chest. He didn't want us to get trampled during the stampede. But we didn't leave. We stood there for a good twenty minutes, even when the crowd kept running back toward us. I don't know why we didn't leave, but I guess I was so anchored in awe and anger and frustration that I couldn't move.

The moment a white boy, dressed in all black, came and crouched behind the car we were standing behind and whispered something to us like, "There's an undercover FBI agent following me. You guys don't mind if I change clothes right here, do you?"—I got the feeling that it was time to go. He switched his hat, took some items out of his pocket, and placed them in his book bag. Then he flung one book bag over his shoulder and another one under the car and walked away. A different white man who was standing next to us said, "We're going to step back because we don't know what he put under there." We stepped back, too, but we didn't leave.

I'm still trying to figure out why we didn't leave immediately after that. It was as if we knew nothing would instantly change in the moment, but we still waited. Perhaps all we needed was to witness the most chilling moment of the day—the people locked up on the inside banging on the walls of the county jail, which is located inside of the Justice Center. This was proof that we all heard each other even though we couldn't see them and they couldn't see us. My chest lightened, and Na-Te' and I left. As we walked about fifteen blocks back to our car, our backs to a part of history we will never forget, Na-Te' turned around and screamed, "Ms. Ali!" I turned around and saw the biggest pyrocumulus cloud I'd ever seen. Thick black puffs inched toward the sky. Something had to be on fire! A police car? My mouth dropped wide open.

Today is June 2, 2020, and the reality is, none of this is new. I'm talking about the chest pains and the panic and the worry and all of America's funky-ass situations. I felt like this two months ago. I felt like this a year ago. Five years ago. Ten years ago. As it turns out, the young man I mentioned at the beginning of this has graduated from high school. My brother ended up being cool. I have yet to run out of medicine. My husband is home safe, and my girlfriends and I are still cracking jokes about Tish's cami.

—JUNE 2, 2020

Letter to Juneteenth

Gregory Pardlo

Dear Juneteenth,

You're a celebrity all of a sudden? Don't get me wrong, I'm happy for you, and for the many Americans who now see how important you are. I don't remember the first time I learned about you, but I do know Black folks have been celebrating you for generations. What took the rest of the country so long to catch on? Coincidentally, one of my daughters had a question along these lines, which is the reason for my letter. *Why did it take more than two years for folks in Texas to get wind that slavery had ended?* I've known the answer intuitively, of course—race is at the heart of just about everything in this country—but I didn't know the details.

You probably get this question all the time. Before the pandemic, I was occasionally invited to speak to schoolchildren for Black History Month. I always had a presentation prepared. Without turning MLK or Rosa Parks into cartoon heroes or abstracting white supremacy into a scheme for world domination hatched by villains in white hoods, I wanted to have nuanced discussions with kids. Instead, I'd end up fielding questions like "Do you think things are getting better?" and "Why is your hair so curly?" I can only imagine the kinds of challenges you must face in getting your message out now that you're being introduced to so many new people. You have to admit you are a complicated historical marker.

Your name, Juneteenth, absorbs and memorializes the very kind of historical obfuscation that has been used to suggest African Americans have no historical relevance in the life of this country. I'm talking about our pathological ignorance of the central role African Americans have played in building the wealth, prosperity, and security that we all enjoy today, but I'm also talking about the practiced obscurantism around basic information that helps us authenticate the stories we tell ourselves about who we are individually and collectively.

Frederick Douglass believed he was "between twenty-seven and twenty-eight years of age" when he wrote his life narrative and lamented that "slaves know as little of their ages as horses know of theirs." This was by design, that is, not merely because there was no column for dates of birth in the livestock ledger. Douglass writes: "I was not allowed to make any inquiries of my master concerning [my birthday]. He deemed all such inquiries on the part of a slave improper and impertinent, and evidence of a restless spirit." What does it mean to be denied, as a matter of principle, anniversaries of any kind? You, Juneteenth, are a brick in the historical foundation upon which our country might reimagine its collective future.

This year, we also met Covid-19, which means, like everyone else's, my kid was homebound for most of the school year. She and I were at leisure to think about you as a historical marker and as a call to reflection. The morning of your arrival found her throwing some plush toy at the door, in my direction. I was trying to tell her about the history of Texas, to tell her that the Republic of Texas seceded from Mexico because Mexico had abolished slavery. "Why do I care about Texas?" is all I could pick out from the words muffled by the duvet she'd pulled over her head. If you had come on a normal school day, I like to think, she'd care about Texas.

By that hour of the morning, she would already have made the 45-minute subway ride from Brooklyn to the West Side of Manhattan and have been sitting in her ninth-grade classroom bursting with questions about Texas. Instead, she had developed a habit of sleeping late and attending—if you count the soundless square displaying her initials as attendance—the optional late-morning Zoom sessions some of her teachers offered for an hour each day before she drifted off into a miasma of headphones and group chats. Things were not normal.

In the quarantine weeks before you arrived, most mornings, including weekends, a school bell would ring in my mind, and I'd leap from bed in a panic. A mash-up of climate and virus anxiety made a further mash-up with my fear of failing my kids, and together they revised that old nightmare where I walk into a class to discover I'm the only one who doesn't know we're having a major exam. In this version of the nightmare, my performance on the exam will determine the physical, financial, and emotional health of my descendants for the next seven generations. That's enough to drive me to turn every space in our home into a makeshift classroom. My kids now avoid me, and they are not at all subtle about it.

Until this year, my oldest daughter spent her entire educational life at a tiny independent school where she knew every student, teacher, administrator, staff member, and in some cases, their extended families. This was her first year outside of the "glass bubble," as she called it. This year, she switched to a public school for multiple reasons, most of them, I suspect, having to do with race. Only recently she told her mother and me that once, in sixth grade, some boys in her class asked her permission to use the N-word. Apparently, they held Black culture in such high esteem that their thirst for Blackness would not be slaked until they could roll that obscenity on their tongues. They called it "privileges," a kind of disposable Blackness that only a Black person could bestow. My daughter alone, as the person of color in the class, could do the honors. The irony—that these most privileged children would amplify that privilege by leveraging cultural sensitivity against the one person it was intended to protect—may have been lost on the children at the time, but it was a formative moment in their developing relationships to race and, it must be specified, gender. The boys learned a toxic etiquette, the transactional logic that will always favor men and people who trade on their privilege.

What did my daughter learn? Hers is the perspective that I care about. I don't want to further privilege the boys and people like them by focusing on lessons in cultural awareness and sensitivity. I want to empower my kid by putting the aggression she will continue to experience into structural and historical perspective. Had she stayed at her private school, she would not have had access to resources for understanding her experiences, nor would she have learned ways to respond that would be useful to her. As long as she lives in this country, she will continue to have these experiences. Call it systemic racism, call it white supremacy, there's a kind of cultural inertia that will yield only to a substantial opposing force like the one that has risen in response to the murder of George Floyd.

Considering the state's history, it's a wonder news of the Emancipation Proclamation reached Black folks in Texas as soon as it did. You know this, Juneteenth, but I was never taught that Anglo immigrant settlers, along with the people they enslaved, had occupied the Mexican territory they would eventually call Texas initially at the invitation of the Mexican government. More settlers occupied the territory illegally. When Mexico abolished slavery, these largely—not to paint them with too broad a brush—illegal settlers ignored the law of the land and kept people in bondage. In a move foreshadowing the Emancipation Proclamation, Mexico granted citizenship to free blacks, and the outraged illegals—the settlers, that is—drafted their own constitution countermanding that citizenship. The settlers were so dependent on slavery that, rather than admit to Black humanity for any reason other than to prosecute Black people in courts of law, settlers would fight and die to maintain their social hierarchy.

By that time, the Anglo immigrant settlers had invaded the Mexican territory in such numbers that the Mexican military could not deport them. I'm choosing my words a little facetiously, but slavery thrived in Texas for good reason. Slave owners in Texas were not inclined to respect any law that would disrupt the social and economic order. Indeed, in response to the Emancipation Proclamation, slave owners from neighboring states spirited their plantations to Texas to keep profits and the fantasy of their dominion alive. Texas would remain a stronghold of slavery even after the Emancipation Proclamation because there had not been a significant enough buildup of Union troops during the Civil War to enforce the new law of the land. In two and a half years, General Gordon Granger would arrive in Galveston with 2,000 troops to make the message clear to everyone that slavery had ended.

If there had been no pandemic and classroom instruction hadn't been disrupted, would you have figured prominently in school curricula? Probably not. The idea that Texas was so remote that the news of Emancipation didn't reach them for two and a half years is deceptive at best. Yet any historical narrative that challenges the image of America as a nation that has always been devoted to fairness and equality gets spun as slander in the larger culture. Sadly, I believe only the murder of George Floyd could clear a space at all for you in the public mind.

If I don't have to practice my special brand of ambush home-schooling next year, it'll be interesting to see how your celebrity holds up in the classroom. Someone will figure out how to Disneyfy your virtues, for sure, but I also hope others will see in you a tradition of resourcefulness in contending with social and economic structures designed to prevent Black people from prospering. That you, June-teenth, have taken shape enough for me to write to you is proof of progress, I admit. It is also evidence of the challenges we face.

—JULY 4, 2020

Letter from Burlington

Major Jackson

Dear JF,

Happy Juneteenth! I am going to pretend that it's a national holiday until the rest of the country catches up. Today is one of those stunning late-spring days in northern New England. I will likely turn on the grill this evening and give respects to those ancestors and elders who made my life possible, who made all our lives possible. I think I can explain.

John, when you gave me this epistolary assignment in the midst of the protests, I immediately reread MLK's "Letter from Birmingham Jail," and sought out his phrase about direct action as presenting "our very bodies as a means of laying our case before the conscience of the local and the national community," followed by this gorgeous assertion: "We are caught in an inescapable network of mutuality, tied in a single garment of destiny." Juneteenth allows us to keep present in our hearts and minds the interrelatedness of our fates as free individuals. I think one of the arguments we miss out on making is that to say "Black Lives Matter" is to publicly acknowledge Black people's extraordinary contributions to the *idea* of America for whom many have benefited, to keep within sight the history of struggle, not just for one set of people, but as King famously notes: "Injustice anywhere is a threat to justice everywhere."

In this light, the tragic deaths of Ahmaud Arbery, Sandra Bland, Rayshard Brooks, Michael Brown, Jr., Philando Castile, George Floyd, Eric Garner, Trayvon Martin, Tony McDade, Tamir Rice, Breonna Taylor (so many in our lifetime) by racialized violence and police brutality amount to a kind of involuntary Black martyrdom that gets us closer to an idealized society. That's a harsh sentence to write, and the phenomenon is wrong. We have to say *No more!* Political leaders, religious leaders, community leaders, artists of all disciplines, people who believe in beauty, decency, and justice: we have to rise above our massive ambivalence and say: No more Black deaths on the altar of our country.

As a Black person, I walk with history within sight, and so it is difficult to not contemplate almost daily what freedom and equality mean; to ask, what does it taste and sound like, for the meek to inherit the earth, for BIPOC to be treated with dignity and respect, afforded the same privileges as those who claim a "white" identity? Black people and immigrant communities have carried forward the vision of America for some time now and yet, ironically, are some of the most persecuted. So, again, Happy Juneteenth!

I am writing from my home in South Burlington, Vermont. I know: an obvious utterance to make during a pandemic. I like those Instagram posts that overtly announce a person's mood with a chosen image that matches their disposition: #cozy (a fireplace and glass of wine), #confusion (green forests), #chilledout (sailing boats tethered to a floating dock on a placid lake). For all the obvious reasons, over the past several weeks I have posted pictures of marches and raised fists and traded out #emotionallyexhausted with high doses of #panic and #resistance. Does it bother you like it bothers me that a young Black Lives Matter activist was found dead in Tallahassee, Florida?

Speaking of Dr. King's notion of "networks of mutuality" in "Letter from Birmingham Jail": last week, amid the grief and rage at the ongoing struggle to affirm the sanctity of Black life against rhetorical and physical assaults that would diminish and extinguish it, amid the disparities of a global health crisis that seem to inordinately target Black and poor folk, a few friends and I, contrary to all sane advice, gathered at one of our homes on a deck early one evening for spur-of-the-moment cocktails. Lately, in correspondences, I have been speaking about the necessity of curating joy.

We were a group of six adults. We were more or less six feet away from each other. Not having seen each other in months, we pained at the inability to properly greet with hugs. Instead, our eyes and the occasional bow sufficiently conveyed the deep joy we felt.

Based on the pitch and volume of rising laughter that became tears, we gathered as much to survive the absurdity of this moment as to break the malaise of weeks of sheltering in place. John, having shared company with you on several occasions, I know you would have fit comfortably among this cabal. The hot temperatures of the day seemed stagnant, the tall pines above the house offered cool shelter, and the leaf-covered creek behind made for a setting that harkened to a pre-pandemic life where such impromptu get-togethers of reveling in banter and solving the world's problems were the norm.

While most of the conversation centered on the good fortune of one of us signing a new book contract while also staring down recent micro-aggressions, several friends delved into discussions of being recruited in the wake of the protests to craft or sign off on antiracist statements by institutions with which we are professionally affiliated.

We commiserated about feeling emotionally on guard unlike ever before while sitting in endless Zoom meetings, addressing the not-so-complicated issue of police brutality that led to George Floyd's and Breonna Taylor's deaths. I complained at hearing a paragraph I authored on a shared Google doc described by a fellow board member as "too strident," the same person who said, "This is not our fight." Also, how many times can one hear oneself and people who look like you (and other people of color) described as "minorities"? Still, for some older white Americans, the world lazily breaks down to two races: "whites" and "minorities." In one exchange, I had to make the obvious argument that "how we treat and regard the environment is inextricably tied to how we treat each other." These are vulnerable and tense moments that add layers of stress for BIPOC, who know just around the corner is the careless remark that sadly illumines how long the road we must travel together, as difficult as that may be, to figure out how to eradicate oppressions of all kinds and how to cherish the earth. But we remain hopeful, undaunted.

Ultimately, most of us conveyed over cheese and crackers feelings of relief to have so many colleagues, neighbors, and local businesses and nonprofits, unlike ever before, show up in meaningful ways that suggest earnest and humane concern for the plight of Black people. It is difficult to ignore the cries of a man calling out for his mother.

One hopes this is the blush of some permanent fever for reciprocity and justice. King reminds us: change is ongoing, the result of persistent action. Antiracist statements are the first leap for many people. One of us joked about terminating their career as an academic and starting a social equity consulting firm to meet high demand. I personally railed at the reality that such voluntary (read: unpaid) contributions to institutional messaging occlude the very work we love and were hired to perform. I imagine many BIPOC at some point in their career make peace with the fact that success in their fields often means, to greater or lesser degree, enlisting in the struggle for social justice, inclusion, and equity.

John, my dear brother poet Patrick Rosal tweeted something that I cannot stop pondering. After reminding us of Kevin Quashie's wonderful scholarship on the inner lives of Black folk as its own beautiful sovereign space in his book *The Sovereignty of Quiet: Beyond Resistance in Black Culture,* Rosal wrote:

> When allies fight for Black liberation, we are fighting for systemic change, but that systemic change is meant to protect the intimacy and interiority of Black life and Black lives. In practical terms, do not check in on your Black friends & expect them to process their feelings with you or worse that they will help you understand your feelings. If they need you, it will be in their time. The part of Black life that you don't actually see, that they don't share with you is the part you must protect. This is love. It is no small coincidence that it is also the thing that whiteness feels so awfully threatened by.

This idea that Black interiority is the threat to white supremacy woke me to a new reality about freedom: that space where we dream, imagine, think, and ponder the world around us is somehow menacing because it is this aspect that defines us as human and that which defies the horrid historic characterization of Black folk as anything but.

I've talked about the sacredness of the interior life, and like you, I teach writing and editing as a craft. Teaching is also a wildly political act when we contemplate especially the high rates of illiteracy in our country that prevent most from thinking independently, let alone expressing clearly their opinions. I understand even more the implication of Patrick's radical understanding: the marches and chants are ultimately for the purpose of guarding and defending our inner lives, even as we urge each other to confront and defy that which separates us.

After reading his tweet, I begin to reflect upon that awful, painful distance between the inner life of Tamir Rice and the officers who killed him, between Ahmaud Arbery and the two men who hunted him down, between George Floyd and Derek Chauvin, whose stance and knee showed how emotionally distant and psychically far he was from the man beneath him.

That gap is what we need to fill; not with fear or outdated lenses that distort, but a reimagining that announces something greater within us and a purpose born of our shared humanity.

—JUNE 22, 2020

Black Prayer

James Noël
Translated by Nathan H. Dize, Nashville

(To the memory of George Floyd)

> Lord forgive me
> I'm almost an atheist
> I address my black prayer
> to all those praying
> in the mosques
> in the churches
> in the monasteries
> in the Vodou temples
> I address my black prayer
> to the women who pray
> and those who cry
> black tears
> through the early morning prayer

a standing prayer
that does not bend
to the rules of engagement
that does not submit
to the catechism of the clock
a prayer that targets
the knees of the police officer
the one who took
Floyd's neck
as a fulcrum

a standing prayer
a gospel song
that aims for the knees
the cold knees of the police officer
that took
Floyd's neck
as a fulcrum
Hurry Lord
I'm almost an atheist
Act so that this man
Can no longer walk

—JUNE 5, 2020

Sense

Dawn Lundy Martin

"Sense," the first sacrifice—that cohesion dispersed. Only
lull left, "pause," they say, no such thing as "culmination"
unless cupping the squeezed-out life, black, a delicate furry
   thing.
Disturbances and gun buying. My mother refuses everything.
Her body is mostly skin, mostly enduring. I hear hope in her
   voice.
She tells me, when the pain ends, when calm comes, she's
   going
to buy me a birthday present and it's going to be a good one.
Remember? Soft to fingers, a thunderous pour, the clean feel of
   snow?
The way a child body can walk through a blizzard unbeknownst
   to anyone and deep inside of her own feeling space.

Somewhere else a cage rattles. In that place, fingers raw
to bone. But, here, gorgeous desolation, and the first
remembered sign of one's selfness. The I emerges, a staff,
a kingdom.

—MAY 2020

Black Motherhood in Sleepless Times

Idrissa Simmonds-Nastili

Sleep Goals: For baby to learn to self-soothe, and fall asleep at night in the bassinet (or Pack 'n Play) without nursing until asleep or rocking over a long time. For baby to have a consistent nap time.

On the evening of the day a video is released of a police officer kneeling on the neck of George Floyd—friend, father, homie, human—until George cannot breathe, until George calls for his dead mother, until George himself slumps and dies, I stay up late tending to my hair. I do this in preparation for sleep-training my son. The practice of combing out the knots in my head feels like both armor and surrender at a time when I cannot bear another thing weighing my body down.

It makes sense, in a time of racial trauma, to crawl back into the lap of my black girlhood and find the ritual that made me feel most seen, loved, and beautiful: sitting at my mother's feet while she sectioned and braided my hair. This walk through my personal history is a portal for my rage. I drench my hair in water, then detangle and comb it out with painstaking slowness. I have not properly combed out my hair since taking out braids following my son's birth. I shed and shed and shed. I think of my own departed father, named George. It is a good, solid name, one of my son's three middle names. Wherever you are from across the black diaspora, I appreciate the way George drawls from the mouth.

As I comb and pull and twist, I think of my father, my brother, my husband, my son, my cousins, my found family, my neighbors. I think of every black man I love and know. I think of all the black mothers I know and the tsunami of our collective grief. I wonder what these mothers are doing with their own hands right now. Some of us are writing, some of us are planting greens in the earth, some of us are essential workers bearing the brunt of both Covid-19 and the grief, rage, and fear that come with racism. Some of us are praying. All the hair that had nowhere to go when braided, all the growth now breaking free four months postpartum, lies in the sink like a soft, small animal. I don't know what to do with so much shedding. Should I burn it? Leave it in the backyard for the birds to find? Bury it? How do I care for the parts of my body that are no longer attached to me?

The goal of the bedtime routine is not to put him to sleep but to prepare him for sleep. Milk and sleep need to become separate functions. The last milk should end at least 20 minutes before he is put into his bed.

For the last four months I have slept most nights with my son's warm body pressed to mine, his steady infant breath a hush landing on my breast. We have established a sort of choreography—both of us awakening throughout the night to find the perfect position for him to latch on. As he sleeps, his mouth moves as if he is still nursing, still tethered to me. I look at his perfect face, watch his mouth dance, and try not to think this is the safest he will ever be. Someday my son may inhabit an America where he will no longer be the sweet baby strangers love to coo over, but the black man they fear. I must use the word *may*: I reject a bleak future as absolute truth.

We had to hire someone to help us help our son sleep. I have paid someone to buffer me from my own tendencies of protection in pursuit of a higher good. I am a black mother living in America. You cannot blame me for wanting to watch my child breathe all night. I am told all the ways that learning to sleep independently helps babies' brain development and leads to happier waking hours. I get it: good sleep hygiene for everybody. But there is only one truth my mind clamps to: My body can keep my child alive. My body tells the story of his life. He slipped from me easily, and I hope this means the world is ready for him.

But in sleeping next to me, my child is getting only light sleep. Light sleep, I have learned, is where newborns spend 75 to 90 percent of their time. This is the sleep that comes in sips. Twenty minutes here, thirty minutes there. "You want him to experience deep sleep," the consultant tells us. My son wakes up every hour or so, eyes still shut, rooting blindly for my breast before latching and relaxing again. He needs to learn how to self-soothe, I am told. He needs to fall back asleep without the aid of my body. At his age, he has everything he needs to do so.

I marvel at this.

I am a grown woman.

I don't have the tools to self-soothe my way to sleep.

Or black people have learned to self-soothe in other ways.

During nursing, the pituitary gland opens like a valve and releases oxytocin. This love chemical flows into my milk and makes both me and my child want to fall into deep sleep. What does it mean for my body to relax and fall into a deep sleep in this era of wokeness, of hypervigilance? To let my guard slip completely away and sleep well is a dangerous thing. If I stay ready, I don't have to get ready.

He is going to cry. He has the right to be angry. His world has changed. Give him space to express himself.

On the first night of sleep training, protests erupt across the country. My son cries and cries for almost forty-five minutes. On a night where my city breaks and burns, his frantic shrieks seem to join the weeping of the world. I have been instructed to sit in a chair beside him, positioned so he can sense my presence and hear me but cannot see my face. I expected this to be stressful and for it to be impossible to fight the urge to scoop him into my arms. But I find myself nodding alongside his tears, shushing him, saying his name and reminding him: "I'm here. You can do this. You are okay." The way church mothers might surround the heaving body of a wayward sinner locked in grief or shame. I can handle his rage and frustration as long as I am alongside him, in the thick of it, too. I channel all the confidence and peace I can muster from my body to his. "You can put in headphones and listen to music if you want," the sleep consultant says. I don't. I will not buffer myself from his cries in order to make myself more comfortable. Just because you choose not to hear the cries does not mean they cease to exist.

All night I listen with one ear for my children sleeping, and with the other for helicopters and police sirens circling my neighborhood. Where I live, black folks are ever ready. Activism is stamped in the bones and blood of native black Oaklanders. I know I am not going to sleep tonight. Being a black mother is its own form of activism. I hear phantom cries throughout the night. I creep up the steps to lay a hand across my son's chest. He is sleeping sweetly, deep in the cocoon of sleep while the world around him seethes.

On the second night, sirens and helicopters circle again. This time, my son falls asleep after only thirty minutes. There is both magic and a touch of grief for me in this. Where previously he needed me to fall asleep, he is discovering his own ability to access rest. And while the city around us and the country we are nestled within breaks itself open and screams *Enough!,* my black child is learning a new superpower. Yes, I will finally have my bed back. Yes, my children sleeping through the night will open up delicious hours in the evening for me to do with what I will. But I want this for him for one reason: I want him to know what it is like to get lost in his dreams. For both of my children, I want them to access the full breadth of the power of their visionary minds. May they imagine the futures we have been too dumb and afraid to actualize. And then may we walk alongside them with enough courage to help them make it so.

I did not birth children to be afraid. I believe their lives are meant to be songs of jubilation, not laments. Most days I can lean into this belief and hold on to it like a mantra. Other days, I need them to believe it when I don't have the strength to.

Note: Language in the last two quotations credited to Arlene Fryling at Gentle Touch Sleep Time.

—JUNE 9, 2020

Letter to a Mother
Who Survived and Thrived

Cynthia Tucker

Mom,

You were right about my neighbors: They are friendly and gracious, just as I would expect southerners to be. Most of them recognize my eleven-year-old and me, even if they don't know our names. They nod and wave when they see us out walking or bike-riding, just as I would expect southerners to do. Besides, we are among two or three black families in the vicinity. Of course they greet us with smiles, not wanting to be perceived as disapproving or hostile or, heaven forbid, racist.

On September 17, 2020, the morning after Hurricane Sally blew through here, leaving Mobile bruised and battered, I heard the noise of chainsaws down the street. With no electricity for blocks around, no radio or TV news to inform me of local damage, I meandered down the street to see who was about. A huge old blackjack oak had fallen across the pavement, blocking the roadway, and neighborhood men were busy sawing it into movable chunks. Their wives stood in a huddle, watching.

I joined the huddle, the only black person there, as women discussed the wind and rain, the fallen trees, the stillness after the storm, with few cars about and no one rushing off to work. I complained that I couldn't even brew a cup of coffee, and a neighbor invited me into her home. She and her husband have a generator, so their electricity was humming and their coffee machine brewing.

She introduced me to her grown daughter, her husband, her mother, and a couple of other neighbors also seeking a hot cup of coffee. We shared more small talk. It was a pleasant interlude, reminding me of the friendliness and simple gestures of goodwill that are commonplace in the South.

But I still don't feel at home here. Though I grew up in this part of the world, I am a stranger in a strange land.

When I returned six years ago to live in LA (Lower Alabama), as I like to call it, I thought I could manage the change to a more conservative political culture, a more traditional world view, a less socially sophisticated ambience. I was wrong.

Even as I was enjoying the cup of coffee my neighbor generously gave me, I couldn't help but think as I looked around at the company in her kitchen: Most of you will vote to reelect Donald J. Trump, won't you? You quietly accept his racism, his sexism, his nativism, his mendacity, his corruption—even if you don't celebrate it overtly. He's your guy.

Mom, I admire the way you've managed to stitch together a pleasant and meaningful life just an hour and a half northeast of here, in an even smaller and more narrow-minded place. You've spent all of your life—except for your college years—in this part of the world, coping with the explicit racism, the constricted world view, the diminished expectations for black folk. You and Daddy did more than survive. You thrived.

You have told me, more than once, that you and he made the decision not to join the Great Migration to the Northeast or Midwest. You made a commitment to stay in a rural area of the Deep South to try and help our people, so that's where I grew up. During my childhood, you and he represented a tiny segment of the population: black Americans with college degrees. And as small-town educators in segregated schools, you were essentially doing missionary work—encouraging black children to stay in school, pointing the way to college, helping them find scholarships, even visiting their parents at home to smooth the passage.

And thanks to you and Daddy, I have options you didn't have. I, too, have spent most of my life in the South—but not this South. My adult years in Atlanta, a blue island in a red sea, gave me the comfort of a large black middle class, racially integrated neighborhoods, and voters who demanded equality for all, regardless of race, religion, or sexual orientation. When I lived there, I was represented by the late great John Lewis, for goodness' sake. I miss that.

Even as Georgia trends toward purple, Alabama remains deeply and miserably ultraconservative, committed to Trump, mean in its hyper-religiosity, suspicious of immigrants, hostile to gays, lesbians, and transgender folk. I don't see any rebel flags on my morning walks—my neighbors are too sophisticated for that—but the Trump yard signs remind me where I am.

So does teaching at the local university. While several of the college professors share my political views, many of my college students are enmeshed in the conservative politics with which they grew up. Some complain about the "government overreach" that requires them to wear masks to class to fight the spread of the novel coronavirus.

I can't stay, Mom. My daughter and I will miss being able to see you as often as we do now. Though the plague has transformed our visits, I've enjoyed sitting on your porch, seeing your flowers still in bloom, sharing the sweet potato casserole that you make better than anyone else I know. While you are in good health for a nonagenarian, I don't know how much more time we will have to share.

But I can't stay. I want something different for myself and for my chocolate-colored child. I love the South, but I want to live in a part of it that is trying to be better, not a part that wants to return to a time that never was. Sometime in the next couple of years, I will have to make my way back to a part of the South that isn't trying to preserve the monuments of traitors, that doesn't deny science or dispute logic, that respects diversity, embraces immigrants, and welcomes refugees.

This is not that South.

—OCTOBER 8, 2020

"Maybe"
(Letter to a Daughter Who Will Wear Two Masks)

Jasmon Drain

Maybe I'll be wrong about this whole thing. It's possible.

So, all right, here goes . . .

Hi there. I realize you don't know me and perhaps never will, but I've always wanted a daughter, a little girl like you. Heck, I spent my life preparing, nervous about the opening of these very conversations. That's sort of embarrassing, since you still haven't come. Yet sometimes, in the early mornings, when I'm jogging in a pickup truck's trail, checking the scenery and all the while assuming I'm alone, I'm rather grateful you haven't. I'll now have this talk with you anyway—before it's too late . . . just in case.

Because you'll certainly inherit the ambition of my eyes, teamed with dangerously darkened skin, my assertiveness, and long, thin toes to carry you through to . . . safety. Don't interrupt. This is difficult enough, so please listen closely. You'll need this. It's the only protection offered us.

Hold on! Wait-wait-wait! Don't do that! Hold it in!

Okay, okay . . . Whew.

With one cough or sneeze that may bleed into a runny nose, you'll be amplified in diseases. One is the vector of color ignorance. The other is known as the Rona. Both magnify your invisibility and make you more untouchable. Here, lemme check your temperature before I continue.

Not too long ago, coughing and sneezing meant very little, merely a nonviolent part of being human. No worries, in these fifty you won't often be considered that. You'll be marked coming from me, delivered fully symptomatic, with these same shining eyes, same rounded ears, the small teeth forming a smile people remember you for. As a result, you'll be born with the first mask.

The dark-skinned one I mentioned? I apologize in advance. I REALLY do. 'Cause along with it, I'll be forced to give you the second before you're not a month old, the one attached to this addled letter. By then, I'm hoping to have a strong enough memory of what you'll look like. It shouldn't matter that you're covered and hidden. You'll eventually get used to that. Hey, guess what? I actually tried to find a pink one for you. Nah, they didn't have any. Sorry. But it's not so big a deal. Now, tighten the straps. Can you breathe in it? Make sure to say it loudly if you cannot.

Huh? No, no, no. It's unacceptable that you don't speak clearly yet. You don't have much time to learn this, so stop mumbling. Nice and plainly. No aggression. Say it slowly, as I do. There you go. Is the filter positioned? Good. In a few minutes, I'll show you how to insert a new one. Yes, you'll have to wear this mask your entire life also. There's no vaccine for who you'll be or how you'll be viewed, for the unseen or visible parts that will ofttimes be assumed of you.

What you say? How does any of this affect you? Or wait, did you say in-*fect*? Is that what you said?

Fine. I'll explain. Less than a year ago, in this Windy City, the second mask would have panicked any of the liquor store owners on 69th and Halsted, and even the white-coated CVS pharmacist with his windows shattered and shelves emptied. Your born mask brought fear. This new one redoubles it. He'd have called "them people" on you immediately. Even while tucked in my arms as I browse the aisles, with a single barrette holding the ponytail choking three or four strands of your curly hair, you'd most likely have gotten stares. They'd have gaped at your saliva as it soaked my wrists like paint from a mural. Yea, I know they're still looking now. Don't be so offended. That's not new. Because you're just as unwelcome as before. As I was. But without this new mask and its germ-blocking apparatus securely intact, you wouldn't even be granted entry. Isn't that odd? One mask keeps you out. The other allows you in. You choose which is which.

Please remember, though, if I'm not around, let someone know if it's hard for you to exhale in it, in either of them. Yell if you have to. Oh, that's right . . . I said no aggression. How hypocritical. I can't lie, my biggest fear is *they* won't pay attention.

Aww, jeez, I'm being terribly unfair. It's a bit much? I'm sorry for confusing you so soon. Shoot, by the time you'll need to know this, that chain-store glass will be swept up. It was only broken in the silly belief that everyone should discard their masks. Was I proud of the attempt? Sure I was. Well, kinda. But I'll be damned if I trust it going forward. With that said, I'll go on wearing mine just to be safe. I'll "yes, suh" and "no, suh" and make "no sudden moves" in the collapse of Chicago's mile of magnificence, or in the Englewood liquor store where your saliva drools into a redder color. Maybe there I could be a tender of help, the second voice in big city wind. Plus, all this I'm dumping ain't really yours anyway. It's mine, you say. From my time? Nope, can't be. What you mean, that's the way it used to be? Impossible. You telling me people won't think like that no more? Things gonna be different for you? Okay then . . . alrighty. I guess I can see it. It's mostly mine. 'Cause when you told me earlier that breathing wasn't very hard with or without either of your masks, I heard. I listened. For your benefit, I'll spend another maybe or two believing you won't have distanced picnics at Gwendolyn Brooks Park; or in your time, jobs for working people wearing the essential and suffered colors of any mask will be aplenty, and not simply in box-shaped and under-waged corporate stores.

I'll be hopeful they'll discover you, fully receive the colors of your masks, then peel them off to hear and envision your delicate chest as it expands, just as I now do. As I've always wished to. *Hmmmmm.* Lemme think on it . . . Maybe I can try and look at it through your eyes. They *are* bright. Yea, there's a small chance it's to be different.

In case, though . . . juuuuuust in case I'm wrong about any of the nonsense we've talked about, put it on as a favor to me. This one favor. Put them both on with the filter I forgot to show you how to insert. Because maybe in the chances I spoke of, they'll be blind to you as well. Possibly even deaf.

And I realize those are the maybes I can't afford.

—JULY 2020

This'll Hurt Me More

Camille T. Dungy

Don't make me send you outside to find a switch,
my grandmother used to say. It was years before
I had the nerve to ask her why switch was the word
her anger reached for when she needed me to act
a different way. Still, when I see some branches—
wispy ones, like willows, like lilacs, like the tan-yellow
forsythia before the brighter yellow buds—I think,
these would make perfect switches for a whipping.
America, there is not a place I can wander inside you
and not feel a little afraid. Did I ever tell you about that
time I was seven, buckled into the backseat of the Volvo,
before buckles were a thing America required.
My parents tried, despite everything, to keep us
safe. It's funny. I remember the brown hills sloping
toward the valley. A soft brown welcome I looked for

other places but found only there and in my grandmother's
skin. Yes, I have just compared my grandmother's body
to my childhood's hills, America. I loved them both,
and they taught me, each, things I needed to learn.
You have witnessed, America, how pleasant hillsides
can quickly catch fire. My grandmother could be like that.
But she protected me, too. There were strawberry fields,
wind guarded in that valley, tarped against the cold.
America, you are good at taking care of what you value.
Those silver-gray tarps made the fields look like a pond
I could skate on. As the policeman questioned my dad,
I concentrated on the view outside the back window.
America, have you ever noticed how well you stretch
the imagination? This was Southern California. I'd lived
there all my life and never even seen a frozen pond.
But there I was, in 70-degree weather, imagining
my skates carving figure eights on a strawberry field.
Of course my father fit the description. The imagination
can accommodate whoever might happen along.
America, if you've seen a hillside quickly catch fire
you have also seen a river freeze over, the surface
looking placid though you know the water deep down,
dark as my father, is pushing and pushing, still trying
to get ahead. We were driving home, my father said.
My wife and my daughters, we were just on our way
home. I know you want to know what happened next,
America. Did my dad make it safely home or not?
Outside this window, lilac blooms show up like a rash
decision the bush makes each spring. I haven't lived
in Southern California for decades. A pond here

killed a child we all knew. For years after that accident,
as spring bloomed and ice thinned, my daughter
remembered the child from her preschool. And now,
it's not so much that she's forgotten. It's more that
it seems she's never known that child as anything other
than drowned. My grandmother didn't have an answer.
A switch is what her mother called it and her grandmother
before her. She'd been gone from that part of America
for over half a century, but still that southern soil
sprang up along the contours of her tongue. America,
I'll tell you this much, I cannot understand this mind,
where it reaches. Even when she was threatening
to beat me, I liked to imagine the swishing sound
a branch would make as it whipped toward my body
through the resisting air. She'd say, this is hurting me
more than it's hurting you. I didn't understand her then,
but now I think I do. America, go find me a switch.

—JUNE 15, 2020

Have I Ever Told You
All the Courts I've Loved

Ross Gay

The very first would be the ones in the apartments where I grew up, where I have the firm memory of my father dunking while still wearing his Pizza Hut duds—my brother confirms this—and where I marked spots (X's with medical tape) to practice for the hot shot competition, shoveling snow from the court (cue little-kid-shoveling-snow-so-he-can-practice-basketball music), which, yeah whatever, Craig won. Sometimes at this court there were two hoops, sometimes one (a hoop can get pulled down by a big kid, you know? I have been that big kid. Who even knows what a big kid is anymore?), always it was crooked, often there were puddles, perpetually there were little craters in the asphalt, which, if the game was serious, someone would probably take a little bit of that asphalt home in their palm or knee.

And then the courts—that's overstatement, it was a hoop—at the public elementary school next to the apartments (where the court, the hoops, had been all the way ripped down by the big kids), where one night a couple kids from Bristol came by to play, and I probably had the very best shooting game of my life. In a two-versus-two, fourteen years old, in the dark as I recall, having a night like Klay Thompson would thirty years later, myself the sole verifier of the feat. (I kid you not, I dreamed of one of those guys a few weeks ago.) Also at that hoop, my buddy Chris and I, burst from our chrysalises into butterflies by a couple tabs of LSD (apiece), leapt until, I swear to you, we got first our wrists, then our forearms, then our elbows above the rusty rims. Oh, fuck it: we got our chins above the rusty rims. Butterflies blending into the Milky Way that night were we. Chimney swifts, too.

And of course those courts at the Philadelphia Bible College up the road we would sneak into through a never-locked back door. Who doesn't love a prohibited court, one you might get kicked out of? And if it has a wood floor and a roof, and soft rims to boot, good lord—you better kick me out. And Delaware, pinned in a floodplain between I-95 and Business Route 1, behind the Denny's and car dealerships and pool hall and ice cream place where I actually might have cried once when they didn't have any chocolate with peanut butter left (or that might have been my mom, though no vanilla with peanut butter would have been her tragedy), the court with the huge metal backboards where that oldhead Gerald (this well before the term oldhead, and Gerald was probably at least twenty years younger than I am now) could make bank shots from anywhere on the court. The sound something between a timpani and a slammed door. This was one of the many courts I have loved where for a few years at least I had to beg a brief pause in the game (as you know, it is a kindness for a game to be paused for you) because I was vomiting once or twice a day for no discernible reason, at least to my folks who were neither therapy adjacent nor mental health literate. I'm saying, the puking was an expression of what we might now call anxiety (or "nerves," in the olden days), which would return in the near future a bit less convoluted. As anxiety, etc., I mean.

Anyhow, I remember running off the court, one finger in the air to indicate *right back!,* finding a big sycamore to lean against, and bending over, getting ready to let loose. And I can remember at least once at that court Mike jogging behind me and rubbing my back as I puked—wait; I think I remember him holding my locks up out of the slurry of chicken tenders and French fries and cheesesteak and gummy bears and salt and vinegar chips (my dad had class!), and rubbing my back—I do remember that!—while everyone else kind of gagged or looked away or took a couple shots or wondered what will it be like in the future to look at a phone in a moment like this or said, "Hurry up, dude," or "Is he okay?" Mike held my hair up and rubbed my back while I puked until I was done and jogged back, the other team's little guard watching me get into the lane before yelling "Ball in!" (Mike and I cried and cried over our Whoppers in the Penndel Burger King when he told me he was moving away.)

And Vets farther up the road, where they had lights, and on good nights the parking lot would be full enough that the adjacent field became a parking lot. Where the games were good enough that when, one time, I broke my nose going for a rebound—someone's elbow accidentally putting a hearty divot on the left side of what had been the bridge of my nose. (Did you all make a tee for kickoffs by kicking your heel against the ground? That's what it looked like.) I couldn't bring myself to leave and stuck around for another couple hours (and had a less pleasant nose-fixing experience thanks to that, which I will tell you about another time). I remember one of the Wilson sisters, part of the Wilson family (all ballers, even Ma and Pa), can't remember which one, ringers from the perimeter and slashers both, seeing my crooked nose and making a face that made me think uh-oh.

And the beautiful old gym where I went to college, which they replaced with an ugly new one. And the beautiful old gym where I went to grad school, which they replaced with an ugly new one (where I became kin with my brother Patrick, who claims to have ripped me—he described it very precisely, which any good liar knows you do to tell a convincing lie—as I was coming down left-handed on a fast break; he poked it with his right and did a 360 dunk, he remembers).

All the beautiful old courts I have known that they have replaced with shitty new ones. All the auxiliary gyms, all the courts under an overpass, that run in Pittsburgh in the big public school that got moved when they were redoing the floor to a beautiful gym at Carlow University (god, I hope they didn't ruin that gym with an upgrade). In my memory, that gym is like a greenhouse. In my memory there are windows and nooks made of low bookshelves and beanbags and long pillows to lounge on reading or napping or stretching luxuriously when you're waiting for your game. The very slight beautiful rank smell of gym and fabric. A Roman-style water fountain burbling very nice water. That gym in my memory is a Christopher Alexander situation if ever there was one.

A couple courts in Jersey City. The White Eagle, now that was a gem. Terry Dehere shot eleven three-pointers in my face there, until my buddy said, "Dude, don't let him shoot! He's Terry Dehere!" And the one down 9th that you had to kick the broken glass from. And that one in Hoboken on Washington and Park, I think. In a big public park, which is usually a good thing. The tight end for the Giants at the time used to get in over there. And that one in Hartford, the courts were a little shiny for my taste, but the runs were good, also in a big public park. Once during some loud debate over a call, some bullshit walk, some bullshit foul, someone said, "Shhh, there's white people around." As Du Bois more or less says, white people can't wait to take your rims down.

And so, so many courts in Philadelphia. Palumbo, just up from Sarcone's, a couple blocks from the fig tree (it's growing back!), where that little girl who I did not know spotted me from across the gym, set up shop behind me with her sort-of-ruthless comb (to be fair, I was the one let it get so knotty), and put my hair in the prettiest braids they have ever been in while I was watching the game before ours. And Seger court, beloved Seger, where I think I started understanding a court as a site of care, ball as a practice of care, a kind of constant practice at working it out (which a ref always fucks up; as does, so often, a coach), which is the point of the game, you know, working it out. You know, together. That's the flight. That's the beauty. The quick eye contact—a kind of touch—between you and the guard whose name you do not yet know. The big man whose name you do not yet know, seeing your eyes touch, sliding into a high back screen to free you up for an alley-oop. A baby who stumbled on the court whisked quickly off by a kid waiting for next. Dude's knee buckled and three people immediately put hands on him. Banging on doors and dragging the youngsters out of bed to the court. Bringing water to share. An old-timer taking a kid to the side, teaching her how to use her hands in the post. Two bruisers in the key who keep touching each other, leaning on each other, holding each other, while there's a looooooonnnnnnng dispute over a call. Show me that Jamal Crawford dance move, would you? Hold my ball till tomorrow, I gotta get to work. Man, just keep it. You okay? You good, baby? You all right? Love you. The whole very busy court paused as a father takes his son and another boy, both of them taller than him, who just got into a quick scuffle, outside the court to work it out. The forty-two times he touched those children while talking. The seventeen they touched him. A good court—maybe this is the definition of a good court—helps you witness the catalog, the encyclopedia, of tendernesses it is.

Which leads me to the court I'm playing on now, a more solitary affair, but a beauty still, tucked into a neighborhood not too far from a coffee joint, up a hill, playground nearby, a couple picnic tables, I think, and a bike path running next to it. They unbroke my heart by taking the Covid-19 bars off the rims a few weeks back. Like many a perfect court, this one's too small—with a running start you could jump from one three-point line to the other—but too small makes it sweet, a touch jenky, nice for the full-court one-on-one, two dribbles and you're in range. One end has a soft rim and the other an obstinate double rim. It's got a side in the sun and a side in the shade. Which means sometimes a side with puddles and a side without. A side with a drop-off that will tweak your ankle, and a side with an edge smooth as sorbet. (Nothing about this court, I am happy to report, is "smooth as sorbet.")

On that same side there is a big, beautiful tree just low enough to bat away corner threes (not that I would ever shoot one), unless you shoot a line drive (not recommended). A few big soft pines nearby whisper when you make a good move. Or dribble off your foot. There is a simple bench beneath one of them. At one end of the court a loose ball rolls down into a playground and then the street (good for those quick sprints to keep it from escaping), at one end into a little mown field. On one side, it rolls beneath a picket fence into someone's yard; on the other side, it rolls into a thicket of honeysuckle, redbud seedlings, that creamily fragrant climber I just learned is a clematis, poison ivy, and autumn olive, which is one of my very favorite berries. Autumn olives are sweet, especially the longer they are on the bush, and they are among the most beautiful flourishes in the kingdom. I don't mean the kingdom. Fuck the kingdom. I mean earth. Little silver speckles on the bright red fruit subtled into shimmering the leaves.

The last time I played here, I didn't want to leave. I kind of couldn't bring myself to. In my head I was kind of begging my friend, my partner in ball, who is no longer here (don't worry, he's alive), to stick around, to stretch the game out. C'mon, man. Five more points combined and we're done. Now five more. Okay, two more possessions apiece. Two more. C'mon. Let's stay a little longer, don't you think? Let's just keep going. Up and back. Your knees okay? The hammy's good? Ankle? C'mon, let's hang around. A couple more shots. Your ball. A couple berries. Clematis in the breeze. Have some of my water. C'mon, my ball. We don't have to be anywhere, do we? We don't have to leave anytime soon? Pack up and leave, do we? This must be the sweetest court in all of Indiana. In all of southern Indiana. In southern Indiana. Autumn olive and clematis and a rim soft as bathwater. Should we stay a little longer? Out here? We don't have to leave, do we? Anytime soon? Do we need to leave now? Is it time now to leave?

Do we need to leave.

—SEPTEMBER 15, 2020

Letter from Exile:
Finding Home in a Pandemic

Samiya Bashir

Oh, Dear.
>Thrown away. Caught mid-toss.
>I tried to write about everything except my own experience.
>Time has come so untethered. Remember Tuesdays?
>Everything remains unresolved.

I'm still, in theory, one of two 2019–20 Rome Prize fellows in Literature. This year marks the 125th anniversary of the American Academy in Rome; a rare two-poet year. Bold and brilliant Nicole Sealey holds the second prize.

We are, together, the academy's first Black women literature fellows. Ever. Being a Negro First™ just feels so last century.

———

I'm almost certain the academy tried not to kick us out.

Remember certainty?

First, they kicked some of us out of our rooms, some out of our studios, some out of both. Word was we'd be shuffled, only temporarily, to maximize social distancing. For our safety.

The days groundhogged and caught. Food was altered. Then adjusted. Then gone. Our lives were pieced apart and jumbled around with an almost-impressive opacity.

We weren't allowed to leave our new shuffle-spaces. We were asked not to see each other. We sang from our rooftops and leaned through our windows to see each other.

Conflicting messages raced toward obsolescence. Now stock groceries, at least three weeks' worth. Now leave your groceries. Leave your belongings. Leave your projects. Leave your work. Just leave.

You ain't gotta go home, but you cain't stay here is what I hear being said when I remember it. We'd stood a meter apart, for our safety, across the steps. Some of us, just away for a day or a few, were told remotely: *You can't come home.*

And it was our home. And where were we supposed to go? Nearly everyone from New York had sublet their places. Someone else had just sold their home. I'd ended my lease months before landing in Rome.

I was given two days—okay, less—to un-home myself. Borders were closing, they said, for our protection. Pack a life. Leave a life behind. Thrown away, one or two of us stayed despite it all. Ghosted the empty city streets in search of shelter. Home.

———

For decades I joked that home was somewhere around 33,000 feet. No more.

Remember planes?

Around dawn on the first day of spring we were flung, stiff-legged and bleary, from frying pan to fire. For our protection. The last fellows in flight. The ways we clutched our rationed masks and overused gloves were, honestly, kinda sketch.

Rome-Fiumicino International Airport lay empty as old-timey Christmas Day. No Prada. No Gucci. No Valentino. Dark windows twinkled all their shiny things. Everyone tried to avoid eye contact.

Onboard we shuffled to separate corners, then again for more social distancing. A flight attendant's ersatz alarm woke me when my mask slipped in my sleep.

Then magic and sisterhood and poetry and love and dreaming and trust all got together and gifted me a place to land by the sea. In one day. By nightfall. Imagine.

Take that, hope.

The first thing I saw as we landed ashore was a big-box store. Home.

At JFK someone tested my temperature on the jet bridge. I guess I passed. Then the constant assault of commercials. So many Cuomos. So many talking heads loudly declaring war. For my protection.

That our isolations showed not violence or oppression but care seemed so basic when I left Rome that it remained unspoken. Now "shelter in place" was a canyon echo.

That language, it mattered.

"I guess a silver lining of all this," I heard so often that I lost count, "is we get a break from school shootings."

The Venetian etymology of *ciao* is one of enslavement. Whether coming or going, one said *s'chiavo*: I am your slave. This was, I guess, in case someone forgot.

So much about home is buried beneath every breath.

I remain your slave. Venice flooded but—dammit—

I wasn't there.

A very fine person met me outside of Logan Airport to take me home. We followed Route 3 to Route 6 talking (mostly him) through politics, through life.

He'd spent years building his livery business, he said. By March he'd already had to let every one of his drivers go. Now he himself was back to driving.

He noticeably avoided praising or defending the president. No one wanted to fight that night. It was so late. I was so tired.

I couldn't say whether it had been moments or millennia since our last masked goodbye outside of customs. Holding each other up. Taking pictures.

Now the house on the hill sat cloaked in new-moon darkness. Like me. Alone.

To matter. To be important. To signify.

So well curated we were an accident. Our hodgepodge had lived together, traveled, studied, worked, and eaten together every single day. Six months. Longer than Covid-19.

At first all I could do was mourn us and all we'd left shattered atop Gianicolo. That our hill was named for Janus—two-faced god of beginnings and endings, doorways and gates, transitions and time—felt ominous after having felt just right.

Exile. Loss. My heart sinks. At least two of us likely contracted coronavirus on those flights back home. I spoke broken Italian for weeks, catching myself *un po' prima*—a little earlier—each day.

This year threads its needle between robbery and gift, horror and beauty. Global trauma and lovely surprises.

To wake up in Cape Cod! Shingles! Whippoorwill winds! A new old-fangled tide clock!

Quarantines require preparation. What do I know from hunkering? Shopping and setup and space and supplies met most of us who went home, but I wasn't home.

The refrigerator was so empty it shone. My phone was hooked up to all the wrong satellites. All day I went out of my way not to touch anything. I covered my face and crept the Cape gathering whatever I guessed I might need.

Yes, toilet paper. Yes, tequila. Yes, flash-frozen soups and every kind of chip I could find.

I bathed in hand sanitizer at every stop. I tried to not be a stranger. I snapped through pair after pair of the latex gloves I'd been using to dip ink. I remembered that I'd left my ink atop Gianicolo.

That was the first day. There was another. And another.

It was good that I didn't have to do anything because I could barely breathe. I made my quarantine phone calls. I attributed my breath, my tight chest, to everything except my own experience.

I was almost sure my life mattered.

The thing about Twenty-First-Century Negro Firsting™ is that racism—the distraction of it, as Toni Morrison warned—is just so boring.

Yet another exhausting lack of imagination.

Most days America screams to anyone who'll listen how it hates me so much it would rather kill us all than let me live. Home.

Our first "reopenings" were met by multiple mass shootings. We barely discussed it.

I want to cry from all this freedom.

Surfing a sandbar in the sea, I confront what *home* means. I don't know. I'm not actually surfing, because sharks, but I confront. I sat through *Jaws* at least twice now.

"My kids are on that beach, too," the mayor of Amity Island said, a bit overdue. He'd been mocking the sheriff for insisting they close the beaches after another deadly outbreak of shark attack. Familiar? This time his kids were on the beach. This time the great white problem mattered.

Biggest protest movement in American history was a phrase that barely survived its own news cycle. No matter the nonstop marching, the nonstop murdering. No time to come home from a police-murder protest before another police murder occurs.

Even in apocalyptic times, when words scarcely even mean anymore, they matter. Asian Giant Hornets become Murder Hornets become Kung Fu Virus become kids in need of a good incarceration camp.

We've needed a bigger boat, like, forever.

So many of us set adrift at once. Either we can't go home, or we can't leave. Crisis after crisis kick-drops all our plans. Virtuality claims even our closest family and friends. All the wrong people keep dying alone. Behind glass.

Since day drinking and night sleeping both became available choices, I've struggled to stay present through the never-ending now. I can't remember the last time I've been this still.

No flights. No road trips. No million places to be. A sweet old house by the sea where whole communities thrive between the walls like jellicle cats.

The thing about *going,* much less *home,* is how it shrinks all the surreal, all the moments, into just some things that happened. Anecdote. Questionable, even.

Winter finally turned to spring sometime around midsummer on the Cape. Everything around me came alive. Difficult as we make it, the land seems to work the best it can for now. And the birds. And their songs.

I'm happy to report, for instance, that the ocean is still here. I've checked. Often. I'm thankful for the tides, at least.

Another great white chomped down a seal too damned near shore the other day, which I know because this one not-a-stranger lady told me that's what happened.

———

Looking east from our mountain of mess to Italy's flattening curve hurts like fractured safety. So many of us saw the nightmare coming and tried like hell to avoid it. But here we are. Kruegered.

Here I am. Locked down. Tensed up. On pause. Uncertain. One whole leap-year season in exile so far with no end in sight. Spent.

A neon sign in my campus office blazes BREATHE. I miss that light. I don't know when I'll see my campus office again.

Everyone here wears a mask. The rare exceptions are, without exception, out-of-towners. You'd think this was Amity Island. Where did they come from? How did they get here? What have they brought? Why are they trying so hard to be strangers?

Days have begun again to take the shape of days. I look around and everyone seems to be doing things.

I'd like to do, for once, not a damned thing. But then how will I matter? I can't always remember why these verbs become so transactional.

Oh, Dear.

I'd been on the road twelve weeks already by the time I landed in Rome. This far below cruising altitude "on the road" is mostly what home has meant.

I've been anxious for months about driving again, Black, from viral coast to stubbornly viral coast. Just to land somewhere that still won't feel like home. Assuming I survive. Then. Finally. No. I won't go.

I'll remember magic. Virtually reimagine my work. Embrace this gifted corner by the sea. Remain thrown away and netted and held and fortunate and terrified.

Everything remains unresolved.

Getting on dusk now. I think how it's always a surprise to find myself exactly where I'm supposed to be. Our lives insist on small miracles despite us.

I went to a restaurant again for the first time. I sat outside. I was as far away as everyone.

—JULY 2020

A Generational Uprising

Héctor Tobar

In the days before the virus arrived, I was falling out of love with my hometown. I'd had enough of Los Angeles and its conspicuous displays of wealth, and the public tragedy of its smoky homeless camps. I was sick of the Teslas and the exotic Porsche SUVs and the gas-guzzling Expeditions cutting me off on the freeway. The thoughtlessness and self-interest of the fit and monied classes disgusted me (in California today, a toned body is a fairly reliable marker of class status). The nouveau riche had set off the insane gold rush of the real estate market, forcing legions of humble folk to flee to the desert in search of affordable housing.

I missed the earnestness and naiveté of the happy, sunburnt, flabby, and unpretentious Angeleno middle class. I missed the feeling that we were all equal, somehow: not just in the constitutional, Enlightenment sense of that word, but also in the backyard California party sense of being comrades in relaxation gathered around barbecues and inflatable kiddie pools. In the new Los Angeles, smart people know we're all not equal, and that we never really were and might never truly be.

And then we heard news of the drama unfolding in Wuhan. The mysterious acronym COVID worked its way across the globe, reaching Seattle and San Francisco. Soon enough our university classes and theaters and restaurants were shut down. We retreated into our homes and a simpler kind of living. I was liberated from my automobile. No more fifteen-mile daily round trips to my daughter's high school; no more forty-two-mile treks across the metropolis to the university where I teach. My teenage daughter, my adult son, and my wife and I hunkered down.

For the first time in years, we ate nightly meals together at the table. We had weekly family-movie sessions, watching scenes from a mask-free past where people gathered in crowds and strangers kissed and breathed in each other's germs. We ate healthier and we saved money. Seventy-five dollars' worth of toilet paper arrived on our doorstep, delivered by a servant of the Jeff Bezos empire. When I had to take to the streets (for groceries, or to visit my housebound father), I guided my car through empty thoroughfares. Intersections that once held me up for two or three stoplight cycles waited for me open and free, and the only bad thing about the traffic-less freeways was that the few cars sharing the highway with me were driving way dangerously *too fast*.

Our sleep patterns changed. Freed of our daily commutes, we slept in and slept longer. And then, after weeks of quarantine, we all got bored and went to bed earlier and rose earlier. One morning my daughter got up before dawn to take a walk, listen to the morning birdsong, and watch the sunrise. We live in a small valley that's just a ten-minute drive (4.5 miles walking) from downtown Los Angeles. It's a community still clinging to its bohemian past, with hillside cottages and a few unpaved roads, and native black walnut trees and scores of transplanted pines and Chinese elms. A deep and unusual quiet settled upon our valley, and this was at once comforting and unsettling.

This is what the birth of the post-Anthropocene epoch will sound like, I thought. If another virus follows this one, and then another one, eventually deer and bobcats and feral parrots will descend over our neighborhood, and they will recolonize it in the name of wildlife and natural selection. And then, one night, at eight P.M., I heard a distant howling. *The coyotes are back,* I thought. A pack is free in the canyon, hunting for dogs and cats to eat. But no. These were people, yelling. In some sort of ritual. My wife explained it to me: "It's for the first responders. To show support for them." The howling was repeated every night at that hour, and each night my daughter joined them enthusiastically, in a high-pitched yell that was a rough imitation of the coyotes, but more joyful than those animals ever sounded. Each night, more neighbors howled, and beat on pots and pans, and one played an electric guitar, and even though we could not see them (and rarely talked to them, even before the quarantine) we were, for the ninety seconds or so the ritual lasted, joined with them in an impro-vised, communal performance of music and human longing.

While we grew content in this simpler, quarantined existence, reports of the suffering around us came to us via our Zoom links. One of the students in the two classes I was teaching reported that her father had lost his job; she feared he would soon lose his home because he couldn't make his mortgage payments. Another student missed class repeatedly because he'd taken a job to help out his family—delivering packages for Amazon. I ventured into downtown and saw the home-less wearing masks. One afternoon I jogged through Chinatown, and the empty streets resembled the landscape of a dystopian video game; like an animated character being guided by button clicks on a game controller, I wove past people-less restaurants, shuttered warehouses, and grim, silent alleyways.

The weeks became months, and the internet brought images of another kind of suffering from the world outside. I saw a black man taking a neighborhood jog, much like my own, being hunted and shot down in Georgia. I witnessed the slow strangulation of another black man, in Minneapolis. Once again these faraway events became a thing creeping closer to us, until, on a warm spring afternoon, we heard the distant wailing of many police and fire sirens. A curfew order arrived on our phones. We were not allowed to venture outside, said the text alert—except for "the homeless, who are sheltering in place." I called my father and took perverse pleasure in speaking the Spanish translation for curfew, "toque de queda," a phrase that defined the Latin American dictatorships of the last century. "Papá, declararon toque de queda."

On the television, I watched another kind of history being replayed: the street theater of the last Los Angeles "riot" or "uprising" I'd lived through. I saw protests, lines of police officers, looting, all photographed from cameras in the sky. A fleet of news helicopters captured groups of people entering a shoe store, grabbing boxes of luxury sneakers; and surging through the shattered safety-glass doors of an Apple store and various apparel retailers. A few buildings and patrol cars were consumed in flames. The glib news anchor inside my head deadpanned: "This happens in Los Angeles roughly every twenty-seven years or so." 1965. 1992. 2020. In my second novel, published some years ago, I wrote: "It's quite a thing to be able to measure the passing of time by conflagrations one had seen, by the looting crowds and the fire-makers." But no two historical happenings are ever truly identical.

The events of 2020 carried a signature that was more generational than anything. I saw youthful black, brown, Asian, and white faces, and I sensed their collective identification with the body of George Floyd—and a deep disgust with the rules of a consumerist, monetized society. They marched through Beverly Hills and carried signs with anti-capitalist messages. "Eat the Rich." My teenage daughter watched a video from the hacker collective Anonymous promising dirt against the Minneapolis Police Department, and she seemed to feel exhilarated at the idea that there was a secret army out there, conspiring against power.

I went to bed one night with images of burning buildings in my head. I imagined the ash from torched stores and patrol cars floating up to my hillside, joining other layers of anthropogenic matter in the soil. The charcoal from the fires set for centuries by the Tongva people in the river canyons nearby; the soot from the annual infernos of our modern brush-fire seasons, and from the Watts riots of 1965 and the "quemazones" of 1992, when dozens of burning liquor stores sent sugary smoke into the air. I thought of all that ash falling on Los Angeles like a delicate gray snow. Layers and layers of ash, the most elementary evidence of human existence, to be studied by archaeologists at work in some future age, when justice reigns.

—JUNE 3, 2020

When the Shadow Is Looming

Oscar Villalon

My understanding of the desperation of being abandoned, of being totally without help, is once removed. It's from family stories, accounts of children dying—babies and kid brothers—sometimes in the arms of a sibling. The cause of death in each case the same: illness, and no money for medicine. It is a wretched thing. These stories were told so we could understand why a man was the way he was. His rages. His anxieties. Living as if one were a fish that at any moment could be plucked from the water, always sensitive to the weight of a hovering shadow, always thrashing when he felt its cast, lest the cruel hand of fate snag him. Added to the pain of losing the blood of your blood this way, there's the degradation.

When there was little money for food, when breakfast would be coffee and cold tortillas, he alone, barely a teen, would leave the house before dawn, jumping over stone walls, raiding meager orchards, carrying back as much fruit as he could for his little sisters and mother. Imagine doing this day in and day out. Imagine knowing nobody was going to help you or even could help you. The only way things might get better would be to leave your family once the girls were old enough to run the house, then find work far away, and send money back to a place you will never call home again. Can you understand what that would do to you?

A few weeks ago, there was a young guy alone in a car parked under a tree on my block in the Mission, in San Francisco. I was walking the dog, and the only reason I took notice of him was because as I went past the car, I could see he was fidgeting in the passenger seat, digging his hands into his pockets as if looking for something. He radiated anxiousness. When I came back from my long loop of a walk, the car was gone, and I thought nothing more of it until my wife told me that after I went outside, as she was working on her laptop in the living room, she could hear a man loudly talking to somebody. He must have been on his phone, and it sounded like he was talking to a government employee of some sort. He was telling this person he had four kids to take care of, and he was running out of time here. Where was his unemployment check? What was he supposed to do? Where was the help that was promised, that was needed? His anger, his fright was palpable.

Was it the same person, the young Black man, that I saw in the car? We can imagine how a person would want to have this conversation at a distance from the people they feel responsible for. To drive your car to a neighborhood some blocks over and make sure your children do not hear their father at his wit's end. But even if you don't hear your dad's voice go raw, even if you don't know your family is in trouble, how well can such a thing be hidden? As of early July, California had yet to make good on 1.88 million out of the just over 5 million unemployment claims filed here since March, April, and May. Rents are coming due and are past due. When time runs out, what then?

Not too long ago, in the early afternoon, an ambulance came to our block. The EMT, wearing a turquoise medical mask and black gloves, trundled out a stretcher that folded into something of a wheelchair. I had never seen a device like that before. The last stretcher I saw was about twenty years ago when paramedics had to come in the middle of the night to take my mother to the hospital. That thing was ridiculous in its bulkiness as the men struggled to wriggle it into my parents' living room. But the elegance of this stretcher, the neat way it morphed from bed to La-Z-Boy, right there on the sidewalk, was such that it took me a moment to absorb that a neighbor, Mexican like me, was being placed into that chair. All I want to say about that is even though he had already been lifted into the back of the ambulance, and even though we live in a second-floor apartment, I could hear him cough and cough.

In the very early days of the pandemic, walking around the neighborhood with leash in hand, careful to avoid coming near the very few people who were out on the street, I knew we weren't going to do well. For far too many of us, especially if you're undocumented, the draconian maxim still applies: you don't work, you don't eat. If you're sick, if your body hurts, you still need to get out of bed. Whatever is out there, when compared to the certainty of bills, is purely theoretical. There are no excuses, because there is no net underneath you. We simply cannot afford to stay at home.

But as bad as I thought it would get, the reality is worse. Though just 15 percent of the population in San Francisco, Latinos account for nearly half of all Covid-19 cases here. The Latino Task Force, an umbrella group made up of dozens of community organizations, has secured funding so that Latinos who test positive can afford to stay at home and in quarantine. So in spite of what gets drilled into us from when we are children, we are not totally alone. We do have one another. But this precious piece of hopefulness loses its warmth for me when other factors are taken into consideration. Tests aren't easy to come by, and the results are taking nearly two weeks to come back. And of course this is a form of triage. Those of us who can't work from home and are not sick still must go out there, assuming we have a job to even go to. The rent is still coming. So many things are heading our way. The shadow falls on our heads.

—JULY 23, 2020

From Plagues to Protests to Wildfires

Manuel Muñoz

March 13, 2020

I'm afraid of lightning. Unreasonably so. During monsoon season here in Tucson, Arizona, my anxiety builds in July, in August, when the height of the storms hit the desert. I've learned to watch the skies and time my movement outdoors. I'll stay in the car if I'm caught in a parking lot during a downpour—I didn't grow up in weather like this, booming skies and rain with weight. All June, we build toward this season. High clouds out in the distance, a stray bolt every once in a while, but nothing holds together to build into a storm. I was out on my evening run and I remember seeing stray strikes here and there in the Catalinas, the range on the north side of town. Not long after, the fires started. It was the first week of June.

I live on the east side of town, a good ten miles from where the fires first began. At night, I was startled to see the rim of a canyon lit up from so far away, a distinct U-shape, a cruel half grin. I got messages from friends on the East Coast because the pictures were making national news. My sister in California asked me about it, passing on my mother's worry. How close was I? Was it true that they were evacuating? Parts of town, yes, I told them, but that was miles away. I didn't want my family to worry, but all they had was what they were seeing on television.

I'd been steady and calm all spring, but the fires broke me. Something about how Covid-19 was forcing us to admit our interdependence was actually comforting to me. The national protests affirmed everything I knew about not only the police, but the migra who had deported my father decades ago. It was a strange relief to see so many people own up to what we'd been saying for so long. I knew my white colleagues were watching the same television news that I was. I wanted them to worry, for once. I hoped one colleague, for their sake, would see deeply enough to spot themselves in Amy Cooper.

I lost sleep in the first few days of the fires, though, as far away as they were. I'd pace the kitchen at three in the morning and look out the back window at the ever-changing shapes of the flames. Sometimes the whole lip of a ridge was outlined in a bright yellow-orange. Other times, fire had dipped so far into a canyon that only a pink-purple glow came up. Once, still awake at near dawn, I mistook the fire for actual sunlight, startled to see it so sharp and fierce in the coming heat of the day. *No more water,* I wrote on my notepad one morning, remembering the Bible verse.

When the fire's edge closest to town was more or less contained, the line moved higher into the mountains, away from homes and infrastructure. In the daytime, the Catalinas were clouded by smoke, a scarlet slash of fire retardant visible on the west slopes. At night, though, the fire's terrible light showed how much higher and deeper it had gone. At one point, it seemed to stretch across the entire length of the range. Uncontrollable. *Cataclysm* was a word I scribbled a few times over coffee as I began my days, trying in vain to concentrate on my week's work.

When I was little, a wave of storms came off the California coast and into the Valley. Our family sat around a kerosene lamp all night in the dark, the uninsulated walls of the house creaking and shifting. My sharpest memory of that night was using the bathroom, which was part of the enclosed back porch, and sensing the storm at its most potent. The lone casement window pressed up against the frame with every blow; I could hold up my fingers to the edges and feel the needling rain pressing inside. The next morning, trees were down across town—to this day, a prima fears the wind because of those storms— and I tried to make sense of my family's joking about the house staying upright. I remember it as a kind of small miracle.

That might be what is bothering me most about the fires right now. It's June 29, and they've been burning all month. When I speak to friends about it, there's a resigned air about the topic—we'll have to wait until the monsoon starts, let nature cancel out nature. Another kind of small miracle, I suppose. I don't know what kind of sense to make of that.

Or maybe I do, given that I usually have a faith in things working out. One sister works for county services and is understandably nervous about going in to work. "Put on your mask, hermana," I tell her, "and just take it day by day." I sense that my voice calms her a bit, but maybe it's enough. When the TV news shows pictures of the protests against police brutality all across the country, I have a sense of relief of not needing to explain much of it to my mother. She has her stories:

the yellow 1974 Duster confiscated in El Centro as she tried to get my father back home, echando madres at the agents rather than getting a lift from them into town once they released her from a couple of hours' custody. She hears my stress and exasperation with my job, with the people at work, but it's too complicated to bother to explain what it's like to get diversity reading lists from white colleagues. It's minor, anyway, in the greater scheme of things. "I still have my job," I tell her because, in times like these, she recognizes that jobs are the first things to go up in smoke.

I speak to her every weekend. This time, I ask her advice about a family member who needs some help and whether or not I should pitch in. In my notebook, I notice a scribble from a meeting: "those of us with family at home," someone had said. *That's most of us,* I had written to myself, single and alone in the desert. For all the new awareness at work, people still say stupid shit. There was still someone worrying about me, I imagined myself saying in a Zoom meeting. Still someone depending on me. My dad in his post-stroke days. A sister who needs daily assistance, whose plans to get an in-home aide through state services are now made impossible by Covid-19 for at least a year. My mom, who helps them both. She told me this story, in Spanish, about the last Social Security check that my grandmother cashed before she died: "She had figured out all the bills and told me to pay this and to pay that, but she told me to keep the last hundred for myself, just for me. I never spent it. I still have it, stashed away, and no matter how bad things got, I never, ever touched it."

That's how it's been, all June. I look out at the mountains and the fires and some story circles in my head. I try to make meaning of it. Tonight, four hot orange spots, more to the east, and high up. I keep coming back to the same words: *resiliency, faith, miracles.* No matter what goes on in the world, I find some way to make it recall my family. I can conjure my mother's face, very young, sitting in the middle of the bench seat of the family pickup, her father on one side, her mother on the other. Stopped by the border patrol and made to wait in the Texas heat, all three of them U.S. citizens.

Once the fires go out—all of them—I hope I can get back to a restful sleep.

—JULY 7, 2020

Postcards from a Quarantined Paradise

Craig Santos Perez

March 13, 2020

It's the last day of my "Food Writing" class before spring break. Several students are out sick, and those present look exhausted. Hawai'i may be one of the most isolated places in the world, but it's also an international hub. All the positive coronavirus cases thus far are travel-related, spreading through Waikīkī. The Honolulu airport is deemed a potential "super-spreader."

We discuss our current topic: grocery stores. How do they function in society? How are they represented in literature and film? What characters and scenes do we encounter there? How does a grocery store tell a story?

I didn't know that would be the last time I'd see my students in person.

March 22, 2020

Today, the governor of Hawai'i issued a work-from-home order. "Community spread."

I nervously drive to Costco in Waipahu. The line to the parking lot extends around the block, and it takes me thirty minutes just to find a space.

I try not to touch my face while navigating the crowded aisles. The water, toilet paper, eggs, and milk are already gone. I grab all the meat and frozen fruits and vegetables I can find.

Bulk panic.

As I wait in the crowded checkout line, I look around at everyone's concerned faces and carts full of canned goods and boxed foods. I feel lucky. My job is safe: online and remote. And I can still afford rent and food in the most expensive place in the world to buy toilet paper. The bill is $450—the most I've ever spent on a single grocery trip. I feel a kind of survivor's guilt.

"I'll visit her tomorrow. Wave through the window."

When I return home, my daughters are sleeping, and my wife is sanitizing every surface. The national news plays on the television. "250,000 cases worldwide." I disinfect and put away the groceries in the pantry and fridge. "10,000 deaths." I freeze enough meat to last months. "Habitats destroyed. Bats and pangolins butchered." I take a hot shower.

How long can we shelter in place?

March 25, 2020

I leave the apartment for the first time. I drive to Longs pharmacy to refill my five-year-old daughter's asthma inhaler and Montelukast prescription. She was hospitalized last year because she couldn't breathe. "Immunocompromised."

March 27, 2020

My mom calls from California, where the virus has spread like wildfire. She's had a dry cough and sore throat, but her doctor said she doesn't qualify for a test. No fever.

"Hopefully, it's just a cold," she says.

I ask about Grandma, who's ninety-two years old, dementia.

"Her care home is quarantined," my mom says. "I called her on the phone, but she doesn't understand why no one visits her anymore. I explain the pandemic to her every day because she doesn't remember. I'll visit her tomorrow. Wave through the window."

I feel an ocean length apart.

April 2, 2020

"Happy birthday to you," I sing to my daughter as we wash our hands together. She doesn't understand this new ritual because her real birthday is months away. She doesn't understand why her school was shut down, why she has to stay home all the time, why we can't go to the playground.

I don't know how to explain the pandemic to her.

So I scrub her fingernails and repeat: "Happy birthday to you . . ."

I close my eyes and make a wish: six lit candles on a chocolate cake, unopened presents, our family who traveled across the ocean to celebrate with us.

I hear them singing.

And no one, no one, is missing.

April 10, 2020

Good Friday. I buy two dozen eggs from Safeway—the per-person limit. I don't want to go back to Costco.

At home, my wife boils a pot of water, mixes vinegar and food coloring in small bowls. We livestream mass from inside the burnt shell of Notre-Dame. "Ave Maria, gratia plena."

On CNN: images of Hart Island in New York, dozens of unclaimed bodies buried in unpainted pine caskets.

We dye the Easter eggs, plan where we'll hide them in our small apartment.

"Et benedictus fructus ventris."

April 12, 2020

Easter Sunday. We wake early. Brew coffee. Cook banana pancakes. On the local news: a procession of cars waits in line at Ala Moana mall. The Salvation Army has donated two tons of potatoes; 4,000 cartons of eggs; 2,000 gallons of milk; and 3,000 loaves of bread. For hours, volunteers wearing masks and gloves load food into every empty trunk. A contactless communion.

We set the table. Butter, syrup, juice. On the national news: farmers dump 2,000 gallons of milk into manure pits; plow ripe vegetables into the soil; break a million unhatched eggs. What if the miracle of

Jesus feeding the multitudes wasn't God's endless provision, but the gospel of human generosity? What if, when we care for each other, we resurrect our bodies, full of grace?

April 15, 2020

Our daughters fall asleep earlier than usual. My wife and I shower, brush our teeth. We've been so busy homeschooling, teaching online, attending Zoom meetings, grocery shopping, cooking, washing dishes, cleaning, watching the news, disinfecting everything.

It's awkward at first. Kissing. Touching. Is it safe? For weeks, our bodies have been nothing more than vectors of disease.

We inch closer, slowly, as if emerging from separate quarantines. Our skin. Tensed. At the vulnerable. Risk. Of reopening.

At least for this night, our bodies become, again, vectors of desire.

April 20, 2020

Hundreds of tourists continue arriving every day. Cheaper flights, discounted hotel rates (reservoirs of disease). Residents protest at the airport. One sign asks: "Why is your vacation more important than our health?"

Under pressure, the governor finally establishes a two-week quarantine for all visitors. However, many tourists break quarantine, post selfies at the beach on social media. Some are arrested and fined.

Not even a pandemic can shut down paradise.

April 25, 2020

My mom calls again. Says the funeral director called. If Grandma dies, we aren't allowed to have a funeral service. Shouldn't grieving together be our most essential business?

May 2, 2020

My wife, who's Hawaiian, tells me about the history of disease here. After the arrival of Captain Cook in 1778, epidemics flood the islands in the wake of foreign ships (reservoirs of disease). Cholera, influenza, mumps, measles, whooping cough, smallpox, leprosy. Ninety percent of the native population dies over the course of fifty years. No immunity, no safe place to hide.

As she tells this story, her voice breaks like waves of intergenerational trauma. Moments of silence between sentences. Each word: a quarantined island.

May 10, 2020

I call my mom for Mother's Day. She visited Grandma in the afternoon, sat outside, talked to her through the window, explained the pandemic again, why she can't come inside.

"Grandma wants to go home," my mom says. "She's so lonely."

I visited Grandma when I was in California for Christmas. I was supposed to visit again this summer, but that trip has been canceled. Will I ever see her again? Will this be her last Mother's Day?

"I want to hug my grandkids," my mom sighs, no longer able to hold her tears at a safe distance.

May 12, 2020

Pacific Islanders in California, Utah, Washington, Oregon, Oklahoma, and Arkansas are contracting coronavirus at disproportionately high rates compared to other racial groups. We suffer from high rates of diabetes, obesity, heart and lung disease, asthma, hypertension, and cancer. Colonial comorbidities.

Pacific Islanders are frontline workers. We live in multigenerational households. In our cultures, elders are essential and unending sources of wisdom, history, memory, and love. If we lose a single elder, we lose a multitude of stories.

I look at maps tracking the pandemic. Our peoples and islands are not even included. Invisibility is a preexisting condition for Pacific Islanders in the United States.

May 16, 2020

My students submit their final creative writing assignment. Nearly all their short fiction stories are pandemic, apocalyptic, survivalist, sci-fi, and/or zombie stories that take place in a grocery store. I give them all A's.

June 1, 2020

Viral videos of George Floyd's death crash against our shores. Videos of peaceful protests and riots. Viral videos of mourning and looting. Videos of tear gas and rubber bullets. Viral videos of police cars and precincts on fire. Videos of countless arrests. Viral videos of the National Guard and private militias. Videos of Trump holding a Bible in front of a church. Viral videos of George Floyd's six-year-old daughter saying: "Daddy changed the world."

It's strange to watch protests and not hear chanted slogans; strange to see looting without the sound of glass shattering; strange to witness police brutality as silent shrapnel.

June 5, 2020

We live in Aiea, which is just a few minutes' drive to Joint Base Pearl Harbor-Hickam and home to military personnel and their families who live off-base. While countless U.S. soldiers and sailors at bases around the world and on aircraft carriers have tested positive for Covid-19, the military here won't disclose to the public the exact numbers of infected soldiers in Hawai'i because of "security" reasons. The Department of Homeland Security recently announced that military members traveling to Hawai'i for the upcoming training and war games known as RIMPAC will be exempt from the state's quarantine guidelines.

Not even a pandemic can demilitarize paradise.

June 6, 2020

It's the hottest day of the summer. We turn on the AC and close the blackout drapes.

More than 10,000 people attend a Black Lives Matter march from Ala Moana Beach Park to the state capitol in Honolulu. We watch a Facebook livestream on our laptops.

Our daughters, tired from playing, lie down to nap. My wife takes their temperature. How long can we shelter each other in a world where children can't play with friends at school, where elders can't breathe without ventilators, where we can't hug without fear?

I turn on CNN but mute the volume. It's strange to watch protests and not hear chanted slogans; strange to see looting without the sound of glass shattering; strange to witness police brutality as silent shrapnel. How long can we shelter each other when there's no vaccine for the virulent outbreaks of human greed and racial violence?

They replay the video: a white cop's knee choking a black man's neck. His lips move, but his voice is an unheard riot.

Our youngest daughter stirs. I gently rub her back. Her body curls like a flattened curve. Breathing, peacefully.

Please, I whisper, don't wake up yet.

—JUNE 6, 2020

Three Liberties: Past, Present, Yet to Come

Julia Alvarez

1

July 4, 1960
Ciudad Trujillo, Nueva York

Papi gave me a little statue
of the patron saint
of the United Estates,
a guardian angel watching
over the land of the free
and home of the brave.
Nuestra Señora de Libertad
sat on a shelf beside a globe
full of snow, *The Arabian Nights,*
La Cartilla del Escolar Dominicano,
el Jefe's manual with rules
for kids to live by.

Nuestra Señora watched over me
with her star halo, her white robe
like a guardian angel's. Instead
of rolling eyeballs on a platter
like Santa Lucía or a flaming
sword like San Miguel
or a baby Jesus in her arms
like la Virgencita de la Altagracia,
Libertad held a big book
for writing down our petitions.
I prayed for toys, candy, snow
from the rich country to our north.

Papi's prayers came true:
we escaped to Nueva York,
refugees from el Jefe. I learned
her English name. Lady Liberty
wore a crown and a long gown
like a beauty queen on *Miss America*.
Carved on the cover of her book
was the birthdate of my new country:
July IV, MDCCLXXVI.
Teacher said no one knew
if the rest of the pages were blank.
She had us take turns guessing.
The American Nights? *A Manual
of Rules for USA Kids to Live By*?

On TV, people were marching
attacked by dogs, bludgeoned
by clubs, hosed down like a fire
inside a blazing building.
I asked Papi, Was it true
we had escaped the dictatorship?

2

———

July 4, 2020
Minneapolis, St. Louis, Houston, Detroit, Austin,
El Paso, Washington, D.C., Omaha, Atlanta,
Oakland, Indianapolis, Philadelphia,
New York City . . .

This year I can't bring myself
to sing *Happy Birthday to You,*
though I've been singing it
for 20 seconds for months,
every time I wash my hands—
new rules to safely live by
in these times of a pandemic,
while another rages on,
a virus of violence against
our darker brothers & sisters,
still marching, still unable
to breathe with knees
on their necks in our name—
8 minutes, 46 seconds:
time enough to wash our hands
of the matter 26 times.

How old will Liberty be
before her tablet runs out of pages,
filling with the names
of brothers & sisters still waiting
for their prayers to be answered,
for enough breath to sing
Happy Birthday, sweet Liberty!
the nameless at her borders
with Papi's brown face & bigotes,
whose América was co-opted,
(the accent erased from the *e*)
as ours is the only America?
Her book has become a graveyard,
her torch the fires raging in cities . . .

3

July 4, 2021

If we celebrate next year,
which Liberty will we sing to?

—JUNE 2020

Letter to John Robert Lewis

Nikky Finney

Dear John Robert Lewis,

There was a colossal sweetness about you that some mistook for weakness. A sweetness that seemed to power your actions and your life. Seems to me it was a particular kind of sweetness that was perhaps given to you, taught to you, perhaps by your large and loving family, and also taught again, perhaps, by all the tambourine-ing and lightning-bolt words you soon discovered in those second- and third-hand books in that small segregated schoolhouse in Pike County, Alabama. Those same books that you soon learned were the perfect size for marching off into battle with.

John Robert Lewis, this sweetness I speak of continued to be nurtured in you, even as you grew from a Black boy, stowed away in a corner of the American South, to a Black man walking the halls of Congress for thirteen terms, from the 5th District of Georgia. Even as men who did not know your powerful sweetness charged at you on bridges with nightsticks and bully punches, intending to beat the love out of you—the love that fragments of which might have been found inside some of those books you always kept close in your backpack. It was never a secret how much you adored books and how they gave you the power to love people back—no matter what.

I've been looking for your Kilimanjaro sweetness everywhere, I need it now more than ever. I don't want it like a pill I might pop when my anger rises with the news of the day. I want it like a backpack. Something I might put on and tighten around my shoulders and not take off until it is time for bed. Something heavy that has the power to pull back my shoulders. A John Robert Lewis backpack, jet pack, power pack. A fueled thing that would lift me away from all this hatred when I need it to. I've been trying to keep what you taught me top of mind because what I really want to do is punch every booming, bombastic, ruthless liar in the mouth. People are *dying* because of lies. Hundreds of thousands of people, dying and losing everything they have ever worked for because some people do not care if they live or die. I have not been feeling very nonviolent since you left, so I decided to begin my new days here on earth, without your marching feet as one of my sonic compasses, here in my trusty writing chair engaged in the great epistolary tradition of reaching out to you in the only way I truly trust.

Tonight I am remembering that story of you wanting to go to school, when you were six or so, your father waking you early that one morning to tell you to go to the fields to work rather than to school to read. That story—and so many others about you—was sent back and forth across the community switchboard during the week of your crossing-over. I can hear the rich inflection of your southern voice as you retell that story of how you hid beneath the porch, waiting for the right moment to hightail it to the school bus in order to sneak a day in with the books before paying back the two days in the field that you owed your father. John Robert Lewis, you are a boy who I daresay would never disobey his father, unless of course there was a book involved.

You and I both know that sweetness can often be attached to disobedience, that it can follow a boy or a girl until they begin to understand its full power—and only then can they heed its call. I am talking about a kind of sweetness that can even rival preaching to chickens in the backyard or staring straight up into the coal-black country sky, dreaming of one day leaving all that never-ending sweat and dirt for the blinking lights of the city. I might be wrong about that. Send me a sign, John Robert Lewis. Let me know for sure. You were a dust bowl boy, born a generation after the boll weevil and the Great Migration, and therefore there were so many reasons you could have but never did leave the South. The South where you were first handed a beat-up book and locked out of every library. But you never left us. We know this like we know our family names.

At seventeen, the story goes, you left the American Baptist Theological Seminary in Nashville and Fisk University and began plotting what to do with all the words and feelings forming inside you like a geyser. They say somewhere along the road you began to fancy the sweet taste of cold water bubbling out of fountains that did not wear name tags of COLORED and WHITE. They say your taste buds grew loud for the sweetness of a cheeseburger served at a lunch counter and not at a side or back door. I never got to ask you how you learned to concentrate so deeply, how you let your legs dangle freely on that red-cushioned swivel chair, and not be distracted by all the hatred swirling around your bowed head as you read your favorite book?

John Robert Lewis, as you know, life is made of opposites. While you were becoming a man of colossal sweetness, the great malignancy of racism was ticking like a bomb. You and the courageous others were spat upon. Cigarettes routinely sizzled out on your heads and hands. Hot coffee was poured on you. You watched water hoses drill their hatred into the breastplates of Black women whose bodies walked and marched and bent toward the sun in a Black woman arc of prayer. But those who had never been taught the power of sweetness could not stop the love you had been raised in, the love you had read about, and the freedom to hold on to that love. I need a lesson, John Robert Lewis. My father named me Love Child, but my Black woman coffer is running low these days.

I was seven when you woke up on what was to be Bloody Sunday, March 7, 1965. Tell me, kind sir, how is sweetness maintained when someone wakes and knows he is about to be beaten and about to go to jail or worse? Is the secret found in what he packs in his bag for that day? Where does one even find and purchase a backpack in rural Alabama in 1965? And why is your coat not the color of war or camouflage? Why is it the color of eggnog or ice cream or the first light that pierces the morning mother-of-pearl clouds? You, ready to march with your one apple, your one orange, your two books (Thomas Merton and Richard Hofstadter), ready to go to jail for the rest of your life—if necessary.

These books you chose were your anchors—there to weigh you down and keep you closer to earth when the random tossing of black bodies began—and you knew it would begin. Your toothbrush and toothpaste, packed and ready, there with you not because you cared so much about your own mouth, which was about to be filled with blood, but because you knew before the night was through that you would be around other people, those who had been fighting alongside you, in a small jail cell, and you thought it prudent, thoughtful, to be able to brush your teeth for those who would be cramped and near.

John Robert Lewis, there is a magnanimous sweetness about you that I never took for weakness. I need it with me now and not tomorrow. I need it now because the rates of Black Americans dying from Covid-19 are twice as high as anybody else. I need it now because they have unhooked and towed away the mail-sorting machines in the post office in hopes that our votes won't arrive in time this November. I need to be able to store tanks of your opulent sweetness for all the days ahead. Tanks filled with your unshakable human understanding of who I need to be when the buckets of human spit start flying my way and the stolen sorting machines that have been rolled away block me from what I need to remember. When the new fire hoses hit me and my brothers and sisters pouring into the streets of cities and small towns of America. When the hot gourmet coffee of today is poured on nappy-headed bookworm screaming heads of today. I need to restudy the molecular design of your sweetness and remember how it did not shrink away under the hooves of horses coming straight at you. You there in your coat the color of Christmas eggnog and oyster shells and moonlight.

On the night you died, I wrote in my journal that Frederick Douglass must have been whispering in your ear when the wave of Alabama state troopers moved in to crush you there in your ice-cream-colored coat, "Power concedes nothing without a struggle." Over the five days of your funeral, I wondered to myself if you were reciting "Invictus" right before the dogs were released and the batons landed on your head.

You were a sweet and powerful man, John Robert Lewis, walking through the fire of your time. You were a man who somehow became sweeter the more fire he ate. Maybe that is the key, the sign you will send me back down through the clouds. I await your reply. Now you are in the arms of Miss Lillian, your great librarian. I know she has been saving hundreds of books for you. Rest now. Read now. We will take it from here.

Nikky Finney

—AUGUST 27, 2020

Kamala Harris,
Mass Incarceration, and Me

Reginald Dwayne Betts

Because Senator Kamala Harris is a prosecutor and I am a felon, I have been following her political rise with the same focus that my younger son tracks Steph Curry threes. Before it was in vogue to criticize prosecutors, my friends and I were exchanging tales of being railroaded by them. Shackled, wearing green jail scrubs that even at size small draped my young body, I listened to a prosecutor in a Fairfax County, Virginia, courtroom tell a judge that in one night I'd single-handedly changed suburban shopping forever. Everything the prosecutor said I did was true—I carried a pistol, carjacked a man, tried to rob two women. "He needs a long penitentiary sentence," the prosecutor told the judge. I faced life in prison for carjacking the man. I pleaded guilty to that, to having a gun, to an attempted robbery. I was sixteen years old. The oldheads in prison would call me lucky for walking away with only a nine-year sentence.

I'd been locked up for about fifteen months when I entered Virginia's Southampton Correctional Center in 1998, the year I should have graduated from high school. In that prison, there were probably about a dozen other teenagers. Most of us had lengthy sentences— thirty, forty, fifty years—all for violent felonies. Public talk of mass incarceration has centered on the war on drugs, wrongful convictions, and Kafkaesque sentences for nonviolent charges, while circumventing the robberies, home invasions, murders, and rape cases that brought us to prison.

The most difficult discussion to have about criminal justice reform has always been about violence and accountability. You could release everyone from prison who currently has a drug offense and the United States would still outpace nearly every other country when it comes to incarceration. According to the Prison Policy Initiative, of the nearly 1.3 million people incarcerated in state prisons, 183,000 are incarcerated for murder; 17,000 for manslaughter; 165,000 for sexual assault; 169,000 for robbery; and 136,000 for assault. That's more than half of the state prison population.

When Harris decided to run for president, I thought the country might take the opportunity to grapple with the injustice of mass incarceration in a way that didn't lose sight of what violence, as well as the sorrow it creates, does to families and communities. Instead, many progressives tried to turn the basic fact of Harris's profession into an indictment against her. Shorthand for her career became: "She's a cop," meaning, her allegiance was with a system that conspires, through prison and policing, to harm Black people in America.

In the past decade or so, we have certainly seen ample evidence of how corrupt the system can be: Michelle Alexander's bestselling book, *The New Jim Crow,* which argues that the war on drugs marked the return of America's racist system of segregation and legal discrimination; Ava DuVernay's *When They See Us,* a series about the wrongful convictions of the Central Park Five, and her documentary *13th,* which delves into mass incarceration more broadly; and *Just Mercy,* a book by Bryan Stevenson, a public interest lawyer, that has also been made into a film, chronicling his pursuit of justice for a man on death row who is eventually exonerated. All of these describe the destructive force of prosecutors, giving a lot of run to the belief that anyone who works within a system responsible for such carnage warrants public shame.

My mother had an experience that gave her a different perspective on prosecutors—though I didn't know about it until I came home from prison on March 4, 2005, when I was twenty-four. That day she sat me down and said, "I need to tell you something." We were in her bedroom in the townhouse in Suitland, Maryland, that had been my childhood home, where as a kid she'd call me to bring her a glass of water. I expected her to tell me that despite my years in prison, everything was good now. But instead she told me about something that happened nearly a decade earlier, just weeks after my arrest. She left for work before the sun rose, as she always did, heading to the federal agency that had employed her my entire life. She stood at a bus stop a hundred feet from my high school, awaiting the bus that would take her to the train that would take her to a stop near her job in the nation's capital. But on that morning, a man yanked her into a secluded space, placed a gun to her head, and raped her. When she could escape, she ran wildly into the six A.M. traffic.

My mother's words turned me into a mumbling and incoherent mess, unable to grasp how this could have happened to her. I knew she kept this secret to protect me. I turned to Google and searched the word *rape* along with my hometown and was wrecked by the violence against women that I found. My mother told me her rapist was a Black man. And I thought he should spend the rest of his years staring at the pockmarked walls of prison cells that I knew so well.

The prosecutor's job, unlike the defense attorney's or judge's, is to do justice. What does that mean when you are asked by some to dole out retribution measured in years served, but blamed by others for the damage incarceration can do? The outrage at this country's criminal justice system is loud today, but it hasn't led us to develop better ways of confronting my mother's world from nearly a quarter-century ago: weekends visiting her son in a prison in Virginia; weekdays attending the trial of the man who sexually assaulted her.

We said goodbye to my grandmother in the same Baptist church that, in June 2019, Senator Kamala Harris, still pursuing the Democratic nomination for president, went to give a major speech about why she became a prosecutor. I hadn't been inside Brookland Baptist Church for a decade, and returning reminded me of Grandma Mary and the eight years of letters she mailed to me in prison. The occasion for Harris's speech was the annual Freedom Fund dinner of the South Carolina State Conference of the NAACP. The evening began with the Black national anthem, "Lift Every Voice and Sing," and at the opening chord nearly everyone in the room stood. There to write about the senator, I had been standing already and mouthed the words of the first verse before realizing I'd never sung any further.

Each table in the banquet hall was filled with folks dressed in their Sunday best. Servers brought plates of food and pitchers of iced tea to the tables. Nearly everyone was Black. The room was too loud for me to do more than crouch beside guests at their tables and scribble notes about why they attended. Speakers talked about the chapter's long history in the civil rights movement. One called for the current generation of young rappers to tell a different story about sacrifice. The youngest speaker of the night said he just wanted to be safe. I didn't hear anyone mention mass incarceration. And I knew in a different decade, my grandmother might have been in that audience, taking in the same arguments about personal agency and responsibility, all the while wondering why her grandbaby was still locked away. If Harris couldn't persuade that audience that her experiences as a Black woman in America justified her decision to become a prosecutor, I knew there were few people in this country who could be moved.

Describing her upbringing in a family of civil rights activists, Harris argued that the ongoing struggle for equality needed to include both prosecuting criminal defendants who had victimized Black people and protecting the rights of Black criminal defendants. "I was clear-eyed that prosecutors were largely not people who looked like me," she said. This mattered for Harris because of the "prosecutors that refused to seat Black jurors, refused to prosecute lynchings, disproportionately condemned young Black men to death row, and looked the other way in the face of police brutality." When she became a prosecutor in 1990, she was one of only a handful of Black people in her office. When she was elected district attorney of San Francisco in 2003, she recalled, she was one of just three Black DAs nationwide. And when she was elected California attorney general in 2010, there were no other Black attorneys general in the country. At these words, the crowd around me clapped. "I knew the unilateral power that prosecutors had with the stroke of a pen to make a decision about someone else's life or death," she said.

Harris offered a pair of stories as evidence of the importance of a Black woman's doing this work. Once, ear hustling, she listened to colleagues discussing ways to prove criminal defendants were gang affiliated. If a manual of racial profiling existed, their signals would certainly be included: baggy pants, the place of arrest, and the rap music blaring from vehicles. She said that she'd told her colleagues:

"So, you know that neighborhood you were talking about? Well, I got family members and friends who live in that neighborhood. You know the way you were talking about how folks were dressed? Well, that's actually stylish in my community." She continued: "You know that music you were talking about? Well, I got a tape of that music in my car right now."

The second example was about the mothers of murdered children. She told the audience about the women who had come to her office when she was San Francisco's DA—women who wanted to speak with her, and her alone, about their sons. "The mothers came, I believe, because they knew I would see them," Harris said. "And I mean literally see them. See their grief. See their anguish." They complained to Harris that the police were not investigating. "My son is being treated like a statistic," they would say. Everyone in that Southern Baptist church knew that the mothers and their dead sons were Black. Harris outlined the classic dilemma of Black people in this country: being simultaneously overpoliced and underprotected. Harris told the audience that all communities deserved to be safe.

Among the guests in the room that night whom I talked to, no one had an issue with her work as a prosecutor. A lot of them seemed to believe that only people doing dirt had issues with prosecutors. I thought of myself and my friends who have served long terms, knowing that in a way, Harris was talking about Black people's needing protection from us—from the violence we perpetrated to earn those years in a series of cells.

Harris came up as a prosecutor in the 1990s, when both the political culture and popular culture were developing a story about crime and violence that made incarceration feel like a moral response. Back then, films by Black directors—*New Jack City, Menace II Society, Boyz n the Hood*—turned Black violence into a genre where murder and crack-dealing were as ever present as Black fathers were absent. Those were the years when Representative Charlie Rangel, a Democrat, argued that "we should not allow people to distribute this poison without fear that they might be arrested" and "go to jail for the rest of their natural life." Those were the years when President Clinton signed legislation that ended federal parole for people with three violent crime convictions and encouraged states to essentially eliminate parole; made it more difficult for defendants to challenge their convictions in court; and made it nearly impossible to challenge prison conditions.

Back then, it felt like I was just one of an entire generation of young Black men learning the logic of count time and lockdown. With me were Anthony Winn and Terell Kelly and a dozen others, all lost to prison during those years. Terell was sentenced to thirty-three years for murdering a man when he was seventeen—a neighborhood beef turned deadly. Home from college for two weeks, a nineteen-year-old Anthony robbed four convenience stores—he'd been carrying a pistol during three. After he was sentenced by four judges, he had a total of thirty-six years.

Most of us came into those cells with trauma, having witnessed or experienced brutality before committing our own. Prison, a factory of violence and despair, introduced us to more of the same. And though there were organizations working to get rid of the death penalty, end mandatory minimums, bring back parole, and even abolish prisons, there were few ways for us to know that they existed. We suffered. And we felt alone. Because of this, sometimes I reduce my friends' stories to the cruelty of doing time. I forget that Terell and I walked prison yards as teenagers, discussing Malcolm X and searching for mentors in the men around us. I forget that Anthony and I talked about the poetry of Sonia Sanchez the way others praised DMX. He taught me the meaning of the word *patina* and introduced me to the music of Bill Withers.

There were Luke and Fats; and Juvie, who could give you the sharpest edge-up in America with just a razor and comb.

When I left prison in 2005, they all had decades left. Then I went to law school and believed I owed it to them to work on their cases and help them get out. I've persuaded lawyers to represent friends pro bono. Put together parole packets—basically job applications for freedom: letters of recommendation and support from family and friends; copies of certificates attesting to vocational training; the record of college credits. We always return to the crimes to provide explanation and context. We argue that today each one little resembles the teenager who pulled a gun. And I write a letter—which is less from a lawyer and more from a man remembering what it means to want to go home to his mother. I write, struggling to condense decades of life in prison into a ten-page case for freedom. Then I find my way to the parole board's office in Richmond, Virginia, and try to persuade the members to let my friends see a sunrise for the first time.

Juvie and Luke have made parole; Fats, represented by the Innocence Project at the University of Virginia School of Law, was granted a conditional pardon by Virginia's governor, Ralph Northam. All three are home now, released just as a pandemic would come to threaten the lives of so many others still inside. Now free, they've sent me text messages with videos of themselves hugging their mothers for the first time in decades, casting fishing lines from boats drifting along rivers they didn't expect to see again, enjoying a cold beer that isn't contraband.

In February, after twenty-five years, Virginia passed a bill making people incarcerated for at least twenty years for crimes they committed before their eighteenth birthdays eligible for parole. Men who imagined they would die in prison now may see daylight. Terell will be eligible. These years later, he's the mentor we searched for, helping to organize, from the inside, community events for children, and he's spoken publicly about learning to view his crimes through the eyes of his victim's family. My man Anthony was nineteen when he committed his crime. In the last few years, he's organized poetry readings, book clubs, and fatherhood classes. When Gregory Fairchild, a professor at the Darden School of Business at the University of Virginia, began an entrepreneurship program at Dillwyn Correctional Center, Anthony was among the graduates, earning all three of the certificates that it offered. He worked to have me invited as the commencement speaker, and what I remember most is watching him share a meal with his parents for the first time since his arrest. But he must pray that the governor grants him a conditional pardon, as he did for Fats.

I tell myself that my friends are unique, that I wouldn't fight so hard for just anybody. But maybe there is little particularly distinct about any of us—beyond that we'd served enough time in prison. There was a skinny light-skinned fifteen-year-old kid who came into prison during the years that we were there. The rumor was that he'd broken into the house of an older woman and sexually assaulted her. We all knew he had three life sentences. Someone stole his shoes. People threatened him. He'd had to break a man's jaw with a lock in a sock to prove he'd fight if pushed. As a teenager, he was experiencing the worst of prison. And I know that had he been my cellmate, had I known him the way I know my friends, if he reached out to me today, I'd probably be arguing that he should be free.

But I know that on the other end of our prison sentences was always someone weeping. During the middle of Harris's presidential campaign, a friend referred me to a woman with a story about Senator Harris that she felt I needed to hear. Years ago, this woman's sister had been missing for days, and the police had done little. Happenstance gave this woman an audience with then attorney general Harris. A coordinated multi-city search followed. The sister had been murdered;

her body was found in a ravine. The woman told me that "Kamala understands the politics of victimization as well as anyone who has been in the system, which is that this kind of case—a fifty-year-old Black woman gone missing or found dead—ordinarily does not get any resources put toward it." They caught the man who murdered her sister, and he was sentenced to 131 years. I think about the man who assaulted my mother, a serial rapist, because his case makes me struggle with questions of violence and vengeance and justice. And I stop thinking about it. I am inconsistent. I want my friends out, but I know there is no one who can convince me that this man shouldn't spend the rest of his life in prison.

My mother purchased her first single-family home just before I was released from prison. One version of this story is that she purchased the house so that I wouldn't spend a single night more than necessary in the childhood home I walked away from in handcuffs. A truer account is that by leaving Suitland, my mother meant to burn the place from memory.

I imagined that I had singularly introduced my mother to the pain of the courts. I was wrong. The first time she missed work to attend court proceedings was to witness the prosecution of a kid the same age as I was when I robbed a man. He was probably from Suitland, and he'd attempted to rob my mother at gunpoint. The second time, my mother attended a series of court dates involving me, dressed in her best work clothes to remind the prosecutor and judge and those in the courtroom that the child facing a life sentence had a mother who loved him. The third time, my mother took off days from work to go to court alone and witness the trial of the man who raped her and two other women. A prosecutor's subpoena forced her to testify, and her solace came from knowing that prison would prevent him from attacking others.

After my mother told me what had happened to her, we didn't mention it to each other again for more than a decade. But then in 2018, she and I were interviewed on the podcast "Death, Sex & Money." The host asked my mother about going to court for her son's trial when he was facing life. "I was raped by gunpoint," my mother said. "It happened just before he was sentenced. So when I was going to court for Dwayne, I was also going for a court trial for myself." I hadn't forgotten what happened, but having my mother say it aloud to a stranger made it far more devastating.

On the last day of the trial of the man who raped her, my mother told me, the judge accepted his guilty plea. She remembers only that he didn't get enough time. She says her nose began to bleed. When I asked her what she would have wanted to happen to her attacker, she replied, "That I'd taken the deputy's gun and shot him."

Harris has studied crime-scene and autopsy photos of the dead. She has confronted men in court who have sexually assaulted their children, sexually assaulted the elderly, scalped their lovers. In her 2009 book, *Smart on Crime,* Harris praised the work of Sunny Schwartz—creator of the Resolve to Stop the Violence Project, the first restorative justice program in the country to offer services to offenders and victims, which began at a jail in San Francisco. It aims to help inmates who have committed violent crimes by giving them tools to de-escalate confrontations. Harris wrote a bill with a state senator to ensure that children who witness violence can receive mental health treatment. And she argued that safety is a civil right, and that a sixty-year sentence for a series of restaurant armed robberies, where some victims were bound or locked in freezers, "should tell anyone considering viciously preying on citizens and businesses that they will be caught, convicted and sent to prison—for a very long time."

Politicians and the public acknowledge mass incarceration is a problem, but the lengthy prison sentences of men and women incarcerated during the 1990s have largely not been revisited. While the evidence of any prosecutor doing work on this front is slim, as a politician arguing for basic systemic reforms, Harris has noted the need to "unravel the decades-long effort to make sentencing guidelines excessively harsh, to the point of being inhumane"; criticized the bail system; and called for an end to private prisons and criticized the companies that charge absurd rates for phone calls and electronic-monitoring services.

In June, months into the Covid-19 pandemic, and before she was tapped as the vice-presidential nominee, I had the opportunity to interview Harris by phone. A police officer's knee on the neck of George Floyd, choking the life out of him as he called for help, had been captured on video. Each night, thousands around the world protested. During our conversation, Harris told me that because she was the only Black woman in the United States Senate "in the midst of the killing of George Floyd and Breonna Taylor and Ahmaud Arbery," countless people had asked for stories about her experiences with racism. Harris said that she was not about to start telling them "about my world for a number of reasons, including you should know about the issue that affects this country as part of the greatest stain on this country." Exhausted, she no longer answered the questions. I imagined she believes, as Toni Morrison once said, that "the very serious function of racism" is "distraction. It keeps you from doing your work."

But these days, even in the conversations that I hear my children having, race suffuses so much. I tell Harris that my twelve-year-old son, Micah, told his classmates and teachers: "As you all know, my dad went to jail. Shouldn't the police who killed Floyd go to jail?" My son wanted to know why prison seemed to be reserved for Black people and wondered whose violence demanded a prison cell.

"In the criminal justice system," Harris replied, "the irony and, frankly, the hypocrisy is that whenever we use the words *accountability* and *consequence,* it's always about the individual who was arrested." Again, she began to make a case that would be familiar to any progressive about the need to make the system accountable. And while I found myself agreeing, I began to fear that the point was just to find ways to treat officers in the same brutal way that we treat everyone else. I thought about the men I'd represented in parole hearings—and the friends I'd be representing soon. And wondered out loud to Harris: How do we get to their freedom?

"We need to reimagine what public safety looks like," the senator told me, noting that she would talk about a public health model. "Are we looking at the fact that if you focus on issues like education and preventive things, then you don't have a system that's reactive?" The list of those things becomes long: affordable housing, the development of job skills, education funding, homeownership. She remembered how during the early 2000s, when she was the San Francisco district attorney and started Back on Track (a reentry program that sought to reduce future incarceration by building the skills of the men facing drug charges), many people were critical. " 'You're a DA. You're supposed to be putting people in jail, not letting them out,' " she said people told her.

It always returns to this for me—who should be in prison, and for how long? I know that American prisons do little to address violence. If anything, they exacerbate it. If my friends walk out of prison changed from the boys who walked in, it will be because they've fought with the system—with themselves and sometimes with the men around them— to be different. Most violent crimes go unsolved, and the pain they cause is nearly always unresolved. And those who are convicted— many, maybe all—do far too much time in prison.

And yet, I imagine what I would do if the Maryland Parole Commission contacted my mother, informing her that the man who assaulted her is eligible for parole. I'm certain I'd write a letter explaining how one morning my mother didn't go to work because she was in a hospital; tell the board that the memory of a gun pointed at her head has never left; explain how when I came home, my mother told me the story. Some violence changes everything.

The thing that makes you suited for a conversation in America might be the very thing that precludes you from having it. Terell, Anthony, Fats, Luke, and Juvie have taught me that the best indicator of whether I believe they should be free is our friendship. Learning that a Black man in the city I called home raped my mother taught me that the pain and anger for a family member can be unfathomable. It makes me wonder if parole agencies should contact me at all—if they should ever contact victims and their families.

Perhaps if Harris becomes the vice president, we can have a national conversation about our contradictory impulses around crime and punishment. For three decades, as a line prosecutor, a district attorney, an attorney general and now a senator, she has witnessed many of them. Prosecutors make a convenient target. But if the system is broken, it is because our flaws more than our virtues animate it. Confronting why so many of us believe prisons must exist may force us to admit that we have no adequate response to some violence. Still, I hope that Harris reminds the country that simply acknowledging the problem of mass incarceration does not address it—any more than keeping my friends in prison is a solution to the violence and trauma that landed them there.

—NOVEMBER 8, 2020

Refuse Fascism, at the Ballot Box and in the Street

Lilly Wachowski

My grams was one of those people I loved to make laugh. She was a mighty woman who left an indelible mark on the women in my family. Myself included. I think of her when I fold a fitted sheet or make "Gramma eggs," our family's name for eggs in a basket. Her atoms can be felt in every one of my and my sister's films and was a huge inspiration for the Oracle in the *Matrix* trilogy. At the very end of her life, one of the things she said that carries wistful weight in our family's lore was, she wasn't afraid of dying, she just wanted to know the rest of the story, to know what was going to happen.

As we approach the crucible that is the 2020 election, this moment of our potential unmaking, I am at a loss when presented with the idea of what happens if Trump denies the will of the people and refuses to honor a peaceful transfer of power.

And then what happens?

That is the question that leaves me tossing and turning in bed at the darkest hours of the morning, my brain in free fall reaching out for purchase, grasping. The strange event horizon of this post-election moment in its unknowableness is unsettling.

When I was a kid playing Dungeons & Dragons with my pals, there would be some crucial moment in the story of the game where we'd all start chanting, "And then what happens?! And then what happens?!" It was a joke we repeated based on some newly initiated player who didn't understand the idea that role-playing requires participation in the story, but would just ask Lana (the GM) what happened next. We always took the joke to absurdist conclusions. "And then what happens? You get hungry. And then what happens? You collapse from starvation. And then what happens? You die. And then what happens? You decompose and become a skeleton. And then what happens? A pack of wild dogs divvy up your bones and bury them. And then what happens? Dung beetles eat your bones . . ." Hilarious stuff at the time.

We played endlessly. It was a game that would hone my imagination to create and understand hypothetical situations and to navigate through them. It helped my young mind in the creation of my own sense of self and my moral universe. It offered a salve to my gender dysphoria with the opportunity to disappear and inhabit other worlds, other bodies, bodies that more closely aligned to the one I yearned to be.

The ability to answer the question "And then what happens?" has served me immeasurably in my career as a filmmaker. To make a film is an impossibly ponderous endeavor, from its inception and ideation, to story, to script, to production, to post-production; a film is a flowchart of a seemingly infinite variety of decisions. And right now, days before the election, the question nags ominously.

Over the last months, that sense of uncertainty, that hole in our story, had me scouring the abyss of the internet, ultimately turning to the hard answers offered time and again by sites like Truthout, "Gaslit Nation," the Indivisible Project, Stand Up America, and Refuse Fascism. These are folks who have been ringing this alarm for the past four years and succinctly put all of my anger, fear, and anxiety into words on the desperate looming cataclysm we face.

The urgency of Refuse Fascism, though, is that we cannot wait until after the election. That we have to mobilize now, to take to the streets now, to preempt the rolling fascist coup that is taking place NOW. Definitely exercise your right to vote, but they posit that this regime will likely have to be forced out under the weight of mass non-violent protest in the streets. And though this premise is full of the promise of direct action, which I like, I still find my mind wanting, grasping.

And then what happens?

If there isn't some kind of Frank Capra ending to this nightmare, if there isn't an overwhelming electoral landslide of the decent, what do we do?

What happens when Trump disputes a close election, then tries to legitimize his coup via his illegitimately packed courts and a corrupt DOJ? The evidence is that he's already doing it.

My pal Aleksandar Hemon has written extensively about this, drawing parallels to his experiences in Bosnia, prognosticating about the impending doom we are all facing. Doom is a specialty of his. As he says: "The moment when we cannot in any way connect what is taking place and what we know is a traumatic one, because the solidity of reality—the belief that its continuity cannot be altered—catastrophically falters."

This knocks the wind from me. Because the "solidity of reality" is that I can't see through the murk of this situation that doesn't end in violence.

Violence. It is the GOP's go-to. The one substantive piece of their political platform.

And while the Democratic Party's habitual calls for bipartisanship make them accomplices in Republican crimes, violence is the core value of the GOP. The violence of 220,000 dead Americans and counting. The violence of exposing voters to grueling lines in this pandemic. The violence of their economic sanctions against their own populace, sadistically starving those with the least. The violence of their gun-crazy militias and white supremacist thuggery of the fraternal order of police. The violence against immigrants and the xenophobic politicizing of our border. The violence against Black and Brown lives facing more brutality and criminalization on top of a racist carceral state and for-profit industrial prison complex. The violence against my queer and trans brothers, sisters, and siblings.

How many more fucking bodies have to pile up?

The truth is, if Trump "wins" this election, I am having a difficult time imagining I am not going to be one of those bodies. This does not make me special. By the inauguration the number of Covid deaths will likely double. "Rounding the corner" to half a million dead Americans. It is a staggering number. A crime against humanity. And it is indicative that one way or another, the violence of the GOP is going to come for us all.

But it doesn't have to be this way. The dung beetles don't have to eat our bones, not if we rise up and participate. By freeing our radical imaginations we can create that Capraesque ending for ourselves. The movements around the world have shown us the way. Black Lives Matter has shown us the way. The courageous citizens that are hurling themselves into the ballot blockades have shown us the way. We must come together and end this fanatically violent regime that imperils our lives and the Earth itself. We are the writers of this story and we get to decide how it's going to end.

I'll see you in the streets.

The world will be watching to see what happens next.

—OCTOBER 30, 2020

Why I'm Getting Out
of the Boiler Room This Election

Monica Youn

Dear Vote,

I've spent years of my life thinking about you, I've written your name millions of times. But this is the first time I've addressed you directly.

Tonight, the red V of your name was writ large on the wall behind the head of the preternaturally calm woman leading Pennsylvania poll observer training. In the Zoom square, the upward diagonals of the letter formed red horns bursting from her temples as she explained what to do if gun-toting Proud Boy wannabes enter the polling station. (Upshot: Flee, then call the incident in to the campaign from a safe location.) Friends hearing that I'm volunteering as a poll observer in Philly have encouraged me to buy some pepper spray. Honestly, I doubt I'll witness anything at all, much less anything threatening. I'm bringing a folding chair and the new Elena Ferrante instead.

I've worked in voter protection in every presidential election and most midterms since 2004. Usually what I do is called *boiler room*—I'm in a roomful of election lawyers at the campaign office, or if I'm taking the nonprofit route, supervising volunteers at some midtown law firm. We drink a lot of cold terrible coffee, eat a lot of cold terrible food, listen to a lot of cold terrible hold music from the board of elections phone lines.

Every election it goes like this. Just after dawn there will be a slew of panicked reports that polling places are still padlocked and dark, that ballots have failed to arrive, that the poll workers can't figure out how to get the machines operational. Around eight A.M., we start hearing the complaints that always hit me the hardest: "I've been in line for three hours, but I have to get to work now"; "I'll lose my job if I'm late"; "I have to get home—there's no one who can watch my kids"; "I can't come back, my shift doesn't end until after the polls close here." Each volunteer frantically improvises, trying to scrounge up transportation or childcare options, offering to intercede with the voter's boss, anything to help, before finally subsiding into guilt-ridden powerlessness.

Later we fall into a steady rhythm of the "normal" complaints—touch screens freezing or glitching, poll locations running out of ballots, poll workers instructing people to vote by provisional rather than regular ballot, registered voters failing to appear on the voter rolls (on one memorable occasion, this seems to have happened because a poll worker had accidentally photocopied only one side of a double-sided poll book). And always always always the endless stream of registration issues: "I sent in my registration months ago, but it still isn't showing up"; "I've been registered for decades, but I must have been purged"; "I didn't reregister after moving." And always students wailing, "But I didn't know I had to register. Isn't there some way I can vote?"

And scurrying around, putting out little fires, I struggle to maintain focus against my own inner whispers of outrage. Why does it have to be this hard? Why are the barriers to voting the highest for those for whom life is already the hardest? Why does the United States make it harder to vote than any other industrialized nation? Questions to which I already know the answer. We all know the answer.

And I find myself donning the same game face as the voter protection trainer this evening, the face that projects: "Outrage is for amateurs. The time for outrage is always yesterday or tomorrow, never today, and especially never election day." I find myself reciting—even through my own gritted teeth—the election lawyer's mantra, Hanlon's razor: "Never attribute to malice that which is adequately explained by incompetence."

But of course the causal link between malice and incompetence is all too easy to trace—where election systems are chronically underfunded and understaffed, poll workers undertrained and underpaid, requirements and deadlines unreasonably burdensome, then the endless flow of voting obstacles, errors, and debacles is no longer an unintended consequence, but part and parcel of an intentional strategy to suppress the vote. Structural voter suppression is one of the key pillars of structural racism, so deeply embedded in U.S. elections that it can't be attributed to one single set of bad intentions, but to geological strata of white supremacy dating back to the founding of this nation.

There are the obvious malicious examples of voter suppression— war stories of which every veteran boiler room lawyer has a store. My personal collection includes: The letters on forged board of elections letterhead instructing voters in Black neighborhoods to report to a fictional polling place rather than their actual one. The deputy sheriff setting up a roadblock on the only road to a polling place and stopping every car. The signs posted in rural communities saying that election day for Democratic voters was on a different date, the day after the actual election. The vigilante squad photographing every voter in line "so they could check with the police for criminal offenders." The hundreds of thousands of robocalls that simultaneously overloaded our voter assistance hotline at 4:30 A.M. on election day, putting it out of commission.

But these obvious and patently illegal "bad apples" are (to belabor this metaphor) the proverbial low-hanging fruit of efforts to protect the vote. They are relatively easily squashed. Patching the leaks in the whole rickety apparatus is the harder part—and the devil's bargain of election protection work is that you've agreed to use only the master's tools within the master's house. At the front lines of voter protection, a soldier is often armed with just a statutory handbook, a cell phone, and a polling place locator. And until recently for me, those flimsy weapons seemed, if not exactly adequate, at least somewhat helpful.

Then came the moment my confidence disintegrated. It was about six P.M. on election day 2016. I had been in the boiler room since five-thirty that morning, helping supervise about fifty volunteer lawyers—together with multiple similar boiler rooms, our hotline had fielded over 300,000 calls that day, and all of us were drooping, running on fumes. Then a call came in: "There's been a shooting at a polling place outside of Los Angeles." My desk faced the rows of lawyers, so I could vividly see faces abruptly crumple, see tears start down the faces of volunteers still on the phone with voters, still trying to make each vote count while trying not to cry audibly. I remember slumping, head in my hands, the words GAME OVER flashing red in all caps across my consciousness.

Someone projected the news feed up on the big screen—an active shooter in a Latinx district, one dead, two wounded, two polling places on lockdown. The helplessness—all this effort, all these good intentions—all shut down by one bad man with a gun. The knowledge that this could herald the start of a new era, a post-democracy era where armed vigilantes intimidate the rest of us out of our efforts at self-governance. In my thoughts I flashed forward to 2020, to swaggering, gun-toting bullies patrolling outside every polling place, supposedly to keep "illegals" or "felons" from voting, supposedly to keep "voter fraud" or "ballot stuffing" from going on, but in reality, of course, to make America white again.

As it eventually turned out, that 2016 shooter was probably a false alarm. There probably wasn't a direct election link, although one of the women shot was on her way to vote. But since that night, there's been an ever-present hum of fear in the back of my consciousness—my sense that the ramshackle shambles of the election system is so brittle, can so easily be toppled by a tiny but well-armed faction of assholes. There's no do-over for an election, no way to count a lost vote, no remedy for a voter who stays home out of even a well-founded fear of death by virus or death by AR-15 or death in custody.

And over the past weeks, that hum has ramped up to a shriek, punctuated by the steady drumbeat of headlines: RNC recruits an "army" (their word, not mine) of 50,000 poll watchers, Trump says "Bad Things Happen in Philadelphia" after dog-whistling white supremacists at the first debate; GOP kicked out of early voting sites in Philly; armed Trump supporters stage "rallies" at early voting sites. A federal consent decree in place since 1982 kept RNC poll watchers out of polling places for decades after armed members of a so-called Ballot Security Task Force harassed and intimidated Black and Latinx New Jersey voters. That consent decree was allowed to expire in 2018, and the RNC has been quick to seize the opportunity.

People don't volunteer for election protection unless they have an overdeveloped savior complex in the first place, and every electoral adrenal gland in my body is flooding my nervous system with the message "Get thee to a polling place!"

There's a sense that the Eye of Sauron has swiveled toward Philly. I'm doubtful that there will be widespread violence there during my daytime shift, but election night, all bets are off. We don't expect absentee votes to be tallied in Pennsylvania possibly for days post-election. I think the daytime voter suppression in Philly will be the legal kind—long lines, lawsuits, some sporadic polling place Trump rallies or voter challenges. I'm much more worried about daytime violence in Arizona and Georgia and Florida and Texas—places without Democratic mayors, places with large Latinx populations. And, along with the rest of America, starting at sundown on election day, I'm worried about armed mobs, about democratic breakdown, about civil war. Of course, now I'm also worried about posting predictions online in advance of the election.

But for now, I'm mostly checking Dark Sky to see whether I should pack an umbrella in my election day backpack, calculating how many Kind bars I expect to consume during my shift. I'm hoping that if enough of us defenseless but excruciatingly earnest folks visibly turn out, it will be some deterrent against overt violence.

Dozing in my folding chair, sporting my lanyard and my paperback and my water bottle, I feel like I'll be dressed for Halloween as you, dear vote. Because this is how I picture you—not in the bold all-caps font beloved of mask designers and fundraising spammers, but in lowercase—a noun rather than a verb, an object contingent and eradicable as a pencil mark, and (like our democracy) forever dependent on the kindness of strangers.

—OCTOBER 29, 2020

Voting Trump Out Is Not Enough

Keeanga-Yamahtta Taylor

Like tens of millions of Americans, I voted to end the miserable reign of Donald J. Trump, but we cannot perpetuate the election-year fiction that the deep and bewildering problems facing millions of people in this country will simply end with the Trump administration. They are embedded in "the system," in systemic racism, and the other social inequities that are the focus of continued activism and budding social movements. Viewing the solution to these problems as simply electing Joe Biden and Kamala Harris both underestimates the depth of the problems and trivializes the remedies necessary to undo the damage. That view may also confuse popular support for fundamental change, as evidenced by Trump's one-term presidency, with what the Democratic Party is willing or even able to deliver.

Today, in Philadelphia, where I live, there is not a single aspect of life that the pandemic has not upended, from work and school to housing and healthcare, pulling poor and working-class African Americans, in particular, deeper into debt and despair. The uncertainty of the moment, let alone the future, feeds fear, frustration, hopelessness, and dread. In Philadelphia, shootings are on the rise, and the murder rate is growing. With two months left in the year, there have been 416 homicides in the city, compared with just over 350 for all of 2019, which was already the highest number of killings in Philadelphia in more than a decade. African Americans make up 85 percent of the city's shooting victims. Even before the pandemic, drug overdoses in Black Philadelphia were on the rise. In the first three months of shelter-in-place orders, 147 Black residents died by accidental drug overdose, 47 percent of the drug deaths in the city. When, last month, police killed a twenty-seven-year-old Black man named Walter Wallace, Jr., in the streets of West Philadelphia, while he was in the midst of a mental health crisis, the frustration of many Black Philadelphians spilled into the streets, just as it did last summer. And now, like then, Pennsylvania's governor mobilized the National Guard to corral demonstrators, to restore one kind of order while leaving palpable social disorder intact. Trump stumbled on some truth when he said, "Bad things happen in Philadelphia."

The dark side of the pandemic in Philadelphia exists in cities across the country, as we cross the threshold of more than 100,000 daily diagnoses of coronavirus cases. It is not a Trumpian slur to observe that many of the cities where Black suffering takes place are also governed by proud members of the Democratic Party. Instead, it illuminates the depth of the bipartisan failure to address the tangled roots of racism, poverty, and inequality. It can also help us understand why Trump captured more votes from Black men and women in this year's election than he did in 2016. Of course, the overwhelming majority of Black voters backed Biden, but the fact is that millions of African Americans experience the daily failures of Democratic officials to respond to the

poor conditions of their public schools, the lack of affordable housing, rampant police harassment and brutality, and usurious loans. The
answer to these legitimate grievances can't simply be to say that they
are Republican talking points.

During this pandemic, the toll of disease and death has been greatest on those who can least afford it. Job losses have overwhelmingly
affected low-wage minority workers. Since May, as many as 8 million
people have been pushed into poverty, with Black families overrepre-
sented among them. Whereas white workers have recovered more than
half the jobs they lost to the downturn, Black workers have recovered
just over a third of them, leaving Black unemployment at more than
12 percent. But the most provocative measure of the failure of our
response to the pandemic can be found in the growth of hunger. In
June, around 29 percent of American households with children were
experiencing "food insecurity," meaning that either they were unable
to get enough food to meet their nutritional needs or they were uncertain of where their next meal would come from. They were hungry.

Where there is hunger, housing insecurity is not far behind. Thousands of people have already been evicted during this crisis, and nearly
one out of six renters have fallen behind on their rent. Nearly one in
four renters who live with children report that they are not up-to-
date with the rent. The Centers for Disease Control and Prevention's
unprecedented moratorium on evictions was too good to be true: the
Trump administration recently signaled to landlords that it would
allow them to challenge the eligibility of tenants. This leaves the viabil-
ity of the CDC moratorium up to the discretion of individual judges,
who may or may not honor it. Local organizers and activists have tried
to fill the gap created by federal neglect with relentless mutual-aid
organizing, but this is hardly sufficient.

In Philadelphia, which, ignobly, has among the highest proportion of poor residents of any big city in the country, thousands stand on the cusp of eviction. Twenty-two percent of households in the city are severely cost-burdened, meaning that they are spending half or more of their income on housing costs, which is well above the national average. Before this downturn, 61 percent of households headed by Black women in Philadelphia were spending at least 30 percent of their income on rent, compared with 53 percent of households headed by white women and 44 percent of households headed by white men. Black mothers and their children "are most likely to be evicted," according to a 2020 report produced by researchers at PolicyLink, and Black residents in general are "most likely to become homeless." Philadelphia's moratorium on evictions has not been extended beyond its November deadline because landlord advocates and the Philadelphia city council could not reach an agreement. Instead, the courts have agreed to "pause" evictions until the new year, while still making exceptions for landlords who ask for an exemption. Even this concession roused the ire of the landlord class, which is poised and ready to evict. As Paul Cohen, a lawyer for the Homeowners Association of Philadelphia, said, "As a society, we recognize you can't steal food from the grocery store or clothes from a department store, so why is it okay to steal the rent?" An estimated 15 percent of Pennsylvania renters will face eviction in January, when the CDC moratorium expires. The disaster is being forestalled, but winter is coming.

Philadelphia served as an outpost for Joe Biden's campaign, in part because of its proximity to his home in Delaware, but also because the Democratic Party loved the backdrop of the "cradle of American democracy," in contrast to the affront to it that pulses at the heart of the Trump administration. Barack Obama delivered his speech for the Democratic National Convention, this past summer, at Philadelphia's

Museum of the American Revolution; more recently, he returned to Philadelphia to stump for Biden in the final weeks of the campaign. Biden made repeated trips to the city for town hall meetings and to make public addresses. Independence Hall and the Liberty Bell were not only pointed backdrops to political attacks on Donald Trump; they were also poignant symbols of the country's founding contradiction: freedom and democracy bound to racism and inequality.

The pressing question for the new president-elect is, what will he do in this fragile moment of popular radicalization and despair? It is true that Biden's plans became more ambitious after the Democratic Party primaries, when he was to the right of most of his opponents, including Kamala Harris. His campaign melded together a fractious coalition of Democrats, folding in those to his left in order to quiet his critics. This was largely done through a "unity task force," which brought together Bernie Sanders's supporters with Biden's campaign, and created a more than 100-page document that was used to revise the Democratic Party platform. Much of the platform now reads like a wish list for the liberal left, hardly reflecting the centrism that has defined Biden's career. It proposes "a new social and economic contract with the American people—a contract that invests in the people and promotes shared prosperity, not one that benefits only big corporations and the wealthiest few." That contract describes housing as "a right and not a privilege," and promises "good-paying jobs," cash infusions to cities and states, and "fundamental reforms" to address "structural and systemic racism" and "entrenched" income inequality.

Winning the White House may have been the ultimate prize, but the uncertainty over control of the Senate and the Democrats' losses in the House have already imperiled the lofty plans of the unity caucus. The pressure among Democrats to close ranks in order to defeat

Trump and win the Senate had dissolved even before the final tally of votes was taken. On a conference call for members of the Democratic House caucus, moderate Democrats blamed the Democratic left for the loss of House seats. "We need to not ever use the word *socialist* or *socialism* again," Representative Abigail Spanberger of Virginia said, according to *The Washington Post*. "If we are classifying Tuesday as a success . . . we will get fucking torn apart in 2022." This is a conflict that cannot so easily be muted, because the liberal left and moderate factions of the party represent different demands and different constituencies. The Sanders faction—organized around Medicare for All, police reform, and the Green New Deal, among other progressive causes—cannot be quietly stuffed in a box until the party leadership calls on the left again to gin up the base and get out the vote. They are fighting to transform the direction of the party.

It is also no small thing that, during his campaign, Biden insisted on unity with Republicans regardless of the composition of Congress, underlining his intentions to work just as hard for those who voted against him as for those who voted for him. In his victory speech on Saturday night, he said, "To those who voted for President Trump, I understand your disappointment tonight. I've lost a couple of elections myself. But now let's give each other a chance." Cindy McCain, the wife of the late senator John McCain, prominently defected from the Republican camp to endorse Biden. According to McCain, Biden will not merely reach out to Republicans as a gesture toward unity. She said, "I've had this very discussion with him and he's absolutely going to not only work with Republicans but bring them into the administration."

Undoubtedly, no legislation will move through Congress next year without Republican input. But that is hardly a cause for celebration; instead it is a recipe for gridlock and small-scale proposals that make a mockery of the enormous suffering across the United States. The insistence on unity between the two parties almost always comes at the expense of those whose needs are greatest. How would a Biden administration incorporate the views of a Republican Party that has supported a white-supremacist president, voted for Trump's plutocratic tax cuts, advocated for the separation of families at the border, and facilitated the heist of a Supreme Court seat in hopes of fulfilling the right's fantasy of ending access to abortion and destroying any hint of government-backed health insurance? We were told that this presidential race was the most consequential of our lifetimes, that it was a contest between democracy and budding fascism. Why would Biden welcome the foot soldiers of Trump's authoritarian politics into his coalition? As the congresswoman Alexandria Ocasio-Cortez said recently, "We very rarely see the results of bipartisanship yielding in racial justice, yielding in economic justice for working families, yielding in improvements to health care . . . Just because something is bipartisan doesn't mean it's good, or good for you." The biggest danger now is that the Democrats' failure to decisively capture Congress will validate Biden's strategy to emphasize moderate reforms and prioritize compromise.

That conclusion may seem to be supported by the shocking fact that upward of 70 million people voted to reelect the most corrupt, venal, and brazenly racist president in modern American history. The reality is more complicated. The outsize power and influence of the Republican Party has fueled the illusion that the country is more conservative than it actually is. This summer, polls found historic shifts in attitudes regarding the acknowledgment of racism in our society; more recent polling has also found widespread desire for big government spending on public programs. In a *New York Times*–Siena College poll released in October, 72 percent of respondents support a $2 trillion stimulus—far more than the $500 billion plan that Republicans halfheartedly support. Another 67 percent of people support a government-backed public option in healthcare. Sixty-six percent support Biden's $2 trillion plan to combat climate change. Around 85 percent of the public believes that making "safe, decent, affordable" housing available to all should be a top national priority. In this election, six states and Washington, D.C., passed drug-policy reforms, and Florida, which voted for Trump, became the eighth state to vote for a $15-an-hour minimum wage. These successes were offset by the failure of other progressive referenda, like the "fair tax" initiative in Illinois, which would have replaced the state's flat income tax with a graduated one, resulting in an additional tax hike for those making more than $250,000 a year. In California, a referendum supporting affirmative action in public employment and college admissions failed, with only 44 percent voting for it. And in a huge blow for the "gig workers" of Uber and Lyft, voters passed a measure that exempts both companies from classifying these drivers as employees instead of independent contractors.

When seen alongside the popular outpouring for Black Lives Matter protests and the support for progressive policies, these electoral successes for the right point to increasing polarization, rather than singular growth on either side. But though the right has effectively used the Republican Party to express its ideas, molding public opinion and transforming public policy, the left has had no such vehicle. Instead, the Democratic Party remains hobbled by cautious and careful messaging intended to hold its fractious factions together in an effort to capture an imagined political center. Not wanting to offend the millions of people who went to the streets to rise up against police brutality, and likewise seduced by the idea that there were Republican suburban women voters repelled by Trump, Biden focused on civility, restoring the "soul of the nation," and other vague and canned political promises. When party leaders talk of winning portions of the Republican base, they intend to do so by reflecting their conservative politics, rather than challenging them. In the end, an airtight 93 percent of those who usually think of themselves as Republicans voted for Trump, with white women increasing their support for Trump from 2016.

More pointedly, the radical demands that emerged from the protests of the summer and the breakthrough of the slogan "Black Lives Matter" brought the simmering tensions within the party to the surface. Whereas few elected officials supported the activist slogan to "defund the police," rising support for Medicare for All as well as calls to cancel the rent and student-loan debt have put the cautious Democratic Party leadership on the defensive. Government-backed healthcare is a radical idea, as is canceling debt and other popular causes supported by tens of millions of people. There is no more radical idea in the United States than seeking to eliminate institutional racism, but although the Democratic Party is willing to wield it as a talking point, it has produced not a single substantive policy or initiative to actually do so. These divisions within the party muddle its messaging, making it an ineffective tool for influencing public debates, not to mention actually convincing those outside of the party's milieu to see the world differently than they currently do. How else will the Democrats stop the bleeding of white workers from their ranks into the Republican Party? As Ocasio-Cortez said in a recent interview, assessing the Democrats' performance in the election, "We need to do a lot of anti-racist, deep canvassing in this country. Because if we keep losing white shares and just allowing Facebook to radicalize more and more elements of white voters and the white electorate, there's no amount of people of color and young people that you can turn out to offset that."

Racial inequality means that the worst consequences of the pandemic will continue to have an outsize impact in the lives of Black families. Covid-19 is now the third-leading cause of death for African Americans. But even the relative advantages that white workers have so far retained in the recovery will not be enough to overcome the material disadvantages imposed by American capitalism. You may keep your job, but it doesn't pay enough to keep up with the bills that continue to come due. White workers may be better off, on the whole, than Black workers, but that is a pyrrhic victory in a race to absolutely nowhere. Our economy is built on jobs that lead to nothing for some and to otherworldly riches for others. And they are usually connected. Those who toil in the low-wage world create the wealth enjoyed in the world of the elite and powerful. To be sure, this is an argument that can be won or lost, but it is not one that Nancy Pelosi will ever entertain.

The most effective tool the left has had in shifting public opinion and debate has been protest, along with interjecting provocative slogans and analysis into stale debates. The most enduring phenomenon during the Trump administration has been public protest and demonstrations: the 4 million people who gathered across the country to protest after Trump's inauguration, the airport protests of his racist Muslim ban, the public school teachers' strikes of 2019, the high school students who have marched since Parkland against gun violence and for climate justice. Then there is the awesome size of this past summer's Black Lives Matter protests. Between 15 and 26 million people participated in the summer uprisings against police brutality and murder sparked by the death, under a policeman's knee, of George Floyd. Despite claims to the contrary by Republicans, the overwhelming character of those demonstrations was nonviolent.

The outpouring of the public into the streets in response to the failures of the American state began during the Trump administration. But the pressures of the pandemic and the absence of any federal unemployment aid since July are not going away. The pandemic is as bad in the United States today as it has ever been, if measured by the daily count of new cases. The pressures created by the absence of federal assistance since July are peaking. After this election, tens of millions of Black voters once again will be praised for saving the party, even as they continue to die by the thousands; they will expect more than congratulations. This past summer, the resurgent Black Lives Matter movement tasted its power and its ability to interrupt the usual political conversations, which have so often left the needs of Black communities behind. The movement that changed the political fortunes of the Democratic Party through fevered efforts to get out the vote is here to stay. Changing a corrupt administration for an inept one will be hard to accept when there is so much at stake. Indeed, one of the surprises of this election was the gains made by Trump among Black and Latino voters, especially in South Texas. If ordinary Democrats begin to believe that it is the Republican Party that can guarantee employment and a booming economy, even when the spoils are unfairly shared, then the Democrats' homey bromides about unity and healing will alienate more than attract.

After the uprising, elected officials across the country claimed to have heard the grievances, describing newfound epiphanies about systemic racism and promising to confront the layers of injustice that inhibit Black social mobility. Fulfilling these promises has been impossible. The problem is in part the cruel refusal of the Republican Party to negotiate a new stimulus package, which would include hundreds of millions of dollars in support for local governments. But it's more than just partisan gridlock and an inability to cut a deal. To reduce American racism and inequality to politics, partisan or otherwise, is to ignore the fact that our economy is organized around human suffering. Whether it is the refusal of the federal government to increase the minimum wage, or a skewed tax code that allows the richest Americans to use loopholes to avoid payments while extracting the maximum amount from the ranks of the working class, or the unrestrained rise in the costs of food, shelter, healthcare, and education because of the valorization of market principles as the ultimate expression of freedom, systemic inequity is not an error but an emblem of American capitalism. The two parties have worked to create a condition under which the spoils of economic exploitation are increasingly concentrated at the very top, and practically everyone else struggles to make ends meet.

The deprivation created by this grotesque imbalance does not self-correct with a redistribution of wealth and resources, so ordinary people have been forced to demand those changes. Police brutality was the precipitating event of this past summer's uprising, but those events were also protests against this economic reality. That is why the demand to "defund the police" resonated so widely with demonstrators and those sympathetic to the movement. Communities of poor Black people in the United States are, by nature, suspect. They warrant particular and excessive surveillance by police, who understand the conditions that create those communities' social disposability as an invitation to abuse them. Political demands to redistribute public money from the police to programs that can address economic inequality and racial injustice are the only way to overcome these disadvantages. That was certainly the case this past summer. It is also what ignited the streets in West Philadelphia in the waning days of October.

The likely gridlock in Congress next year will lead to more stagnation in local government, as communities become hamstrung by a lack of federal funding. But the failures of electoral politics create fertile ground for organizing. Last June, around the time that the National Guard left Philadelphia, activists from Occupy Philadelphia Housing Authority (PHA), the Workers Revolutionary Collective, Black and Brown Workers Cooperative, ACT UP Philadelphia, and other groups organized an encampment of homeless people alongside the Benjamin Franklin Parkway. On a baseball field set between high-rise condominiums and Philadelphia's cultural epicenter, multicolored tents became a symbol of the city's summer-long struggle against racism and inequality. The field was just steps from where, two weeks earlier, thousands of Philadelphians had gathered to honor George Floyd and protest police brutality.

Within a few days, fifty people had arrived to stay in the camp, where residents and activist organizers quickly assembled a list of six demands, among them the provision of permanent low-income housing and the firing of police officers who treat the homeless poorly. Shortly thereafter, two other camps were established: one behind the Philadelphia Art Museum, near the main encampment, and another near the headquarters of the Philadelphia Housing Authority, in Sharswood, a Black working-class neighborhood. Sterling Johnson, an attorney and one of the organizers of the direct action, made the connection between the broader Black Lives Matter movement and the many different assaults on Black life in Philadelphia, including the dearth of affordable housing. The housing encampments were safe havens for those who are particularly vulnerable to assault when living on the streets. "Talk about Black Lives Matter," Johnson said. "We're talking about Black disabled people, we're talking about Black drug users, we're talking about Black sex workers, and we're talking about Black women."

For 126 days, the encampments provided space for people to live safely outdoors during the summer months and, at the same time, dramatized the crisis of affordable housing in the city. On August 25, the city received the legal go-ahead to commence evictions, but officials were reluctant to follow through with the removal of the residents. After the events of the summer, Mayor Jim Kenney seemed wary of sparking a new confrontation with the homeless and their allies, and instead negotiated unprecedented concessions to clear the encampments. As part of a settlement, the city agreed to provide social services for many of the people who had been living in the encampments and to transfer ownership of fifty viable properties to former encampment residents, who will in turn create a community land trust ensuring that the properties remain low-income housing. The settlement also allows about fifty people, mainly mothers and their children, to remain in twelve Philadelphia Housing Authority properties that they have taken over since the pandemic struck.

The activists in Philadelphia will tell you that the housing that they have secured is a drop in the bucket, but the fact that overwhelming housing need still exists should not detract from their achievement. These local activists have provided tangible tactical options in the ongoing struggle to secure safe, sound, and decent housing for the poor and working class in Philadelphia and beyond. And they have brought attention to the ways in which the local public housing authority fails to do its most basic task: provide housing to those in need. The terms of the Philadelphia agreement are not only a jolt to a burgeoning local movement for housing justice. The activists occupied green spaces and abandoned homes—and the imagination of those wondering what housing justice could look like amid the glacial response of local and federal governments. As millions face eviction and other forms of dispossession and displacement, the question of what to do hangs in the air. Philadelphia activism is only one node in the web of what ordinary people may be willing to do to defend themselves as public officials waste precious time.

Of course, the tumult across the country has had some effect on the composition of Congress. Over the past several years, young candidates of color have been motored into political office by the desire for our elected officials to reflect our greatest ambitions. The so-called Squad, whose members are congresswomen Ilhan Omar, Alexandria Ocasio-Cortez, Ayanna Pressley, and Rashida Tlaib, has two newcomers on the way: Cori Bush, from Missouri, and Jamaal Bowman, from New York. They represent the best in electoral politics today. There are now democratic socialists on city councils across the country; in Chicago, they are numerous enough to have organized a socialist caucus.

These are important developments and will be crucial in pushing for reforms at the local and national level. But the limits of electoral politics are what have brought us to this moment. The left never leads in the Democratic Party, no matter how much it preaches "accountability" and pledges to hold the feet of party leaders to the fire. The reality is that as long as we have a two-party system, where the winner takes all, the reactionary politics of the Republican Party will always create the right amount of pressure to discipline activists to go with the old guard, as we have all done with Biden. The stakes will always be too high. The real levers to hold liberal leadership accountable can't exist within the party but must exist outside of it—or the left needs its own party reflecting its actual politics and priorities.

The need in this country dwarfs the best of what Biden has put on the table for changing our current condition. But the demonstrations of the summer, the ongoing campaigns for mutual aid, and the growing movement against evictions are demonstrable proof that power is not only generated in mainstream politics but can be garnered through collective organizing and acts of solidarity. They also foretell a future in which the country does not return to a long-forgotten normal but is animated by protests, strikes, occupations, and the ongoing struggle for food, medicine, care, housing, justice, and democracy.

—NOVEMBER 9, 2020

The Fall of Trump: On Presidents, Dictators, and Life After a Regime

Francisco Goldman

It was 1986, late afternoon and snowing pretty heavily in Crown Heights, Brooklyn, and people were pouring out onto Eastern Parkway, charging up and down through the snow in their long winter coats, shouting with joy and triumph, some carrying and waving half blue/half red banners, the flag of Haiti. The neighborhood, back then, was a center of New York's Haitian community; in the massive apartment building on the avenue that I was living in, many of our neighbors were Haitian. The date must have been February 7, the day the dictator Baby Doc Duvalier fled into exile, ending a family stranglehold of the country that had spanned thirty years. Rather than via CNN's Magic Wall, the news would have reached them by long-distance telephone calls or over the radio, triggering what somehow could only be expressed outside on the avenue, with other people. I went out and ran and jumped around in the snow, too.

That memory came back to me last Saturday, when the networks finally called our election, and so many—on social media or the news shows, friends texting—were comparing the jubilant celebrations filling the streets of American cities to the fall of a dictatorship, calling up media images of scenes of similar outbursts, perhaps with statues being toppled, images of the Berlin Wall swarmed. Watching on television at home in Mexico City, and looking at photos and videos sent by friends in New York and Washington who were taking part, I ached to be there. (Even Azalea, our two-year-old daughter, had caught the spirit, lifting her arms into the air, gleefully chanting her new children's rhyme: "Joe Biden, Joe Biden.")

Likewise, the day before, on Friday, when Trump delivered his televised rant from the White House, insisting that he'd won the election and won it easily, alleging a vast conspiracy of electoral fraud— mostly centered in American cities with large black populations, of course—it seemed like a first reaction of many, myself included, once we'd shaken off the initial shock, was to compare Trump to a dictator. Like one of those stereotypical strongmen derived from certain Latin American, Caribbean, and African novels, or cartoonishly outlandishly satiric movies: deranged, paranoid, a monster of violent ego and autosuggestion, but sinister and dangerous, blustering mendacity and buffoonery an essential part of his show, a deception, or maybe not a deception (maybe he really *is* that fucking crazy).

I thought of General Efraín Ríos Montt, the most notorious of the string of military dictators who ruled Guatemala for thirty-plus years following the 1954 coup against that country's last democratically elected president. Guatemala is my mother's country, but I've spent parts of my life there, including much of the 1980s, a decade during which Ríos Montt headed the military junta for two years. Ríos Montt, an Evangelical Christian in a mostly Catholic country, was regarded as divinely anointed, a "chosen one," by his fervent followers. During his years in power, the Guatemalan military waged a campaign, against the rural Maya especially, of relentless massacres and atrocities, resulting in tens of thousands of civilian deaths. When 200,000 attended a Protestant gathering that Ríos Montt presided over, the dictator boasted that not even the Pope would draw as big a crowd when he visited Guatemala. On Sundays, Ríos Montt gave television sermons on morality. "The guy who has a gun should be shot, not assassinated," was the kind of moral edification he proffered. In the Guatemala City cemetery, young delinquents were being rounded up and, without court trials, executed by firing squad.

People don't always need to see a tyrant fall, to be ousted, to realize that our hopes of a better world have finally been realized, triggering an ecstatic outburst. Sometimes a democratic election—perhaps even regardless of who wins it—in itself can be a celebration, as much a release as any statue-toppling street carnival, though it can also be like the sacred destination of a pilgrimage, a long line, stretching for city blocks and village squares, of pilgrims who've finally arrived. An election can be at least as much an expression of hope and optimism as what follows the toppling of a demagogue or tyrant. That was certainly the case during the Guatemalan presidential election in the summer of 1986, when Guatemalans finally got to elect a civilian president for the first time in over thirty years, though the country's long civil war wouldn't formally end for another decade. It's the longest I've ever gone without sleeping, two nights and three days, catching some occasional naps in the car as, with a couple of journalist friends, we tried to cover as much of the country as we could, from the city to Maya villages still shrouded by war and military repression, out to Puerto Barrios, on the Atlantic Coast.

Everywhere we went we found excitement and hope for an end to terror, death, and injustice and for the start of a new era, during which Guatemala would get to be a normal country, one with problems, of course, its staggering poverty and inequality, but at peace, with some degree of justice at least, and where citizens would have a voice, and a chance to make things better, because they got to vote for their government. The Christian Democrat Vinicio Cerezo won the election. He frequently remarked that as president he would possess only "70 percent" of the political power; he meant that the military and its allies would retain the rest. When my friend Jean-Marie Simon interviewed him in the National Palace, he pointed to a nearby potted plant, suggesting that an eavesdropping device was planted there, that the National Palace wasn't a place that he, the president, was free to converse. Seventy percent was wildly optimistic; whatever it actually was—25 percent?—amounted in reality to almost nothing. The military had agreed to elections only because the dictatorship's human rights violations had made Guatemala a pariah state; the brutal war had essentially been won, and now they wanted, for obvious economic reasons, to be accepted by the community of nations.

In many ways, the dictatorship in Guatemala has never ended. The cold war years, when the military and right-wing economic elites held power through complicity with the CIA, evolved into a military and political narco-kleptocracy. The cause of democracy and justice had some successes in the ensuing years, but under the last exceedingly corrupt government, fiercely supported by the Trump administration, those forces were routed, driven from the country, crushed. So it goes, as Billy Pilgrim would say.

Trump isn't a dictator, of course. He just acts like and reminds us of a dictator. Trump is like a dictator. A sub-headline in the November 10 *New York Times* read: "President Trump's iron grip on his party has inspired love for him among many Republican lawmakers and fear in others." Usually we think of dictators—"Dear Leader"—inspiring love and fear with their iron grip, not democratically elected leaders. Trump's circle of advisors, his supporters in government, act like the advisors and supporters in a classic dictatorship, utterly subservient, but also conniving and corrupt sycophants, fattening off the dictator's delusions and lies. His most fanatical followers remind us of the fanatical followers of a dictator, worshipful, credulous of every lie, fevered by his rhetorical poison, because every dictatorship presumes a pact with violence and hatred of an enemy that needs to be stigmatized, subjugated, defended against, crushed. Otherwise, there would be no need for a dictator, or a dictator-like president. There would merely be an opposition, with its competing vision and ideas about how to govern. After an election, the winner would win, the loser would accept his or her defeat, and peace and civic seriousness, an essentially agreed-upon common public reality, would reign. Obviously that's not even close to what is happening in the United States of America today.

One of the reasons that Trump fired Secretary of Defense Mark Esper was that he stood up to the president, refusing to invoke the Insurrection Act to send American military troops into the streets to repress this summer's Black Lives Matter–led protests. Imagine the protests we'll see in the streets if Trump succeeds in deploying his power, if cowed and servile Trump-appointed judges attempt to overturn the election on false charges of fraud. Now imagine the ensuing bloodshed in our streets. Does anyone believe that Trump's most feverish supporters, the most extreme of whom like to parade military trappings and weapons of war even when they gather outside centers where votes are being counted, are not eager to see that happen, or that they wouldn't swell with a sated righteousness if it did?

_____

The fall of a dictator, the end of a dictatorship, is a release from suffering, fear, hopelessness. That's why people flood into the streets to celebrate the way they do. The suffering is going to stop now, and so is the fear; a heavy darkness is dissipating, and that's why we practically feel like we're floating, and need to dance and raise a liberated clamor in the streets. The smothering pollution of lies and hate is lifting, and it's our joy that is helping to drive it away. What we saw in the streets of so many American cities on November 7, 2020, was a genuine release. These aren't really emotions that can be faked. (Did Republican voters break into such spontaneous outpourings of joy when Trump was elected to succeed Barack Obama? Not that I recall. No doubt they felt vindicated, now that their own chosen one, representing their own values and desires, would be running the country. But even Trump's inaugural crowd was famously subdued. The closest Trumpian expression of carnivalesque public expression came months later, when the white supremacists and neo-Nazis held their Charlottesville tiki torch parade.)

Such pivotal moments don't inevitably lead to disappointment and disillusion, even if they usually do. But sometimes, almost instantly, they mark the start of a true change for the better. I was there the night, in 1997, that Cuauhtémoc Cárdenas became the first democratically elected mayor of the Distrito Federal, or Mexico City. Before that, the Mexican president appointed the mayor, who, like the president, was always from the Party of the Institutionalized Revolution, the PRI, which ruled Mexico "with an iron grip" for seventy years. The Perfect Dictatorship, Mario Vargas Llosa memorably termed the PRI, in part for their mastery of "demonstration elections" that were rigged so that the ruling party would win while providing the veneer, the illusion, of a functioning democracy.

Cuauhtémoc Cárdenas headed an opposition center-left party, and his victory was the first breaching of that Perfect Dictatorship—three years later the PRI would finally lose a presidential election, too, this time to the candidate of a right-wing party—but that night the streets of Mexico City overflowed with jubilation. Yellow PRD banners were everywhere, streaming from the honking cars circling the Angel of Independence monument; my friends and I went that night from riotous party to party in homes thrown open to strangers. At the time Mexico City was notorious for being one of the most dangerous and corrupt cities in the world; rife with violent insecurity, kidnappings, holdups, carjackings, rampant sexual abuse, practically bankrupt, and its citizens, if they could afford to, were fleeing to the provinces.

Under Cárdenas and a succession of left-leaning mayors, Mexico City became an oasis of progressive reform; while much of the country—ravaged by the narco war and the corruption that remains the Perfect Dictatorship's seemingly ineradicable legacy—grew ever more violent under succeeding national governments, including the disastrous PRI restoration of 2012–18, Mexico City became much safer, with a resilient and feisty civic spirit that made it a much better place to live and transformed it into a cosmopolitan world city. By standing apart from the way the rest of Mexico has been governed, perhaps Ciudad de México (CDMX) points the way to a better national future?

Guatemalans often strike outsiders, and even themselves, as a taciturn, dour, mistrustful people, and those deformations of character are usually attributed to decades of living under repressive dictatorships; but those same fearsome pressures also account for the chapines' defiant black humor and the incredible warmth, loyalty, and generosity of their spirits, at least once you've won their trust; I can tell you that there are no better friends on the planet.

During my first visits to Chile, I was struck by how sour, testy, and closed-off older people seemed to be in that country—it made sense to me that Chile has more pharmacies per capita than any other country in Latin America, if not the world—compared to the younger people, who seemed just the opposite: friendly, open, charming, and funny, as well as free-spirited and rebellious. This was just a general impression. But my good friend the Chilean writer Alejandro Zambra has written brilliantly and movingly about the strange sense of distance that separates the generations of Chileans who'd lived to survive as adults, working, raising families, under the decades-long Pinochet dictatorship, the corrosive moral compromises so many of them were forced to accept as a consequence, the relentless grind and drama of daily fear and humiliating conformity they lived with, as opposed to the generations that at most witnessed the dictatorship from the vantage point of children, mostly sheltered from those fears, pressures, and inner struggles.

In Guatemala, including around my own family, I was always noticing how people normalize their acquiescence to and silent complicity with horror. People don't want to acknowledge, even to themselves, that they are being debased; they greatly resent anyone judging them as morally deficient because they, in order to live their lives and keep their families safe, have had to go along with evil. They are right to resent it, especially when such judgments come from people who haven't had to endure what they have! Normal people need to feel that their lives are normal and acceptably good even when they are living in the shadow of human cruelty and injustice, of such murderous evil that, were they ever to act or speak out too emphatically against it, could cost them, and their family, everything. (Of course many Guatemalans did courageously rebel; most were killed, or if they were fortunate, eventually escaped into exile.) I love my middle-class Guatemalan family and learned to live with their conformity, their discomfited silences about all that I—an American, after all—was free to rail against, privately, and even in print.

There's another side to this: people who need to feel that they were right in supporting the dictatorship, whatever its crimes. These are the people who to this day, decades after the disappearance of the Soviet Union, still revile any even slightly liberal person as a Communist. They are everywhere in Guatemala, though especially among the rich and powerful, going around even now in 2020 menacingly quacking, Communist Communist Communist!

It takes many years for a dictatorship, or even existence borne under a demagogic president who acts like a dictator, to finally damage the human spirit in the ways I've been describing. What would happen in the United States if Trump had been given another term to go on dismantling and subverting our democratic institutions in the way he has been, and now, unrestrained, probably even more radically and punishingly than before? The foundational rhythm to which Trump moves his followers is cruelty. Racial cruelty, cruelty against immigrants from poor ("shithole") countries, manifold cruelty against women, cruelty against anyone who is not like the people Trump and Trumpians approve of. Trump's America dances and marches to cruelty, derision, mockery. Lies are his weapons in buttressing and justifying his various cruelties.

Evil dictator—that's a normal collocation, *evil* and *dictator*. We don't easily say *evil president*. It drags back on the tongue. The words aren't supposed to go together. Our country elected him, how can he be evil? If he's evil, does that mean we're evil, too? But thank God, he's not a dictator, and at least now, this second time, we didn't elect him, we dodged that bullet.

And so now we need to come together, Joe Biden and so many others are saying. Come together, Americans, it's the new consensus. Forgive and come together with people who disagree with us about what should be done about the economy, NATO, the Covid-19 pandemic, and so on; even come together with those who don't believe in climate change! But of course that's feasible. After all, a functioning democratic government includes the possibility that even parties holding extremely divergent opinions on the most crucial issues can somehow find a way to move forward. I can "forgive" someone for holding a view I disagree with, that I even detest, on any of those issues, and would expect the same in return. Our side just has to argue and persuade better, I suppose that's what I tell myself in these circumstances.

But how are we supposed to forgive evil? How do you compromise with racism? It's not possible to reach a halfway point of common agreement on racism. Or on denigrating and punishing immigrants. Or on unimaginable cruelty to children, carried out in our name.

It's hard for a society to rid itself of the effects of an evil dictatorship, I've seen so many try and fail. Some of these effects can be institutional. In Chile, for example, the Pinochet dictatorship survives through a constitution absurdly contorted in such a way as to guarantee to right-wing parties an outsize share of power in any government, and through the extant, despised, repressive Pinochet-era militarized police colloquially known as Los Pacos. A decade of nonstop protests by students and other young people, especially, seems now finally to have led to the chance to write a new Chilean constitution. Maybe that will sweep away the other remaining vestiges of Pinochetism that survive, whether institutional or embedded in human spirits.

In Guatemala, after peace negotiations put an end to its three-decade-long internal war, with a blanket amnesty for human rights crime, the victors—the army, the rich, the establishment political parties—called for forgiveness. It's time to heal. Our long nightmare has ended. Forget the past and forgive. But the Catholic Church's pre-eminent human rights leader, Bishop Juan Gerardi, knew that really there can't be forgiveness without some accountability, without justice. Standing up for that principle cost him his life. He was bludgeoned to death in his parish house garage days after presiding over the release of a Catholic Church–sponsored human rights report that exposed military officers to possible war crimes trials. In Guatemala, despite some victories, despite its at times laughable democratic facade, the haphazardly disguised iron grip of dictatorship survives.

Of course the United States has committed horrible crimes "in our names" before Trump. For years, when the United States was directly supporting the military dictatorship and the slaughter of civilians in Guatemala, few things tore at me as much as the indifference of U.S. citizens to the role of their government in these crimes, which were partly enabled by their tax dollars, their silence nearly as painful and infuriating as conscious implicit support. People could name many other countries where the same or maybe even worse has been done "in our name." Our presidents and governments always have their jus-tifications, ludicrous and exaggerated as they often are. We're fighting communism, Islamic terrorism; we're keeping our country safe. Such are the disagreeable responsibilities of being an imperial power. Would you rather be ruled by Russia, China, a caliphate? Out of sight, out of mind—that's certainly a big part of why people go along, too.

Trump's "Muslim ban" was carried out in our name. So was the abrogation of long-held laws granting migrants fleeing lethally dangerous circumstances the right to petition for political asylum. The child-separation policy on our southern border was also carried out in our name. Families who'd arrived at the border, mostly from Central America, seeking asylum, were often separated, the children, including infants, taken from their parents, who were sometimes deported, while the children were infamously even "kept in cages." All done in our name. Nothing about the child-separation policy was essential, or even strategically sound, for putting a stop to illegal immigration. It was pure cruelty. Contempt for poor migrants, not just a lack of respect for the sacred dignity of their family units, but an active, aggressive policy to cause suffering, to do harm, to abuse and traumatize children. No other of the Trump administration's crimes carried out in the name of the American people so befouled us.

And we are supposed to just forgive that? It's time for Americans to come together, so let's not talk about the family separations on the border anymore. Except only yesterday it was revealed that we now know that 666 of the separated children have not been reunited with their parents, and that those parents cannot be found.

In *A Lexicon of Terror,* her classic book about the Argentine military dictatorship of the 1970s and '80s and its disappearances of "subversives" and secret prisons, Marguerite Feitlowitz wrote: "The regime's depravity reached its outer limit with pregnant detainees." The Trump regime's depravity reached its outer limit with what it did to the children of those detained migrants.

The Argentine dictatorship had a policy of keeping those pregnant detainees alive until they could give birth in secret birthing wards. Afterward, the mothers would be murdered, and the children were secretly given away for adoption, usually to childless supporters of the dictatorship. The children of detained subversives were regarded by the dictatorship as "seeds of the tree of evil" that needed to be "replanted" in healthy soil. Ever since the fall of the Argentine dictatorship, Argentinian society has been reckoning with the repercussions of those crimes.

The group known as the Grandmothers of the Plaza de Mayo have relentlessly searched for the missing offspring of their own disappeared children. Of the approximately 500 children believed to have been taken in that way, the Grandmothers have managed to identify and recover 130, restoring to them their original identities, at least. Argentina is one of the countries that have been most successful in bringing the criminals of the former dictatorship to justice. But it took longer to hold members of the former military junta and their accomplices accountable for their "systemic plan" to steal babies.

Back in 2011, when I was in Buenos Aires reporting on another case involving the Grandmothers and missing children, I attended some sessions of the trial being conducted in the enormous, chilly, and bleak federal courthouse on Avenida Comodoro Py. On the left side of the courtroom, three groups of prosecution attorneys, including one from the Grandmothers, sat at their own tables facing the tribune of judges; the defense sat on the right, and behind them, in a sort of box of pews, sat the accused military men, including former junta leader General Jorge Rafael Videla; some of the former military men had been brought to the trial from prison, where they were already serving sentences for other crimes of the dictatorship. Separated from the courtroom by a high wall of bulletproof glass were two areas for the public, one atop the other. Upstairs was reserved for relatives and supporters of the defense. Journalists could sit downstairs with other spectators.

That day I listened to a witness, a former physician, testify about how the illegally detained women were brought to give birth in a small epidemiological area in a military hospital. Civilian physicians participated in the secret births. Newborns were entered as *NN*—no name—in the official birth ledger; the secret-prisoner-mothers were *NN*s, too. A nervous woman in late middle age, in a bulky sweater and a thick white wool scarf, who testified that same day was Sister Felisa, from a Franciscan order of nuns who'd worked at the hospital until 1983. She served meals to patients and managed a dispensary where soldiers received and exchanged their bed linens. In 2007, when the Grandmothers had first called her to testify, she'd spoken of being told to write down *NN* in her ledger for bed linens handed out to people with "no name," but now she told the court that she didn't remember that. "I ask you to think back now," said Judge María del Carmen Roqueta. "Why did they use *NN*? Who could those people be, who could not be named?" "I don't know, doctora," answered the nun in her timorous manner.

In 2007, Sister Felisa had vividly described her encounter with three small children who'd turned up in a corner of the hospital one night in 1976, whom the Croatian Mother Superior had ordered her to feed, but now she insisted that she didn't remember those children either. Incredulously, Judge Roqueta read Sister Felisa's 2007 testimony back to her. There had been a boy of about six, who was the cousin of the two younger children, another boy of about four and his little sister, who the nun had guessed was about two. The little girl was crying for her mother, the nun had testified, and the older boy had told the girl that her parents "aren't here anymore." Their parents, he'd told the nun, had hidden them all under a bed and thrown a mattress over the little girl. This had apparently occurred on the night the parents had been abducted by the military; afterward, the children, separated from their parents, had been brought to the military hospital. And now Sister Felisa didn't remember that? No, doctora, she did not remember.

"You were never told what happened to the three children?" Judge Roqueta asked, her voice exasperatedly rising. "You never wanted to know what happened to them?" The judge demanded, "Do you understand that you are testifying in a federal court? Has someone pressured you? Are you under a threat? Do you want us to clear the courtroom so that you can speak?" The nun, grinning nervously, said no.

Later, during the recess, I approached a group of lawyers huddled in the grimy vestibule outside the courtroom—all of them young, scruffy, in dark suits, looking almost like a gaggle of English public school boys—and asked, "So how could Sister Felisa have remembered so much in 2007, and nothing now?" A tall, gangly young lawyer with a shock of black hair falling over his forehead said, "Because one of those two times she was lying." It was obvious that he thought she'd been lying today. A man thought to be Sister Felisa's lawyer had attended the trial that day, too, he explained. The man had identified himself as a lawyer and had arrived with two other nuns and they'd sat upstairs, and he'd stared at Sister Felisa throughout her testimony that day.

So even now the dictatorship survived in that nearly ghostly manner, in the person of that man, whoever he was, who'd come to stare from the balcony at Sister Felisa, delivering a silent message, intimidating her into retracting her testimony.

The aftereffects of an evil dictatorship are hard to get rid of, to scrub clean. It usually involves a steadfast struggle, and justice is the only remedy. A post-dictatorship never manages to bring everybody who might deserve it to trial, I've learned, but it's crucial that at least some of the official evildoers, hopefully the most prominent, be held to account. That means everything.

I try to picture Stephen Miller, allegedly the main architect of Trump's child separation policy, standing in the defendant's box instead of the Argentine former military men, in that bleak, chilly courtroom. I picture Trump standing alongside him. Up on the stand someone is testifying, perhaps a woman who worked in one of the ICE migrant detention centers on the border. She is white, and both she and her husband, a border patrolman, worked for ICE. She had earlier described for investigators an incriminating act she'd witnessed, something done to a Guatemalan child separated from her parents. Can she repeat that testimony now for the court? Hesitantly, she raises her eyes to the second balcony. Is the evil presidency, some incarnation of "the evil done in our name," still somehow present in that courtroom? Or can we be symbolically cleansed of that stain?

—NOVEMBER 12, 2020

Thunder Song

Sasha LaPointe

In 2006, I watched my great-grandmother address a sold-out crowd at Benaroya Hall in downtown Seattle. She climbed the wooden steps of the stage, her small frame draped in her wool shawl. I watched as her father's painted drum was handed to a percussionist in the orchestra. My great-grandmother, my namesake, spoke about the first people of this land. She talked about a need for healing. "People have lost their way," my great-grandmother said when her heart broke over a wounded world. Her father's drum sounded. The first powerful beat reverberated like thunder.

Fourteen years later, my mom sits at her desk, a mosaic of script pages laid out around her. She's studying the opening scenes, the interviews, and the movements of music. She's finalizing what will become the documentary of my great-grandmother's symphony. She looks up from her tiles to tell me, "This has to happen now. People need to hear this music again." The footage for the documentary has sat unused, dormant for all these years. Until now.

That spring, George Floyd was murdered by police officers in the streets of Minneapolis in the middle of the Covid-19 pandemic. Protests erupted around the country, and cop cars were burning in the streets of Seattle.

My great-grandmother was eighty-three years old when she commissioned *The Healing Heart of the First People.* She had been troubled by the world. Back then the news was all about fighting George W. Bush's war on terror. She saw beyond the fear to the country divided, the wars across the ocean, and the violent injustices in her own streets. She saw the people had lost their way. She believed so deeply in our people's stories, the teachings inherent within them. She knew that no one would listen to an old Indian woman, that she would have to reach them another way. Somehow she arrived on what she called highbrow music, symphonies. This came as a shock to us, for my great-grandmother hadn't grown up with this kind of stuff. She loved square dancing and Elvis. But she believed this was the way, that if people could hear our beliefs through song it could heal this wound with music. She wanted something that everyone would hear. She called a famous composer. "I need you to commission a symphony," she demanded, "and perform it at Benaroya Hall." The composer turned her down. But weeks after the call he couldn't get this eighty-three-year-old Indian woman's voice out of his head. He called her back, and together they collaborated on a symphony, the first to ever include Coast Salish spirit songs and the traditional language.

In our longhouse ceremonies, we believe songs hold a spiritual power. There are certain songs for prayer, for healing. My great-grandmother had a cassette tape. On it were recordings of two spirit songs, one belonging to a beloved cousin, the other Chief Seattle's thunder spirit song. She entrusted the tape to the composer, instructing him to listen, but not to share them. She wanted the songs to guide him as he wrote the symphony. She hoped that if the healing power of these spirit songs could somehow take shape in the symphony, people might understand how we could be better. She was hoping for medicine, for a world that could change.

On a hot summer day in 2020 I stood thronged in protest, in the collective grief and anger. We yelled, we chanted, we demanded justice. I raised my cardboard sign that read in bold letters INDIGENOUS SOLIDARITY WITH BLACK LIVES MATTER. This didn't feel like enough, would never feel like enough.

Weeks of flashbangs and tear gas went by. Weeks of protesters being arrested and assaulted, even run over, and finally the people took the precinct. With the police gone, the organizers secured six Seattle city blocks, declaring it the Capitol Hill Autonomous Zone. There were medical tents and tables of free books on political education. People brought crates of food to share, while others held demonstrations. My partner and I walked the streets of a free Seattle, watching the films being projected onto buildings, seeing murals painted over boarded-up windows. There were large plastic bottles of hand sanitizer duct-taped to telephone poles. It seemed as though the people had created a utopia. Until it didn't. We turned a corner to find the park in the center of the autonomous zone in full-blown festival mode. Kids in droves wielded glow sticks. It looked like Coachella. It looked like Burning Man. People were drunk with selfie sticks, wearing angel wings and carrying Hula-Hoops. *Is this what change looked like?*

But in the middle of the intersection, we found a huge gathering of Coast Salish people. I watched as men laid out large cedar boughs in a circle. Then women carried burning bundles. The cedar smoke wafted over the crowd, the tents, the abandoned precinct. They were sharing their medicine.

When the first speaker approached, he asked that any and all Coast Salish and Indigenous people come forward to the edge of the circle. He asked that the white people step back for us. I looked at my partner, who looked at me, then gently let go of my hand. A young woman stepped away from her girlfriend and together we both stepped forward, away from our white partners.

"Before we begin here today," the man with the mic yelled, "I want to honor our elder, Vi *taqʷšəblu* Hilbert. It's important we remember her, here on her land for the work she did for the Coast Salish People." The man spoke in Lushootseed and in English. He introduced a group of Coast Salish singers. They made a half-moon around the burning cedar and hit their drums hard. I closed my eyes to my great-grandmother as she stood on stage at Benaroya Hall fourteen years ago. I saw the painted drum, heard its heartbeat as it boomed like thunder, as it called out for change. I hadn't heard my great-grandmother's name, her Skagit name, the name we shared spoken into a microphone, in a very long time. The symphony had been her last project; she passed away before the documentary could be made. But right up until the end she went to gatherings, to speaking events, events like this. I had seen her small and frail but still so powerful when she spoke. I thought of her here today in this crowd and shuddered at the imagined worry. Even in the threat of this pandemic, she would have been here. I let the drums wash over me as I cried, transporting me to the memories of the smoke in the longhouse, my grandmother's hand on my shoulder as we listened.

Throughout this pandemic I have returned to the books my great-grandmother made, the ones that house our language and our stories.

Some days are spent crying, curled in the crook of my partner's lap as the cats and dog wander the house, charged with an animal anxiety. Some days I make salmon and black coffee, simply to fill the house with the familiar aroma of my great-grandmother's kitchen. All these white women on Pinterest are baking loaves of sourdough, and I am trying to time-travel. We have climbed out onto the roof of my house and watched the sky change. The world has stopped, but somehow it feels more frozen on the reservation. I have had good days and bad days. We have made a game out of our once-a-month grocery shopping. We call it the Hunger Games. We call it the Soft Apocalypse as we wait in line outside Trader Joe's, masks on and six feet apart from anyone but each other. We dress up at night just to light all the candles in the house, eat the fanciest meal we can muster, and drink wine like we were in Paris. I had a panic attack in the middle of one of these nights, suddenly overwhelmed with worry about the elder I bought the smoked salmon from. "What if he gets Covid?"

We've spent the summer locked inside, able to spend time outdoors only in fifteen-minute intervals. Beyond that, it becomes too dangerous because of the smoke from the fires and my asthma. I have been boiling pots of cedar and rosemary. This is to help me breathe. People are still dying in record numbers. We are losing our elders. I have tried to find my breath. I've looked for a mountain I could no longer see, its peak enveloped in smoke. A thick blanket of haze has vanished the islands that I know are out there.

On election night, my partner and I sat barefoot on the floor, nervously checking our phones. We scrolled. We put them down. We anxiously picked them up again. We did this until I couldn't take it anymore. "How is this even an option?" I held up my screen showing the closeness in the numbers. I was afraid as a Coast Salish woman, a female-bodied person, a queer person. I was afraid for the people still being murdered by police, for the elders still threatened in the face of this pandemic. I was afraid for how many times I might have to endure another aggression from a person who refused to wear a mask but clung to their MAGA cap like it was a prayer. Would I feel safe again? Would the world feel safe again?

My partner picked up his guitar and strummed the opening chords of one of my favorite Ramones songs. I joined in off-key and giggling. By the time we reached the chorus, we were hysterical, barely able to get the lines out. We made it through the song only to roar with laughter and begin again. There was a power in the repetition. We let the song transport us.

In her own home on election night, my mom is not scrolling the news. She is pressing play, pause, and rewind, busy transcribing interviews, busy sorting through the raw footage of that day at Benaroya Hall. Again and again, her grandmother illuminates the screen, paused in smile, in speaking. Occasionally the music floats through, the symphony inspired by a Coast Salish spirit song. In the interviews my great-grandmother talks about her anxiety for the world in 2006, her rising concern, but there is something confident in her smile, some glimmer of hope when she speaks about the power of song.

"People have lost their way," she said. "They need to be reminded to take care of one another."

There is a belief in my Coast Salish culture that songs have the power to heal, that they can be medicine. My great-grandmother wanted to share that knowledge, she wanted to remind people to have compassion, she wanted to change things. I don't know anything about symphonies or orchestras. I don't know any spirit songs. But as we sang out loud until two in the morning on election night, we weren't checking our phones anymore. We weren't thinking about the president or the pandemic. We were laughing, lost in the music, lost in trying to get it right, lost in a brief moment of hope. We were singing, we were dancing.

We were trying to heal.

—NOVEMBER 15, 2020

On Motherhood
and Ancestral Resistance

Kirsten West Savali

My dearest Walker,

My son, my love, my heart. I don't know why I'm writing this now. Perhaps because I'm struggling to breathe beneath the crushing weight of my own mortality. Perhaps it's the unfathomable grief that haunts me until I surrender to it over and over again. Perhaps it's desperation, or maybe it's hope—hope that something I say will protect you, keep you safe so that you always, wherever you are, come home to me.

There have been days since your dad died that I'm terrified you'll want to escape this house as soon as you can. How could you not when so much pain lives here, threatening to smother the joy we so carefully nurtured for you and your brothers. I try to do better, be better, for you. I'll never forget the day you found me sobbing in bed, wrapped in your father's jacket. You asked me why; do you remember that? I told you that I missed your dad every second of every day and that sometimes I felt broken. You looked at me and said, "See, Mom, that's why I don't want to love anyone like that because I don't want to feel . . . like that." But you will, baby. You will love and you will mourn like so many others before and after you. The only thing I can tell you is that you're not alone in that inevitability and never have been.

It's been 598 days since your dad died and 593 days since we laid him to rest next to your grandfather, your grandmother, and your great-grandmother at Pine Hill—the hallowed burial ground that holds all of the loved ones we no longer can. Though we've lived in Texas since he was diagnosed with cancer three years ago, my soul is tied to the sacred soil of Natchez, Mississippi, 341 miles away. Still, it is here, in this reddest of red states, that the grit, wisdom, and determination of our Mississippi ancestors have sustained us.

It is here, in this Houston suburb, that a white teacher kicked your little brother out of class for taking a knee in solidarity with others for standing up against police brutality. It is here that a white teacher called the police on him and his friends for not moving far enough away from the basketball courts at school during a track practice. And it is here that our white neighbors—one of whom told me that your friends are lucky they didn't get shot running through his yard—take any opportunity to plant the U.S. flag into their freshly manicured lawns, professing their love and allegiance to a nation that has spilled Black blood for centuries with neither apology nor regret.

I worry about you more in this community—surrounded by the smiling faces and trigger fingers of people who don't see color—than in any place we've ever lived; but I'm not ready to move somewhere your father has never called home.

Sometimes, though, I think our very presence here is a reckless rebellion. Brian Encinia—the Texas state trooper who pulled over Sandra Bland and physically assaulted her before booking her into the Waller County jail cell she was found hanging in three days later—once lived in this town. The long nights of driving the highway between your dad's hospital room and our home were filled with many thoughts, but two pounded like fists in my brain over and over:

The love of my life has to live.

I have to live to get home to my babies.

There's a revolution outside, my love. Do you remember the sign you wrote when you were seven years old to show support for Trayvon Martin, the long nights I spent reporting on the Ferguson uprising after Ferguson police officer Darren Wilson murdered Mike Brown, or going with your father and me to the Triple S in Baton Rouge to pay your respects to Alton Sterling? Well, here we are again, protesting against white supremacist and state-sanctioned violence against our people.

Police officers may have lynched George Floyd 1,194 miles away in Minneapolis, but 25 miles from our front door Houston's Third Ward residents have painted murals and flooded the streets in righteous protest seeking justice for the "gentle giant" of Swishahouse's Screwed Up Click. He was loved as you are loved, Walker. He called for his mama with his last breath.

This violence is not new, baby. No, it's not new in this nation; it's not new in Houston and it's not new where you come from: Natchez, Mississippi, a town where, in 1967, the Silver Dollar Group, an arm of the Ku Klux Klan, murdered NAACP treasurer Wharlest Jackson because he received a promotion at the old Armstrong Rubber and Tire Company. They placed a bomb under his car that exploded a block away from his home. When his wife, Exerlena, heard the deafening sound, she knew in her heart they had finally killed him.

Not too far from there lies the Forks of the Road, once the second-largest human chattel market in the United States, where enslaved

Africans were traded, bought, and sold. It sits across the street from my old Catholic elementary school, the wicked place where Sister Pat told me that even though I was smart, I shouldn't reach too high for a Black girl. This, too, is violence.

Across town, a stone's throw from your great-grandmama's home on Cemetery Road, is the Devil's Punchbowl. According to elders, after the Civil War, Union Army soldiers created a concentration camp there for our recently freed ancestors. They were left to die, starving, as the conquering heroes marched away. Legend has it that no one would eat the wild peaches that once grew there—strange fruit, indeed.

Your hometown is a place where the Mississippi Sovereignty Commission investigated and surveilled your great-grandparents, who were members of the NAACP, for registering people to vote; where white supremacists threw rocks at your great-grandmother; where a bomb was placed under your great-uncle's car when he integrated the all-white high school; where state troopers harassed and assaulted your grandfather and his basketball teammates because they thought they were Freedom Riders; and where a white police officer arrested me after claiming I tried to run him over, his lips twisting into a grotesque smile as he said, "I don't care who your daddy is. You're going to jail."

You probably just remember your granddaddy as the man who spoiled you, loved you, and showed you off to any and everyone who came into his office. But like his father and mother before him, he was a business owner who served on the board of aldermen in a town uncomfortable with and resentful of Black power. That police officer, drowning in his own white fragility, wanted just for a moment to make me feel as if I had none.

He failed.

Our family's legacy is too deep and our love too strong for a badge-wearing coward to strip away. It was that power that helped me rise up from the hell in which I'd been cast when your dad was diagnosed. It was that power that sustained me when I uprooted our family to move to Houston for his treatment. It was that power that protected us when Hurricane Harvey flooded us out of our home and into a shelter, then into a hotel. And it is that power, fueled by ancestral resilience, community solidarity, and love—always love—that lives in and surrounds you always.

It is five A.M. now, Walker, and I can't sleep. I hear you in your room laughing and talking to friends you haven't seen in person since the beginning of the Covid-19 pandemic. Your baby brothers are nestled against me. I'm on your dad's side of our bed writing you this letter, with his socks on my feet and his wedding ring over my heart. We thought he had more time, that we had more time. We thought he'd be here to raise you into manhood, and I'm terrified that I can't keep you safe. Where in the world is safe for you, my beautiful, beautiful boy? These are a mother's fears.

There's a revolution outside, my love. And as empires and tears fall, you need to know that you come from a tradition of Mississippi warriors who have resisted despair's siren song and remixed it until it sounded like freedom. You need to know that yes, one day you may feel "like that," and I'm so sorry that I can't protect you from it all. You may grieve and mourn and scream from the depths of your soul as so many of our people are doing now—not just in streets across this country and around the globe, but in bedrooms and around kitchen tables where there are no cameras or lights or hashtags.

If that should happen, baby, I promise you this: You will see your pain in others, as I see my pain in you. You will see your power in others, as I see my power in you. And now, right now, I call on all of our ancestors to guide my steps in such a way that I'm still alive to love you through it.

My son, it is my honor to bear witness to your journey. I live in gratitude for you. I am in awe of you, you who made me a mother. Your dad and I dreamed of you; we dreamed for you. And I will fight for your joy and your freedom all the days of my life.

With my whole heart,
Mom

—AUGUST 6, 2020

About the Authors

Julia Alvarez left the Dominican Republic for the United States in 1960 at the age of ten. She is the author of six novels, three books of nonfiction, three collections of poetry, and eleven books for children and young adults. *In the Time of the Butterflies,* with over a million copies in print, was selected by the National Endowment for the Arts for its national Big Read program, and in 2013 President Obama awarded Alvarez the National Medal of Arts. *Afterlife,* a new novel, and *Already a Butterfly,* a new picture book for young readers, were published in 2020. Visit her at juliaalvarez.com.

Samiya Bashir is the author of three books of poetry, most recently *Field Theories* (2017), winner of the 2018 Oregon Book Award. A multimedia poetry maker, she sometimes makes poems of dirt. Sometimes zeros and ones. Sometimes variously rendered text. Sometimes light. Her work has been widely published, performed, installed, printed, screened, experienced, and Oxford comma'd. She theoretically lives in Portland, Oregon, with a magic cat who shares her obsession with trees and blackbirds and occasionally crashes her classes and poetry salons at Reed College. However, having been flung from Rome into COVID exile, the 2019–20 Joseph Brodsky Rome Prize Literature Fellow Bashir is currently in pandemic exile far from Italy and farther yet from wherever home might be.

Joshua Bennett is the Mellon Assistant Professor of English and Creative Writing at Dartmouth. He is the author of three books of poetry and criticism: *The Sobbing School* (2016), winner of the National Poetry Series and a finalist for an NAACP Image Award; *Owed* (2020); and *Being Property Once Myself* (2020), the winner of the Thomas J. Wilson Memorial Prize. Bennett earned his PhD in English from Princeton University, and an MA in theater and performance studies from the University of Warwick, where he was a Marshall Scholar. Bennett's writing has been published in *Best American Poetry*, *The New York Times*, *The Paris Review*, *Poetry*, and elsewhere. He has received fellowships from the National Endowment for the Arts, the Ford Foundation, MIT, and the Society of Fellows at Harvard University. His first work of narrative nonfiction, *Spoken Word: A Cultural History*, is forthcoming from Knopf.

Reginald Dwayne Betts is a poet and lawyer. He created the Million Book Project, an initiative to curate libraries and install them in prisons across the country. His latest collection of poetry, *Felon*, explores the post-incarceration experience.

Ali Black is a writer from Cleveland, Ohio. She is the recipient of the Academy of American Poets University & College Poetry Prize for her poem "Kinsman." Her work has appeared in *December*, *jubilat*, *Literary Hub*, *The Offing*, and elsewhere. Her first book of poetry, *If It Heals at All,* was selected by Jaki Shelton Green for the New Voices series at Jacar Press.

Claudia Castro Luna is Washington's State Poet Laureate (2018–2021) and served as Seattle's inaugural Civic Poet (2015–2017). She is the recipient of an Academy of American Poets Laureate Fellowship and the author of *One River, a Thousand Voices* and *Killing Marías,* finalist for the Washington State Book Award 2018, and the chapbook *This City.* Her nonfiction has appeared in *YES! Magazine,* the anthologies *This Is the Place* and *Vanishing Points: Contemporary Salvadoran Prose.* She is currently working on a memoir, *Only the Stars Remain,* about growing up against the backdrop of war in El Salvador. Learn more at www.castroluna.com.

Edwidge Danticat is the author of several books, including *Breath, Eyes, Memory; Krik? Krak!; The Farming of Bones; The Dew Breaker; Create Dangerously; Claire of the Sea Light;* and *Everything Inside.* She is also the editor of *The Butterfly's Way: Voices from the Haitian Dyaspora in the United States, Best American Essays 2011,* and *Haiti Noir* and *Haiti Noir 2.* Her memoir, *Brother, I'm Dying,* was a 2007 finalist for the National Book Award and a 2008 winner of the National Book Critics Circle Award for autobiography. She is a 2009 MacArthur fellow, a 2018 Ford Foundation "Art of Change" fellow, the winner of the 2018 Neustadt International Prize, and a 2020 winner of the Vilceck Prize.

Jasmon Drain is a 2010 and 2011 Pushcart Prize nominee. His book, *Stateway's Garden,* was published by Penguin Random House in January 2020. Drain grew up in the Englewood neighborhood of Chicago, and currently resides in the Kenwood neighborhood.

Camille T. Dungy is the author of four collections of poetry, most recently *Trophic Cascade,* and the essay collection *Guidebook to Relative Strangers: Journeys into Race, Motherhood, and History*. She has edited three anthologies, including *Black Nature: Four Centuries of African American Nature Poetry*. Her honors include a Guggenheim Fellowship, National Endowment for the Arts Fellowships in both poetry and prose, and an American Book Award. She is a University Distinguished Professor at Colorado State University.

Nikky Finney was born by the sea in South Carolina and raised during the civil rights, Black Power, and Black Arts movements. She is the author of *On Wings Made of Gauze*; *Rice*; *The World Is Round*; and *Head Off & Split*, which won the National Book Award for Poetry in 2011. Her new collection of poems, *Love Child's Hotbed of Occasional Poetry*, was released in 2020 from TriQuarterly Books/Northwestern University Press.

Nyle Fort is a minister, activist, and PhD candidate at Princeton University. He lives in Newark, New Jersey.

Ross Gay teaches poetry at Indiana University and is the author of the poetry collections *Against Which, Bringing the Shovel Down, Lace and Pyrite: Letters from Two Gardens* (with Aimee Nezhukumatathil), *River* (with Rose Wehrenberg), *Catalog of Unabashed Gratitude,* and the essay collection *The Book of Delights*. His latest book is *Be Holding*.

Francisco Goldman is the author of *Say Her Name* (2011), winner of the Prix Femina étranger, and *The Interior Circuit: A Mexico City Chronicle* (2014), which was awarded the Premio Azul in Canada. His first novel, *The Long Night of White Chickens*, was awarded the American Academy's Sue Kaufman Prize for First Fiction. His novels have been finalists for several prizes, including the PEN/Faulkner and the International Dublin Literary Award. The *Art of Political Murder* won the Index on Censorship TR Fyvel Book Award and the WOLA-Duke Human Rights Book Award. In December 2020, the documentary film of that book was shown on HBO. He has received a Cullman Center Fellowship, a Guggenheim, a Berlin Prize, and was a 2018–19 Fellow at the Radcliffe Institute for Advanced Study at Harvard. He is a member of the American Academy of Arts & Sciences. He was awarded a 2018 PEN Mexico Award for Literary Excellence. He co-directs the Premio Aura Estrada and teaches one semester a year at Trinity College in Hartford, Connecticut. His work has appeared in *The New Yorker*, *Harper's*, *The New York Times*, *The Believer*, and numerous other publications. *Monkey Boy*, his latest novel, will be published in 2021. Francisco lives with his wife Jove and their daughter Azalea in Mexico City.

Su Hwang is a poet, activist, and the author of *Bodega*, published by Milkweed Editions, which received the 2020 Minnesota Book Award in poetry. Born in Seoul, South Korea, she was raised in New York, then called the Bay Area home before transplanting to the Midwest. A recipient of the inaugural Jerome Hill Artist Fellowship in Literature, she teaches creative writing with the Minnesota Prison Writing Workshop and is the cofounder, with poet Sun Yung Shin, of Poetry Asylum. Su currently lives in Minneapolis.

Major Jackson is the author of five volumes of poetry, including *The Absurd Man*, *Roll Deep*, and *Leaving Saturn*, which won the Cave

Canem Poetry Prize for a first book of poems. He has edited *Best American Poetry 2019* and is a recipient of fellowships from the Guggenheim Foundation, the National Endowment for the Arts, and the Fine Arts Work Center in Provincetown. He has been awarded a Pushcart Prize and a Whiting Award, and his work has appeared in *American Poetry Review, The New Yorker,* and *The Paris Review,* among other publications. The poetry editor of the *Harvard Review,* Jackson lives in Nashville, Tennessee, where he is Gertrude Conaway Vanderbilt Chair in the Humanities at Vanderbilt University.

Honorée Fanonne Jeffers is the author of five poetry collections, including *The Age of Phillis: Poems* (2020), which was longlisted for the National Book Award. She is the recipient of fellowships from the American Antiquarian Society, the Aspen Summer Words Conference, the National Endowment for the Arts, and the Witter Bynner Foundation through the Library of Congress, among others, and she has been honored with two lifetime achievement notations, the Harper Lee Award and induction into the Alabama Writers Hall of Fame. Jeffers is critic-at-large for the *Kenyon Review* and professor of English at University of Oklahoma.

A former Wallace Stegner fellow in poetry at Stanford University, Amaud Jamaul Johnson is a winner of the Hurston/Wright Legacy Award, the Edna Meudt Poetry Book Award, a Pushcart Prize, the Dorset Prize, and fellowships from the Bread Loaf Writers' Conference, the MacDowell Colony, and Cave Canem. Born and raised in Compton, California, he is a professor of English at the University of Wisconsin–Madison, where he teaches in the MFA Program in Creative Writing. His most recent poetry collection, *Imperial Liquor,* was named a finalist for the 2020 National Book Critics Circle Award.

Randall Kenan (1963–2020) was a chancellor of the Fellowship of Southern Writers and a professor of English and comparative literature at the University of North Carolina–Chapel Hill. He was the author of the collections of short stories *If I Had Two Wings* (finalist for the National Book Critics Circle Award and the Aspen Prize, and long-listed for the National Book Award) and *Let the Dead Bury Their Dead* (a *New York Times* Notable Book and finalist for the National Book Critics Circle Award), the novel *A Visitation of Spirits,* and a number of nonfiction works, including *Walking on Water: Black American Lives at the Turn of the Twenty-First Century* and *The Fire This Time.* Kenan was the recipient of a Guggenheim Fellowship, a Whiting Award, and the John Dos Passos Prize.

Michael Kleber-Diggs lives in St. Paul, Minnesota. He is a poet, essayist, and literary critic. Michael's writing has appeared in *Lit Hub, Hunger Mountain, Poetry Northwest, Potomac Review, Poem-a-Day, Memorious, McSweeney's Internet Tendency, Water-Stone Review, Poetry City,* and a few other journals and anthologies. Michael is a past fellow with the Givens Foundation for African American Literature and a past winner of the Loft Mentor Series in Poetry. His debut poetry collection, *Worldly Things,* was selected by Henri Cole for the Max Ritvo Poetry Prize and will be published by Milkweed Editions in 2021. Michael is married to Karen Kleber-Diggs, a tropical horticulturist who makes art with flowers. Karen and Michael have a daughter who is pursuing a BFA in dance performance at SUNY Purchase.

Sasha LaPointe is a Coast Salish author from the Upper Skagit and Nooksack tribes. Her work has appeared in *Hunger Mountain, Literary Hub, Huffington Post,* and *Indian Country Today.* Her book *Red Paint: An Ancestral Autobiography* is forthcoming from Counterpoint Press.

Layli Long Soldier holds a BFA from the Institute of American Indian Arts and an MFA from Bard College. She is the recipient of an NACF National Artist Fellowship, a Lannan Literary Fellowship, and a Whiting Award. She is the author of *Chromosomory* (2010) and *Whereas* (2017), which received the 2018 PEN/Jean Stein Book Award and the 2018 National Book Critics Circle Award and was named a finalist for the 2017 National Book Award. She resides in Santa Fe, New Mexico.

Dawn Lundy Martin is an American poet and essayist. She is the author of four books of poems: *Good Stock Strange Blood,* winner of the 2019 Kingsley Tufts Poetry Award; *Life in a Box Is a Pretty Life,* which won the Lambda Literary Award for Lesbian Poetry; *DISCIPLINE;* and *A Gathering of Matter / A Matter of Gathering;* three limited-edition chapbooks; and a cowritten chapbook with Toi Derricotte titled *A Bruise Is a Figure of Remembrance.* Her nonfiction can be found in *n+1, The New Yorker, Ploughshares, The Believer,* and *Best American Essays 2019.* Martin is the Toi Derricotte Endowed Chair in English at the University of Pittsburgh and Director of the Center for African American Poetry and Poetics.

Sofian Merabet teaches sociocultural anthropology at the University of Texas at Austin. He is the author of *QueerBeirut* (2014), the first ethnographic study of queer lives in the Arab Middle East.

Indigo Moor's fourth book of poetry, *Everybody's Jonesin' for Something,* took second place in the University of Nebraska Press's Backwaters Prize in Poetry. *Jonesin'*—a multi-genre work consisting of poetry, short fiction, memoir pieces, and stage plays—was published in spring 2021. His second book, *Through the Stonecutter's Window,* won Northwestern University Press's Cave Canem prize. His first and third books, *Tap-Root* and *In the Room of Thirsts & Hungers,* were both part of Main Street Rag's Editor's Select Poetry Series. Moor is the Poet Laureate Emeritus of Sacramento. He is an adjunct professor at Dominican University of California and visiting faculty for Dominican's MFA program, teaching poetry and short fiction. He is also co-coordinator for Open Page Writers.

Manuel Muñoz is the author of a novel, *What You See in the Dark,* and the short-story collections *Zigzagger* and *The Faith Healer of Olive Avenue,* which was shortlisted for the Frank O'Connor International Short Story Award. He is the recipient of fellowships from the National Endowment for the Arts and the New York Foundation for the Arts. He has been recognized with a Whiting Award, three O. Henry Awards, and an appearance in *Best American Short Stories.* His third collection of short stories, *The Consequences,* will be published by Graywolf Press.

James Noël, born in 1978 in Haiti, is an award-winning writer and the author of fifteen books. His poems have been translated into several languages. A former Villa Medici fellow and leader of the journal *IntranQu'illités*, he also edited *Éditions Points—Seuil,* an anthology of contemporary Haitian poetry bringing seventy-three poets together. In 2017, he published his first novel, *Belle merveille,* whose German translation received the HKW Prize from the Haus der Kulturen der Welt in Berlin in June 2020. Les Éditions Diable Vauvert published his latest book, *Brexit suivi de la migration des murs.*

Gregory Pardlo's collection *Digest* won the 2015 Pulitzer Prize for Poetry. Other honors include fellowships from the New York Public

Library's Cullman Center, the Guggenheim Foundation, the New York Foundation for the Arts, and the National Endowment for the Arts for translation. His first poetry collection, *Totem,* won the APR/Honickman Prize in 2007. He is poetry editor of the *Virginia Quarterly Review* and director of the MFA program at Rutgers University–Camden. His most recent book is *Air Traffic,* a memoir in essays.

Daniel Peña is a Pushcart Prize–winning writer and an assistant professor in the Department of English at the University of Houston–Downtown. A graduate of Cornell University and a former Picador Guest Professor in Leipzig, Germany, he was formerly based out of the UNAM in Mexico City, where he was a Fulbright–García Robles Scholar. His writing has appeared in *Ploughshares, Gulf Coast, The Rumpus,* the *Kenyon Review,* NBC News, and *The Guardian* among other venues. His novel *Bang* is out now. He lives in Houston, Texas.

Craig Santos Perez is an Indigenous Chamoru from the Pacific Island of Guam. He is the author of five books of poetry and the coeditor of five anthologies. His work has received the American Book Award, the PEN Center USA/Poetry Society of America Prize, and the Hawai'i Literary Arts Council Award. He works as a professor of English at the University of Hawai'i at Mānoa.

Kirsten West Savali is senior content director at iOne Digital, Urban One's family of digital properties. She formerly served as executive producer at *Essence* magazine, most recently serving as the magazine's senior editor of news and politics. As both a writer and cultural critic, she explores the intersections of racism, social justice, Black feminism, and politics. She is the recipient of the Vernon Jarrett Medal for Journalistic Excellence, which honors exemplary reporting on Black life in

America, and an NABJ Award for Journalistic Excellence. She was also named to *Ebony* magazine's Power 100 List, and was awarded a John Jay College of Criminal Justice/Harry Frank Guggenheim Fellowship for her work focusing on criminal justice.

Idrissa Simmonds-Nastili is a poet, essayist, fiction writer, coach, and facilitator. Her work has appeared in *Black Renaissance Noire, The James Franco Review, Fourteen Hills, Room Magazine, Adirondack Review,* and elsewhere. She has been the recipient of fellowships and residencies from Hedgebrook, Bread Loaf Writers' Conference, Poets House, and VONA/Voices. She is coeditor of *The BreakBeat Poets Vol. 2: Black Girl Magic*. She curates Brunch & Word, a bicoastal literary salon.

Patricia Smith is the author of eight books of poetry, including *Incendiary Art,* winner of the 2018 Kingsley Tufts Poetry Award, the 2017 Los Angeles Times Book Prize, the 2018 NAACP Image Award, and finalist for the 2018 Pulitzer Prize; *Shoulda Been Jimi Savannah,* winner of the Lenore Marshall Poetry Prize from the Academy of American Poets; and *Blood Dazzler,* a National Book Award finalist. Her work has appeared in *Poetry, The Paris Review, The Baffler, The Washington Post, The New York Times,* and *Tin House,* and in *Best American Poetry, Best American Essays,* and *Best American Mystery Stories.*

Tracy K. Smith is the author of four books of poetry, including *Life on Mars,* winner of the Pulitzer Prize. *Such Color: New and Selected Poems* will be published in October. She is also the editor of an anthology, *American Journal: Fifty Poems for Our Time,* and co-translator (with Changtai Bi) of *My Name Will Grow Wide Like a Tree: Selected Poems* by Yi Lei. Smith's memoir, *Ordinary Light,* was named a finalist for the National Book Award. From 2017 to 2019, Smith served two terms as the twenty-second Poet Laureate of the United States. She is currently a chancellor of the Academy of American Poets.

Pitchaya Sudbanthad is the author of *Bangkok Wakes to Rain.* The novel, published by Riverhead Books (U.S.) and Sceptre (UK), was selected as a notable book of the year by *The New York Times* and *The Washington Post,* as well as a finalist for the Center for Fiction's First Novel Prize. He has received fellowships in fiction writing from the New York Foundation for the Arts and the MacDowell, and currently splits his time between Bangkok and Brooklyn.

Keeanga-Yamahtta Taylor is a contributing writer at *The New Yorker.* She is an assistant professor of African American studies at Princeton University and the author of several books, including *Race for Profit: How Banks and the Real Estate Industry Undermined Black Homeownership,* which was a 2020 finalist for the Pulitzer Prize for history.

Héctor Tobar's new novel, *The Last Great Road Bum,* was published in August 2020 by MCD/FSG. Tobar is a Pulitzer Prize–winning journalist and novelist. He is the author of the critically acclaimed *New York Times* bestseller *Deep Down Dark,* as well as *The Barbarian Nurseries, Translation Nation,* and *The Tattooed Soldier.* Tobar is also a contributing writer for the *New York Times* opinion pages and an associate professor at the University of California–Irvine. He's written for *The New Yorker,* the *Los Angeles Times,* and other publications. His short fiction has appeared in *Best American Short Stories, L.A. Noir, Zyzzyva,* and *Slate.* The son of Guatemalan immigrants, he is a native of Los Angeles, where he lives with his family.

Cynthia Tucker is a Pulitzer Prize–winning syndicated columnist. Her weekly column, which appears in newspapers around the country, focuses on political and cultural issues, including income inequality, social justice, and reform of the public education system. Tucker has spent most of her career in newspapers, working as a reporter and an editor. For seventeen years, she served as editorial page editor of *The Atlanta Journal-Constitution,* overseeing the newspaper's editorial policies on everything from local elections to foreign affairs. She also worked as a Washington-based political columnist for *The Atlanta Journal-Constitution.*

Oscar Villalon is the managing editor at *Zyzzyva.* His writing has appeared most recently in *Freeman's, Zócalo,* and *The Believer,* and he's a contributing editor to the *Literary Hub.* He lives with his wife and son in San Francisco.

Lilly Wachowski is a trans woman filmmaker who has collaborated on a myriad of moving picture cinematics, including the *Matrix* trilogy, *V for Vendetta, Speed Racer, Cloud Atlas, Sense8,* and *Work in Progress.* She is a board member of Brave Space Alliance and cosigner of A Pledge to the People of the World: In the Name of Humanity, We Refuse to Accept a Fascist America.

Monica Youn is the author of three books of poetry: *Blackacre, Ignatz,* and *Barter.* She has been awarded the Levinson Prize, the William Carlos Williams Award, a Guggenheim Fellowship, a Witter Bynner Fellowship, and a Stegner Fellowship, and she has been a finalist for the National Book Award, the National Book Critics Circle Award, and the Kingsley Tufts Poetry Award. The daughter of Korean immigrants and a member of the Racial Imaginary Institute, she teaches at Princeton and in the MFA programs at New York University and Columbia. She was formerly senior counsel at the Brennan Center for Justice.

Permissions

"Salutation in Search Of" by Patricia Smith first appeared as "Salutations In Search Of" in *Literary Hub* on July 16, 2020, and has since appeared in *One-Way Street Magazine*.

"Learning from the Ghosts of the Civil War" by Randall Kenan first appeared as "Letter from North Carolina: Learning from the Ghosts of the Civil War" in *Literary Hub* on August 18, 2020.

"Mourning" by Edwidge Danticat first appeared as "Mourning in Place" in *The New York Review of Books* on September 24, 2020.

"Why the Rebellion Had to Begin Here" by Su Hwang first appeared as "Letter from Minneapolis: Why the Rebellion Had to Begin Here" in *Literary Hub* on June 8, 2020.

"On the Complex Flavors of Black Joy" by Michael Kleber-Diggs first appeared as "Letter from St. Paul: On the Complex Flavors of Black Joy" in *Literary Hub* on August 11, 2020.

"Letter from the Fault Lines of Midwestern Racism" by Amaud Jamaul Johnson first appeared as "The Fault Lines of Midwestern Racism Run Deep" in *Literary Hub* on September 22, 2020.

"I Cannot Stop: A Response to the Murder of George Floyd" by Layli Long Soldier first appeared as "Layli Long Soldier on Wounded Knee and the Murder of George Floyd" in *Literary Hub* on June 3, 2020, and will also appear in a forthcoming collection by Radius Books in collaboration with the San Francisco Museum of Modern Art titled *American Geography*.

"Be Safe Out There (And Other American Delusions, Rhetorical and Otherwise)" by Sofian Merabet first appeared in *Literary Hub* on August 20, 2020.

"I Hated That I Had to See Your Face Through Plexiglass" by Nyle Fort first appeared as "Letter from Newark: I Hated That I Had to See Your Face Through Plexiglass" in *Literary Hub* on July 1, 2020.

"Let These Protests Bring Light to America" by Daniel Peña first appeared as "Letter from Houston: These Protests Bring Light to America" in *Literary Hub* on June 16, 2020, and has since appeared in *One-Way Street Magazine*.

"Letter from a Seattle Protest" by Claudia Castro Luna first appeared as "Letter from Seattle: A Season of Peaceful Protest" in *Literary Hub* on September 17, 2020.

"Finding Justice in the Streets" by Pitchaya Sudbanthad first appeared as "Letter from Brooklyn: Finding Justice in the Streets" in *Literary Hub* on June 12, 2020.

"A Riotous Anodyne" by Indigo Moor first appeared as "Letter to Sacramento: A Riotous Anodyne" in *Literary Hub* on June 23, 2020.

"A Letter to Black America" by Tracy K. Smith first appeared as "Dear Black America: A Letter from Tracy K. Smith" in *Literary Hub* on July 2, 2020.

"Where Is Black Life Lived?" by Joshua Bennett first appeared in *Literary Hub* on July 21, 2020, and part of it will appear in *Best American Poetry 2021*.

"On the Endless Mourning of the Present" by Honorée Fanonne Jeffers first appeared as "Letter from Oklahoma: Honorée Fanonne Jeffers on the Endless Mourning of the Present" in *Literary Hub* on June 4, 2020.

"On Protest, Laughter, and Finding Breath" by Ali Black first appeared as "Letter from Cleveland: On Protest, Laughter, and Finding Breath" in *Literary Hub* on June 3, 2020.

"Letter to Juneteenth" by Gregory Pardlo first appeared in *Literary Hub* on July 30, 2020.

"Letter from Burlington" by Major Jackson first appeared as "Letter from Vermont: Fighting for Black Interior Lives" in *Literary Hub* on June 22, 2020.

"Black Prayer" by James Noël first appeared in English translation in *Literary Hub* on June 5, 2020.

"Sense" by Dawn Lundy Martin first appeared in *Literary Hub* on August 25, 2020.

"Black Motherhood in Sleepless Times" by Idrissa Simmonds-Nastili first appeared as "Letter from Oakland: Black Motherhood in Sleepless Times" in *Literary Hub* on June 9, 2020.

"Letter to a Mother Who Survived and Thrived" by Cynthia Tucker first appeared in *Literary Hub* on October 8, 2020.

"'Maybe' (Letter to a Daughter Who Will Wear Two Masks)" by Jasmon Drain first appeared in *Literary Hub* on August 6, 2020.

"This'll Hurt Me More" by Camille T. Dungy first appeared in *Literary Hub* on June 15, 2020.

"Have I Ever Told You All the Courts I've Loved" by Ross Gay first appeared in *Literary Hub* on September 15, 2020.

"Letter from Exile: Finding Home in a Pandemic" by Samiya Bashir first appeared in *Literary Hub* on July 23, 2020.

"A Generational Uprising" by Héctor Tobar first appeared as "Letter from Los Angeles: On a Generational Uprising" in *Literary Hub* on June 5, 2020.

"When the Shadow Is Looming" by Oscar Villalon first appeared as "Letter from San Francisco: When the Shadow Is Looming" in *Literary Hub* on July 28, 2020.

"From Plagues to Protests to Wildfires" by Manuel Muñoz first appeared as "Letter from Tucson: From Plagues to Protest to Wildfires" in *Literary Hub* on July 7, 2020.

"Postcards from a Quarantined Paradise" by Craig Santos Perez first appeared in *Literary Hub* on August 4, 2020.

"Three Liberties: Past, Present, Yet to Come" by Julia Alvarez first appeared in *Literary Hub* on July 2, 2020.

"Letter to John Robert Lewis" by Nikky Finney first appeared as "To John Lewis, Whose Strength and Sweetness Never Faltered" in *Literary Hub* on August 27, 2020.

"Kamala Harris, Mass Incarceration, and Me" by Reginald Dwayne Betts first appeared in *The New York Times Magazine* on November 8, 2020.

"Refuse Fascism, at the Ballot Box and in the Street" by Lilly Wachowski first appeared in *Literary Hub* on October 30, 2020.

"Why I'm Getting Out of the Boiler Room This Election" by Monica Youn first appeared as "Dear Vote, or Why This Election Day I'm Coming Out of the Boiler Room" in *Literary Hub* on October 29, 2020.

"Voting Trump Out Is Not Enough" by Keeanga-Yamahtta Taylor first appeared in *The New Yorker* on November 9, 2020.

"The Fall of Trump: On Presidents, Dictators, and Life After a Regime" by Francisco Goldman first appeared in *Literary Hub* on November 12, 2020.

"On Motherhood and Ancestral Resistance" by Kirsten West Savali first appeared as "A Letter to My Son: Kirsten West Savali on Motherhood and Ancestral Resilience" in *Literary Hub* on August 13, 2020.